LIFE IN A RELIGIOUS COMMUNITY:

THE LUBAVITCHER CHASSIDIM IN MONTREAL

William Shaffir

Cultures & Communities: A Series of Monographs
Community Studies
General Editor: Gordon B. Inglis
Holt, Rinehart & Winston of Canada, Limited
Toronto   Montreal

Printed in Canada
1 2 3 4 5 78 77 76 75 74

Cover Design: Carol Noel. Photograph courtesy of the
                              Lubavitch Foundation. Used by
                              special permission.

ii

Foreword

The Series

The Community Studies series is intended to provide a body of original Canadian case materials suitable for students of the social sciences and for the interested general reader. The term "community" in the title is used in the broadest sense; books in the series may focus upon a village, town, neighbourhood, region, economic or occupational category, ethnic group, or other societal unit. Authors from various disciplines will be encouraged to treat their subject matter from perspectives that seem appropriate to their context rather than being bound by traditional models. Although the focus will be upon issues of contemporary interest, historical studies may well find a place.

It is hoped that the series will contribute both to the understanding of Canadian society and to the development of Canadian social science.

G. B. Inglis
Memorial University of Newfoundland

Foreword to this study

If I qualified, at present, as a Canadian sociologist, and were working at my trade, I think I would ask myself this question: In addition to the things which could be done anywhere to add to the knowledge of human societies, what are the features of Canadian life to which the "more-so" principle might apply—those things which are high-lighted somewhat in Canadian life, and from which one might learn something more about some aspect of human society than one would elsewhere?

(Everett C. Hughes)

This "more-so" principle applies with special emphasis to the study of minority groups in Canadian society. Ironically nothing is more typically Canadian than the presence and life of her many ethnic groups: not only the "new Canadians" but the two (or three) native "hyphenated" Canadians as well. Only a dictionary of Canadian English could define the word "Ethnic" as "people who are neither English nor French".

But who are these ethnic Canadians? The most recent Canadian census listed more than 70 foreign language groups. How many of them have we studied? Not more than a handful. The present volume not only fills one of the gaps in the the ethnic mosaic, but it also provides an admirable model for future students. It is both ethnographic and analytic, describing the customs and routines of the community and putting them into a broad interpretative framework. A general understanding of the Canadian ethnic situation can only be built on a foundation of many such case studies of individual ethnic enclaves.

At the same time, Professor Shaffir points out, that for all their differences, the boundaries of the Lubavitch community are not all that clear and distinct, neither to the analyst nor to the members themselves. At what point does the new recruit become a member of the community? The members and the recruits themselves don't know for sure or they disagree. Professor Shaffir's analysis of establishing a relationship with the *Rebbe* is I think a sensitive answer to this question. Similiarly, the economic ties between the Lubavitcher and the larger Jewish community belies the simple distinction between insiders and outsiders. In return the Lubavitcher uphold and provide a model of Jewish practice for less observant Jews who also desire it but are not willing to expend the effort to maintain it. Here Professor Shaffir argues persuasively that the relationship between the Lubavitch and the larger Jewish community is a two way street.

The story of the inner life of a tiny enclave such as the Lubavitcher Chassidim, also says much about the larger community. Can they have their own schools? Can they live wherever they want? Do they have to take extreme measures to isolate themselves from prejudice? Is their different way of life merely tolerated or, perhaps encouraged and nurtured? The answers to these questions say much about Canadian society itself.

Within the study of minority groups, the Lubavitcher are

"atypical" in several respects. First, while many religious based communities seek a rural way of life and discourage contact with outsiders, the Lubavitcher live in Canada's largest metropolis and actively seek contact with members of the larger Jewish community. Professor Shaffir pays special attention to this aspect of community life and his analysis and interpretation of the Lubavitcher strategy warrants close attention. His conclusion that proselytizing activities primarily serve to control the context on interaction between Lubavitcher and other Jews, is quite original and questions traditional assumptions about the functions of recruitment into relgious organizations or communities.

Second, the case of the Lubavitcher raises interesting questions about ethnic, linguistic, and religious distinctiveness. In what ways are Jewish communities different from other minority groups? Many students of ethnicity, and many Jews themselves play down the "religious" definition of Jews, emphasizing ethnic, national or cultural definitions. Professor Shaffir gives us a case where these religious elements are strongly emphasized and insisted upon. This study should be of interest to those interested in the extent to which patterns of Jewish life, assimilation and insulation depart from those of other kinds of minority groups. On this issue, I would point out that the majority of every foreign language minority group has opted for English Canada except one: Yiddish is the only maternal language group more numerous in Québec than in Ontario.

The portrait of the Lubavitcher in this monograph is a striking success. This I attribute to Professor Shaffir's willingness to invest the vast amounts of time, energy and emotion necessary to observe social life at very close range over an extended period of time; his unwillingness to be bound in his thinking by popular beliefs or preconceived "theories" of community life; his mastery and purposive use of Yiddish and Hebrew both in the conduct of the research and in the monograph itself.

His abundent use of field notes, interviews, and the language of the Lubavitcher in the analysis are a model for students using qualitative methodology. They insure that the reader comes away with an intimate understanding of the life and dilemmas of one small Canadian ethnic community.

Malcolm Spector
McGill University

The Book

This study deals with a community of religious Jews—Lubavitcher chassidim—and how they manage to persist in an urban setting. It is argued that in order for the community to maintain itself it must create a distinctive identity for its members and provide them with a tenable way of life. The first few chapters are addressed to how this is accomplished. As do other chassidic communities, the Lubavitcher define the outside world as threatening to their distinctive lifestyle but, unlike other chassidic communities, the members of this group do not attempt to isolate themselves from contact with outsiders. Instead, as the study shows, the Lubavitcher chassidim actively seek out contacts with the larger Jewish community. The latter part of the study examines why they do this and how they cope with the challenges and threats of assimilation posed by such contact. As the data suggest, to offset the potential distraction of assimilative contact with outsiders, the community constantly seeks to control the contexts of its members' contact with outsiders. Proselytizing activities, characteristic of the Lubavitcher chassidim, while seemingly endangering the community's tenability serve, in fact, to provide interactional contexts with a religious base, making religion the explicit focus of attention. Such activities, far from eroding the strength of the community actually reinforce and strengthen the community's distinctive identity.

The data for the study were collected by means of participant observation during which time the researcher spent time within the chassidic community and participated in a variety of activities. While this study focusses on the Lubavitch community in Montreal, the ever-present influence of the Lubavitcher *Rebbe*— the leader of this chassidic group—is emphasized throughout.

The Author

Bill Shaffir completed both his undergraduate and graduate degrees at McGill University, receiving his PhD in Sociology in 1972. He is presently an assistant professor in the Sociology Department at McMaster University, and has recently co-edited *Decency & Deviance: Studies in Deviant Behaviour.* Dr. Shaffir's present research includes co-editing a text in Introductory Sociology and participating in a study focusing on student socialization at the McMaster medical school.

Preface

This study, which is both an extended and compact version of my doctoral dissertation on the Lubavitch chassidic community in Montreal, examines how such a community of orthodox Jews persists in an urban setting. It is not an exaggeration that chassidic Jews and their way of life have been and continue to be misunderstood by the larger Jewish and Gentile community. I have attempted in this study to present the lifestyle of one such chassidic community from the viewpoint of the participants, with the hope that the reader will begin to better comprehend this peoples' way of life. While I have spent considerable time researching two other chassidic communities in this city—specifically the Satmarer and Tasher—I have utilized data from that research sparingly and mainly for purposes of contrast and comparison with the Lubavitch community. The city of Montreal contains within its borders several chassidic groups. Hopefully, additional research will examine the manner in which these other chassidic communities organize their way of life, the relationships between them, the problems they encounter and the strategies used to deal with them. An excellent beginning in this regard has been made by Jacques Gutwirth (1973) whose recent analysis of the chassidic communities in Montreal should lay the groundwork for more intensive and detailed studies.

As the reader will note throughout the study, I have chosen to leave many Yiddish and Hebrew terms in their original form rather than trying to translate them. The reason for this is that, although a roughly equivalent English term might have made it easier for the reader, it would not, I believe, have provided a faithful rendition of Lubavitchers' use of language and, consequently, their view of the world. Lubavitcher seldom use such words as "pray" and "Sabbath" except when speaking to outsiders, and among themselves normally use *davn* and *Shabbess*. For Lubavitcher and those close to them these words assume a certain intuitive and consistent meaning. To replace them with their closest English equivalent would violate this meaning and therefore, has not been attempted.

A major reason for the above editorial decision relates to the impossibility of translating the exact meaning of Yiddish and Hebrew words into English. The meanings of these words change as the contexts in which they are used differ. Two examples are the words *bocher* and *Yiddishkayt*. A literal translation of the first word would be "a young boy, an unmarried male." In the Lubavitch community, however, this word is primarily used to designate students—more specifically, students in the *Bays Medresh*. When a Lubavitcher mentions "the bocherim", he is referring to those students. When he singles out a middle-aged man as a *bocher* this indicates the person's marital status. It is also impossible to translate the word *Yiddishkayt* unequivocally. As with the word *bocher* its meaning is altered by the circumstances in which it is used. When a Lubavitcher says about someone: "He knows about *Yiddishkayt*", *Yiddishkayt* refers to a familiarity with the Torah's laws governing Jewish life. When, however, this same Lubavitcher inquires: "Do you learn about *Yiddishkayt* in that school? " the word refers to the degree to which the Torah's commandments are practised. The word can also refer to matters pertaining to Judaism and to Jews, viewed from an orthodox perspective, as when a Lubavitcher once remarked to me: "People sit around talking about *Yiddishkayt*— young people putting on *Tefillin*, eating kosher food . . ." It should, therefore, be possible to appreciate the difficulties involved in organizing the glossary in which the Yiddish and Hebrew words used in this study are translated into English.

Although the YIVO Institute of Jewish Research has published rules governing orthography, they are generally ignored in this study. The spelling I have used follows the pronunciation of the Lubavitcher themselves. The reader will notice, however, that in several instances the spelling of Yiddish and Hebrew words quoted from Lubavitch publications differs from that used in this study. Lubavitcher, for instance, spell *Shabbos, Mitzvoth*, and *Yiddishkeit*, while I have decided to spell these words *Shabbess, Mitzvess* and *Yiddishkayt*. This spelling, I argue, reflects Lubavitcher's pronunciation of these words more accurately. I have tried to spell the words phonetically and in so doing have used "ch" instead of "kh" to spell such words as *brocheh, chossid* and *Chumesh*. When a word is so widely used as to have become standardized, I conform to the popular spelling as, for example, in the case of *Yeshiva* and *Torah*.

William Shaffir

Acknowledgements

My experiences with the Lubavitcher chassidim will always be treasured. Lubavitcher chassidim have acquired a well-deserved reputation for being hospitable and sincere in their encounters with other Jews. These attributes were clearly reflected in the manner in which they were both interested and tolerant of my research activities. To the many who gave of their time to speak with me, I owe thanks. To those individuals in the Lubavitch community with whom I frequently consulted about my ideas and intentions, I owe a special debt of gratitude.

Those who know me know the high esteem in which I regard Malcolm Spector who was my supervisor in Graduate School at McGill University. His constant encouragement and enthusiasm were mainly responsible for my completing the dissertation and thus for the appearance of this book. I also wish to thank Gordon Inglis, the general editor of this series, for his highly insightful comments.

I wish to acknowledge the financial support of the Canada Council under whose sponsorship the research was begun. A research grant provided by the Canada Council to Malcolm Spector in 1969 permitted me to begin my research for my Master's thesis, and a doctoral fellowship awarded me a few years later allowed me to devote myself completely to writing the doctoral dissertation. I also wish to thank the Faculty of Graduate Studies at McGill University for awarding me with a summer research scholarship for two years.

Other people deserve to be mentioned at this point. First, my father, M. M. Shaffir, who read the manuscript, provided helpful comments and is responsible for the unique spelling of the Yiddish and Hebrew words. By continually asking when the book will be published, my family and friends forced me to commit myself to completing the manuscript. Their interest and concern was continually appreciated. I am especially thankful to Abe Fuks who generously gave of his time to ensure that I had available a choice of photographs of the Lubavitcher chassidim.

Finally, for sharing both the exciting and discouraging aspects of this work, I thank my wife Rivka without whose understanding and patience this study could not have been completed. It is to her that I dedicate this book.

Contents

To Rivka

Chapter One

The Chassidic Movement

The chassidim are a religious movement within the framework of Jewish laws and practices, but with their own unique customs and traditions. Their everyday way of life is circumscribed by religious ideas and principles which differentiate them from other Jewish minority groups, both orthodox and non-orthodox. Although the chassidim are orthodox, all orthodox Jews are not necessarily chassidim. The distinction between chassidic and non-chassidic orthodox Jews lies primarily in the "intensity and emphasis in beliefs, varieties of Rabbinical allegiance, and social structure and organization." (Mintz, 1968:25) Chassidic Jews are viewed by the larger Jewish community as ultra orthodox and fanatical, for their observance of the Code of Jewish Law (*Shulchn Orech*) is far more zealous and meticulous than that of most Jews. Non-chassidic orthodox Jews also zealously perform and adhere to the prescribed commandments in every detail, but they differ in that the *Rebbe*[1] is the central figure to chassidic Jews whereas non-chassidic orthodox Jews have no comparable religious leader.

What commonly is referred to as the chassidic community is, in fact, a number of chassidic groups, each with its loyalty and devotion to its own *Rebbe* (leader of a chassidic group). While it is true that these groups share the desire to maintain the integrity of orthodox Judaism, they are sometimes sharply divided on practice, points of philosophy, and the personality of their leaders. It is a mistake to view chassidim as a unified sub-division of Judaism, as the important dissimilarities among the various groups result in different social organization and techniques of insulation.

In Montreal, where the research for this book was conducted, there are followers of several chassidic groups, including Lubavitch, Satmar, Belz, Klausenburg, and Tash. All of these groups and other, smaller, chassidic courts share at least the one common feature that they attempt to insulate themselves socially and culturally from the larger community in order to maintain their distinctive way of life. The strategies utilized to achieve this goal vary among the different groups. The Tasher chassidim, for example, have established their Yeshiva (school of religious study) in the rural setting of Ste. Therese, eighteen miles north of Montreal. The reason for selecting this site was stated in a Tasher pamphlet:

> The concentration of thoughts, which is the basic require-
> ment for efficient studies, could only be achieved in the
> undisturbed atmosphere of a small town, outside the tur-
> bulent life of a large city.

The physical distance of this community from the larger city ensures that its way of life will be only minimally disturbed by outside influences.

Although the Satmar community is situated in the city, its followers strongly discourage any form of unnecessary interaction with outsiders, regardless of whether or not they are Jewish. Satmarers' reputation for not extending friendly welcomes to strangers and their constant efforts to condemn practices in the larger Jewish community that they believe detrimental to the persistence of orthodox Judaism serve to maintain the community's social boundaries.

Lubavitch, the chassidic community studied in detail in this book, is known for its greater adaptability to Western customs. Of all chassidic groups in the city, Lubavitch is unique in its efforts to impress upon Jews of varying degrees of religious belief the importance of adopting orthodox Jewish principles as a guide to everyday life.

History of the Chassidic Movement

The first *Rebbe* and founder of the chassidic movement was Rabbi Yisroel Baal Shem Tov (Master of the Good Name), a native of Podolia which, at the time, belonged to Poland but is now part of the Soviet Union of the Ukraine. Chassidism arose in the second quarter of the eighteenth century and from its founding to the present day has remained the most influential social and religious movement within Judaism. From Podolia it eventually spread to White Russia, Lithuania, Roumania, and Hungary. Later, through the mass immigration of Eastern European Jews to America between 1881 and 1914 and after the Second World War, the chassidic movement was established on the North American continent.

The early success and growth of the chassidic movement was undoubtedly a direct result of the social, cultural, and economic conditions of Eastern European Jewry around the turn of the eighteenth century. (Minkin, 1935; Mindel, 1969; Rabinowicz, 1970; Dubnow, 1918) Some knowledge of the conditions pertaining in Poland at this time is therefore of help in explaining both how the movement originated and why it spread so rapidly.

The scheme of communal government organized by Polish Jewry resulted in it being the most highly organized Jewish community in Europe by the middle of the sixteenth century. The cornerstone of this organization was the *Kahal* (council) in each community to which the elders were elected. The Polish Government, used the *Kahal* as a convenient tool for collecting taxes from Jews, and supported its efforts to regulate the everyday life of its community members. The Local and District Councils were, in turn, subject to the authority of the highest body, known as the "Council of Four Lands," (*Va'ad Arba Aratzot*). This elaborate organization in Poland and Lithuania gave great impetus to Torah education in the first half of the seventeenth century:

In no country . . . was the study of Torah (the Pentateuch) so widespread among the Jews as in the Kingdom of Poland. Every Jewish community maintained a yeshibah, paying its president a large salary, so as to enable him to conduct the institution without worry and to devote himself entirely to the pursuit of learning. . . . Moreover, every Jewish community supported college students, . . . giving them a certain amount of money per week, so that they might study under the direction of the president. . . . The (poor) boys obtained their food either from the charity fund or from the public kitchen. A community of fifty Jewish families would support no less than thirty of these young men and boys, one family supplying board for one college student and his two pupils, the former sitting at the family table like one of the sons. . . . There was scarcely a

3

home in the whole Kingdom of Poland where the Torah was not studied and where either the head of the family, or his son or his son-in-law, or the yeshibah student boarding with him, was not an expert in Jewish learning; frequently all of these could be found under one roof . . . (Dubnow, 1918; 116-117)

This golden epoch only lasted for a short time. Polish oppression of the Ukraine resulted in a Cossack insurrection that directly affected the Jews, many of whom were employed as stewards by Polish noblemen and were responsible for collecting taxes from the Ukrainian peasantry. Since the Polish magnates were absentee landlords, the Cossacks encountered the Jews more frequently than they did their noble and clerical masters. (Graetz, 1967) It was little wonder then, that, in reacting to their intolerable oppression, the Cossacks unleashed their anger upon the Jews. Led by Bogdan Chmelnitzski in 1648, the Cossacks organized their revenge against the Poles and the Jews whom they regarded as the agents and allies of their oppressors. "These tragic up- heavals throughout the second half of the seventeenth century left the Jewish population of Poland fearfully decimated, eco- nomically ruined, and spiritually quite dazed." (Mindel, 1969:10)

It was more than a mere coincidence that 1648, which marked the wholesale murder of Polish Jewry, also marked the first public appearance of Sabbatai Zvi (1626-1676). His declaration that the Chmelnitzski massacres were the birthpangs of the Messiah and that he himself was the Messiah, gained him many followers. Dubnow writes that:

When, in the year 1666, the whole Jewish world resounded with the fame of Sabbatai Zvi as the messianic liberator of the Jewish people, the Jews of Poland responded with par- ticularly keen, almost morbid sensitiveness.

The Jews—says the contemporary Ukrainian Galatovski —triumphed. Some abandoned their houses and property, refusing to do any work and claiming that the Messiah would soon arrive and carry them on a cloud to Jerusalem. Others fasted for days, denying food even to their little ones, and during that severe winter bathed in ice-holes, at the same time reciting a recently composed prayer . . . (1918:205)

News eventually reached Poland that on his journey Sabbatai Zvi had been arrested in Constantinople and, when brought before the Sultan, was offered the choice between death or becoming a Moslem. Sabbatai Zvi chose to live, but not even his conversion to Islam could erradicate the messianic expectations that had been so firmly implanted in the minds of many Jews. By 1772, a number of Rabbis representing various communities were so alarmed by what they considered a dangerous heresy that they proclaimed that all Sabbatians who failed to return to the ways of orthodox Judaism would be excommunicated. Although partly successful, the excommunication threat failed to erradicate completely Sabbatianism which finally evolved into the movement known as Frankism. Led by Jacob Frank (1726-1791), who also proclaimed himself to be the Messiah, the followers of this movement eventually embraced Christianity.

The material impoverishment of the Jewish communities in Poland after 1648 soon was followed by a decline in their cultural level. The nature of this deterioration and its effect on the Jewish masses was important to the early acceptance and growth of the chassidic movement. Those parts of the country that suffered most from the "terrible decade"—1648-1658—also witnessed a decline in the intellectual level of the Jewish population. "Talmudic learning,[2] which was formerly widespread among the Jews of those provinces, now became the profession of a narrow circle of scholars, while the lower classes were stagnating in ignorance and superstition." (Dubnow, 1916:199) Class divisions became more inflexible and although scholars and ignorant masses worshipped the same God, they had little else in common and walked different ways. (Rabinowicz, 1960:18)

Although the *kahal* had survived the Cossack massacres, their power was declining by this time. As the Jewish masses were too impoverished to provide free education for themselves, the majority of Jewish children were uneducated, "and the gulf between the unlearned masses and the learned minority widened considerably. This cleavage extended to every facet of the social and religious life which greatly added to the miseries of the masses." (Mindel, 1969:13) Describing this cleavage, Rabinowicz writes:

The rabbi in Poland was a salaried official. His status was

high and his economic position relatively secure. Yet there was no bond, no communication between him and the lowly members of his community. He lived in their midst, but was not one of them. They consulted him on ritual matters, but he played no part in their day-to-day life. He rarely preached to them. The sermon was reserved for Shabbat HaGadol (the Sabbath preceding Passover) and Shabbat Shuva (the Sabbath before the Day of Atonement). It was neither on a theme they could understand, nor in a language they could follow. (1960:20)

Rabbinical Judaism at that time neither reflected the needs of the people, nor was concerned with the reality of their situation. The historian Graetz put it this way:

Rabbinical Judaism, as known in Poland, offered no sort of religious comfort. Its representatives placed the highest value upon the dialectic, artificial exposition of the Talmud and its commentaries. . . . Fine-spun decisions of new, complicated legal points occupied the doctors of the Talmud day and night. Moreover, this hairsplitting was considered sublimest piety, and superceded everything else. If anyone solved an intricate Talmudic question, or discovered something new, called Torah, he felt self-satisfied, and assured of his felicity hereafter. All other objects, the impulse to devotion, prayer, and emotion or interest in the moral condition of the community, were secondary matters, to which scarcely any attention was paid. The mental exercise of making logical deductions from the Talmud, . . . choked off other intellectual pursuits in Poland. Religious ceremonies had degenerated, both among Talmudists and the unlearned, into meaningless usages, and prayer into mere lip-service. (1939:385)

The need for spiritual uplifting and guidance, which the formalities of Rabbinism failed to satisfy, remained alive among the Jewish masses. Such was the general state of Polish Jewry when the Baal Shem Tov—founder of the chassidic movement—appeared on the scene.

Yisroel Baal Shem Tov (Besht, an acronym, as his name was commonly abbreviated) was born about 1700 in Okup, a small town on the borders of Volhynia and Podolia. Orphaned at an early age, he was cared for by some of his charitable townsmen. He had left school at an early age but as he was fond of children became a teacher's assistant and later occupied the position of a synagogue beadle. In the year 1736, the Baal Shem Tov revealed himself as the leader of the new chassidic movement. Wandering through towns and villages, he became acquainted with the condition of Jewish life, and won the reputation of a miracle worker. In time he was regarded as a man of righteousness and saintliness by the Jewish masses.

A basic teaching of the Baal Shem Tov was that it was everyone's duty to serve God and that this duty was not confined exclusively to the study of Talmud. It embraced, on the other hand, every aspect of one's daily life. The Besht's ministry stressed the joyful affirmation of life "and the hallowing of all passions and delight in the service of God" and counselled against asceticism and self-affliction. (Newman, 1963:xiii) The Baal Shem Tov's philosophy and teaching is best captured in the following excerpts:

> Originally a healer of the body, he imperceptibly grew to be a teacher of religion. He taught that true salvation lies not in Talmudic learning, but in whole-hearted devotion to God, in unsophisticated faith and fervent prayer. When he encountered men of learning, Besht endeavored to convince them of the correctness of his views by arguments from the Cabala. But he did not recognize the ascetic form of Cabala which enjoined upon the Jew to foster a mournful frame of mind, to kill the flesh, and strive after the expiation of sin in order to accelerate the coming of the Messiah. He rather had in mind that Cabala which seeks to establish an intimate communion between man and God, cheering the human soul by the belief in the goodness of God, encouraging and comforting the poor, the persecuted, and the suffering. Besht preached that the plain man, imbued with naive faith, and able to pray fervently and whole-heartedly, was dearer and nearer to God than the learned formalist spending his whole life in the study of Talmud. Not to speculate in religious matters, but to believe blindly and devotedly, such was the motto of Besht. . . . Communion with God is and must be the principal endeavor of every truly religious man. This communion may be attained by concentrating one's thoughts upon God, and attributing to

Him all happenings in life. The essence of faith lies in the emotions, not in the intellect; the more profound the emotions, the nearer man is to God. To render this communion perfect, prayer must be ecstatic and fervent, so that he who prays may, as it were, throw off his material film. To attain to this ecstatic condition, recourse may be made to mechanical contrivances, such as violent motions of the body, shouts, shaking, and so on. The study of Jewish religious legislation is of secondary importance, and is useful only when it succeeds in arousing an exalted religious disposition. From this point of view the reading of ethical books is preferable to the study of Talmudic casuistry and rabbinical folios. (Dubnow, 1916: 224-225: 226)

In the tradition of the Kabbala, the Besht taught that the end of Divine worship is attachment to G-d[3] (*devekuth*), which is essentually a service of the heart rather than the mind. For, ultimately, G-d cannot be apprehended rationally, and it is by means of emotional commitment and obedience to the Divine Will, rather than by intellectual speculation, that the human being can come closest to his Creator. ... To attain *devekuth*, the Besht preached, it is not even necessary to know the meaning of the prayers and psalms, or the significance of the religious precepts; the sincere recitation of the holy words and the simple performance of the precepts are in themselves sufficient to establish contact with G-d, provided the desire for communion was the object of the worship. This was a concession to the most illiterate, the *am ha-aretz*, as the Besht taught that none is excluded from Divine service. ... Above all, the Besht endeavored to instill the quality of joy in Divine service. To "serve G-d with joy" is a biblical precept which the Besht made a cornerstone of his popular religious philosophy. Indeed, being conscious of the proximity of the Creator everywhere and at all times, being aware that G-d is the essence of goodness, whose benevolent Providence extends to every individual and every particular, and having the opportunity to serve the Creator in so many ways in every-day life, the Besht could not see how any Jew sharing these feelings could experience anything but a perpetually happy frame of mind. (Mindel, 1969: 15-17)

"I have come into this world," maintained the Besht, "to

show man how to live by three precepts: love of God, love of Israel and love of the Torah." According to the Besht, there are no divisions between the sacred and the secular, God is everywhere. "No place is free of Him," and there are no veils between Man and his Creator. ... His radiance might be glimpsed anywhere and everywhere. For those who have eyes to see, the world is a mirror in which is reflected the glory of God. ... Though a child of the Cabbalah, the Besht rejected its asceticism. In his eyes, self-mortification was devised by Satan to afflict men both physically and spiritually.

Joy was the keynote of the Besht's philosophy. "Our Father in Heaven hates sadness and rejoices when His children are joyful. And when are His children joyful? When they carry out His Commandments." This immediate, this wordly joy is the true reward, the greatest reward, for the performance of a good deed or the fulfilment of a commandment (Mitzvah). ... Tears of joy are permitted and are even desirable. But a man should subdue sadness and raise himself to the higher realms of joy . . . .

Worshipping with sponteneity was more important than worshipping at prescribed times. *Hitlahavut* ("enthusiasm") and ecstacy replaced formalism. (Rabinowicz, 1970:34-37)

It was only after the Baal Shem Tov's death that the systematic dissemination of chassidism began. Rabbi Dov Bear—popularly known as the "Preacher of Mesritch"—succeeded the Besht and, developing his doctrine, surrounded himself with a "trained staff of apostles, who eventually became the founders of *Tzaddik* [an extremely righteous man] dynasties in various parts of Poland and Lithuania." (Dubnow, Ibid.:230) Chassidic houses of worship suddenly appeared in numerous communities. However, efforts to implant the chassidic philosophy among the Jewish masses did not always meet with immediate success.

The opponents of the chassidim, the *Misnagdim*, viewed the former as a dangerous element in Judaism. The first violent attack upon chassidim was made by Elijah of Vilna (1720-1797) who "beheld in the Chassidic aberration a continuation of Frank's excesses and corruptive influence." (Graetz, Ibid. 1939:391) A letter addressed to all the large communities directed them to excommunicate the followers of chassidism unless they abandoned their different and erroneous views. (Graetz, Ibid.:392) In many towns of Lithuania the chassidim became objects of persecution, being referred to as the "godless sect." (Dubnow, Ibid.:237) The chassidim, however, remained firm not submitting to their opponents, and formed themselves into groups, each with a leader called *Rebbe.*

By 1781, another *chayrem* (excommunication) was proclaimed against the chassidim. They were declared to be heretics and were to be totally ostracized by all orthodox Jews. Intermarriage with them was to be avoided, their meat and wine were outlawed, their literature was not to be studied, and no community could permit them to hold a position as cantor, rabbi, or teacher. (Rabinowicz, 1970:64) In time, the opposition to the chassidic movement subsided and was accepted as an integral part of traditional Judaism. "While warring with one another, Rabbinism and Hassidism found a point of contact in their common hatred of the new Enlightenment . . . " (Dubnow, Ibid.:238)

The Lubavitcher Chassidim

Chabad (Lubavitch) chassidism was founded in Lithuania in 1773 and in time developed into one of the strongest and most dynamic branches of chassidism. The term "Chabad" is an acronym of three words which signify the intellectual powers— *Chochmoh* (wisdom), *Beenoh* (understanding), and *Daas* (knowledge). These are the three basic principles of the *Alter Rebbe's* (Rabbi Schneur Zalman, the first Lubavitcher *Rebbe*) interpretation of Judaism as a way to God.

The historical centre of Chabad chassidism was the town of Lubavitch, situated in White Russia. For more than 102 years Lubavitch was the seat of four generations of Chabad *Rebbeim* (plural of *Rebbe*) and the centre of Chabad chassidism. It was only in 1915, when Lubavitch was evacuated during the First World War that the seat of Lubavitcher *Rebbeim* and the centre of the Lubavitcher chassidim was moved.

One of the main tenets of the Lubavitcher *Rebbeim* and their chassidim is *Ahavas Yisroel*, love for the Jewish people. To love a fellow Jew, taught the *Rebbeim*, means to love him completely, body and soul. The work of Lubavitch among Jews therefore, aims "to improve both the material conditions of their people as well as their spiritual standards." (Outline Of The Social And

10

Communal Work of Chabad Lubavitch :6) The chain of social and community work both for the physical and spiritual welfare of the Jewish people was carried on by each of the Lubavitcher *Rebbeim*.

The first Lubavitcher *Rebbe* to visit America was Rabbi Jacob Isaac Schneerson. At the end of the first summer after the outbreak of World War II, Rabbi Schneerson was forced to flee Poland and at the beginning of 1940 he, together with his family, came to New York. Upon his arrival in America, the *Rebbe* immediately began to arrange the rescue of his students caught in war-torn Europe. A few days after arriving in New York he founded the Central Yeshiva, Tomchei Tmimim, in Brooklyn, New York. Two years later he helped establish a Yeshiva in Montreal. A Lubavitcher describes the state of American Jewry during the 1930s before the Lubavitcher *Rebbe's* arrival:

Only one who was here during the thirties can appreciate the bland hopelessness that characterized Torah Jewry in America before the terrible War. Yiddishkeit was a vestige, maintained almost entirely by immigrants and repudiated almost without exception by their American-born children. Yeshivos, few but valiant, boasted sons of *Klai Kodesh* (the lay parents could not speak English yet) as their student body. Pessimism about the future seemed quite realistic. Yiddishkeit was a transplant from the Old Country, and the years would take their inevitable toll, until there would simply be no Torah Jews born and raised here.

During that blackest hour, when physical destruction hovered over European Jewry, and spiritual dissolution threatened American Jewry, the *Rebbe* n'e, before he actually set foot on these shores, was making firm plans for his American Yeshiva, resolved that this country can and will be a home for Torah. In America the *Rebbe* demonstrated that the spark hidden within every Jewish soul can be kindled. Distressed by the deplorable study of Torah education here, the *Rebbe* founded the first Yeshivos Ketanos in the smaller communities of the East that never knew of such schools before. The *Rebbe's* pioneering was soon emulated, the *chinuch* trails he blazed in America have become highways today, as witness the Yeshivos and Day Schools that are American Jewry's brightest hope. (*Di Yiddishe Heim*, Vol. 6, No. 3:3)

During his years in America the Lubavitcher *Rebbe* did much to strengthen the Jewish religion, establishing Yeshivess and Talmud Torah's (schools) and other institutions of Jewish learning. He was responsible also, for founding a network of organizations and institutions, among them the United Lubavitcher Yeshivas *Tomchei Tmimim*, in the United States and Canada, the *Merkos L'Inyonei Chinuch*—the educational branch of the Lubavitch movement—schools for Jewish girls called *Bays Rivkeh* and *Bays Sorreh,* and the *Kehot* Publication Society "dedicated to issuing books in the true spirit of Torah and traditions."

The Lubavitch Community in Montreal

The Lubavitch community in Montreal dates back to the arrival of nine Lubavitch students in 1941, although the effects of the *Rebbe's* social and community work already had been felt in the Jewish community there. Before 1941 there were a few Lubavitcher chassidim and Lubavitch sympathizers in Montreal but until the arrival of these students there was no organized Lubavitcher community or Yeshiva in the city.

The nine Lubavitcher were refugees from the Polish Lubavitcher Yeshiva near Warsaw. With the outbreak of the Second World War, many Yeshiva students from all over Europe fled to Vilna, the capital of Lithuania, which, between the two World Wars, was an independent country. Among these refugees were thirty-nine Lubavitcher students. The Japanese Consulate in Vilna generously granted visas for many of the refugees and obtained permission for them to travel across Russia to Japan. Most continued to Shanghai and from there applied to the Canadian Government for permission to emigrate to Canada. The Canadian Government responded by issuing eighty visas to Jewish refugees.

These events were well publicized in the Montreal Yiddish newspaper, *Der Keneder Odler.* On September 28, 1941, a front-page article stated that:

> As our readers already know, permission was granted to bring to Canada eighty Yeshiva students and scholars . . . who were for quite some time in Japan and are presently in Shanghai. According to a cable received from Shanghai, forty of them . . . will depart either today or

already departed yesterday, and will hopefully arrive in Montreal in approximately twenty days. The remaining forty are expected to leave Shanghai one week later (translated from the Yiddish).

On October 17, in another front-page article we read:

> ... a number of Yeshiva students have already reached San Francisco, and they are presently en route to Montreal. We are presenting the entire name list of the expected arrivals. ... The remaining group of Yeshiva leit is expected in the immediate future. They voluntarily remained behind as their poor health would not permit them to observe the two-day fast for the Yom Kippur holiday while they were travelling.
>
> It is expected that the eighty Yeshiva students for whom the Canadian Government issued visas will arrive in Canada shortly, and that a Torah centre will be established in our city, perhaps the largest on this continent.

On October 24, twenty-eight Yeshiva students and Rabbis arrived at the Bonaventure railroad station and were brought to the Talmud Torah school on St. Joseph Boulevard for a breakfast reception. A Lubavitcher Rabbi, sent from New York to greet the students, wrote:

> Friday morning ... there was a big breakfast reception for the newcomers in the Montreal Talmud Torah. ... The interest of the city's Jews was intense; the Talmud Torah was packed with rabbis, representatives from synagogues, organizations and just ordinary concerned fellow Jews. Everyone competed for the honor of having one of the refugees as a guest till permanent arrangements could be made for them. (*Di Yiddishe Heim*, Vol. 10, No. 3:4-5)

The Jewish community planned to establish one united Yeshiva in Montreal. However, the Lubavitcher considered themselves different from the rest of the community, especially in terms of their philosophy, and, as the previous *Rebbe* had instructed his followers to found a Yeshiva, the Lubavitcher were determined to open their own separate Yeshiva. Although the consensus in the Jewish community was that it was financially impossible to support two Yeshivas, the Lubavitcher persisted and opened their

Yeshiva in the basement of the Nusach Ari synagogue on 100 Pine Avenue East.

Lubavitchers' zeal to obey their *Rebbe's* instructions is best reflected through their monthly newspaper publication, *Der Chaver.* The paper, which was started in May, 1942 and ran for just over a year, included stories and articles both in Yiddish and English and gave Lubavitcher the opportunity to publicize their activities to the larger Jewish community. The paper was written to appeal to both adults and children and focused on the importance of pursuing one's daily life in an orthodox Jewish manner. *Der Chaver's* first issue included the following statement of purpose:

In these days when the Jewish population is flooded by periodicals of all kinds, for the old, the young, and even small children, there is sufficient reading material in all three languages—Yiddish, Hebrew and English. It is, therefore, imperative to clarify what our aims are in publishing this monthly magazine.

In order to clarify the aims of the periodical it is necessary to provide a short description of the youth organization, *Oineg Hoirim* (Pleasure For Parents) which, in fact, is the sponsor of this periodical. Since youth organizations in general are, thank G-d, in abundance . . . the name of a new youth organization does not make an impression, and does not lead people to become interested in the nature of the organization and its organizers and goals. In our case, however, immediately upon hearing the name *Oineg Hoirim* . . . one is quick to recognize that this is a unique kind of movement, with specific ideals. . . . The organization's affiliation with the Yeshiva Tomche Tmimim Lubavitch testifies to its uniqueness.

Thanks to the energetic endeavours of the students of the Lubavitcher Yeshiva which, in turn, were guided by their great *Rebbe* Shlita, the elementary Yeshiva has made great progress both quantitatively and qualitatively in spite of the fact that it has been in existence only a short time. During the several months since it was established, the Yeshiva has managed to recruit close to 100 students, *kayn yirboo* (may their numbers increase). In addition, the Yeshiva has acquired great popularity among all the Jews in Canada, and especially in the Montreal Jewish community, as a place where the Torah is taught in order to preserve its

14

holiness, and where fear of G-d and love of the Torah, as well as good qualities of character, are embedded in the student body.

The leaders of the Yeshiva aim to ensure that the pupil will be absorbed in the Yeshiva lifestyle, not merely during his regular study classes, but also throughout the day. . . . He should still be influenced by the Yeshiva's teachings during his playtime. It was for this reason that the Yeshiva organized the *Oineg Hoirim* organization, for its purpose is to give parents joy in seeing their children's righteous behaviour in fearing G-d, as this is the primary joy that parents should receive from their children.

At the meetings of the *Oineg Hoirim* Club, lectures are given on honouring one's parents, love for the Torah, love for one's fellow Jew, etc. The lecturers are the leaders of the Yeshiva. . . . Students are also entertained by and participate in joyful chassidic melodies. Chassidic stories are recounted and the atmosphere is one of love and brother-hood—which is, incidentally, one of the main essentials of a Yeshiva in general, and especially of the Lubavitcher Yeshiva. This is the manner in which these virtues are inculcated into the student body. . . .

Unfortunately this movement has not expanded in accordance with the efforts expended—it has remained con-fined to the pupils of the *Oineg Hoirim* Club and a small number of their friends.

In order to improve the situation, this periodical has been established to serve as a platform from which our voice may be heard among a large mass of Jewish youth. This periodical should serve as a powerhouse from which electrical currents will be generated to reach those places where people live in spiritual poverty.

The periodical should also unite the pupils and their friends and serve as a channel of communication. (trans-lated from Yiddish)

In most issues there was one section of articles in English and Yiddish written by Lubavitcher Yeshiva students. It was hoped these would impress younger readers and their parents with the contentment and satisfaction the students experienced through their affiliation with the Lubavitcher Yeshiva.

A TURNING POINT IN MY LIFE

Have you ever felt that some incident has marked a turning

point in in your life? Well, I have.

It happened one night about 5 months ago. My father came home that night excited and thrilled. When I asked what it was, he told me that nine refugees from the Lubavitcher Yeshivas in Poland had arrived and were going to make a Yeshiva in our city. On hearing this I was not even excited or thrilled about the idea, but just passed it up, thinking it did not concern me. Then at supper my father told me all about them and asked me to come down and see how these young Rabbis studied the Talmud. I would have none of it. After much arguing my father persuaded me to go down and I agreed to it.

On arriving at the synagogue my heart began to beat a little faster. I could feel that this was going to be an experience I would never forget. I am an average Canadian orthodox boy. On seeing this sight for the first time in my life a change came over me. I was attracted to these Rabbis who, although young, were wearing payes and beards and sitting so proudly studying the Talmud. They talked to me in a very friendly way and like a magnet they pulled me towards them and soon I began to feel as if I had known them all my life. Then they asked me to become a Talmid in the Yeshiva and I felt that I would be the only Talmid, but finally I was persuaded and now there are 80 Talmidim in our Yeshiva.

and:

WHY I JOINED THE YESHIVATH

. . . For a long time now, my friends at English school have been asking me: What's the use of your going to the Yeshivath after school and learning Chumosh, Rashe, Gemoreh, Tanach, etc., for while I sit learning, they play football, baseball and many other games. . . . It is true that in childhood you enjoy playing games and spending your time at leisure but this is limited. Now you are playing but as you grow older you stop playing baseball or football, your leisure days will be over, then what will you have left from your childhood? Your older days will be empty without religion, Torah, or knowledge. You will not even be able to say Kaddish for your parents "after 120 years" (after their death). But as for me, even though I do spend less time now in play, I will grow up—if God is willing—a proud Yeshivath student, a Talmud-Chacham, like all my other fellow students, who learn with me at the Yeshivath.

It was hoped that *Der Chaver* would impress upon the larger Jewish community the importance of living an orthodox Jewish life. It printed news about the Yeshiva's progress, articles relating to the Lubavitcher *Rebbe's* activities in New York, and articles emphasizing the significance of the Jewish holidays.

The Lubavitcher Yeshiva in Montreal was founded immediately after the nine Libavitchers' arrival. They affiliated themselves with the Nusach Ari synagogue on Pine Avenue E. and were allowed to use the building's basement as their headquarters for little over a year. Although the school was only open from 4:30 p.m. to 7:00 p.m., the Yeshiva attracted approximately eighty students within a few months. The curriculum centred on religious instruction and special attention was devoted to instructing students how to behave in an orthodox manner. The Yeshiva was divided into sections, according to age and background knowledge of Judaism, with three sections located at the Nusach Ari synagogue and the remaining two in synagogues on Clark St. and Fairmount. Tuition was free as the Lubavitcher did not want lack of finances to deter any parents wishing to provide their sons with a Yeshiva education. The Yeshiva began charging tuition only when it moved to a new location on Park Avenue in 1943. Even then, however, students were readily admitted regardless of their parents' financial circumstances. In 1942, Gan Israel, a summer camp, was founded so that the Yeshiva activities could continue throughout the summer in the pleasant surroundings of Ste. Agathe in the Laurentian Mountains. Classes were also continued at the Yeshiva's branches in Montreal throughout the summer vacation, but at Gan Israel the campers could follow their religious instruction along with a varied recreational program. As one Lubavitcher wrote:

> The decision to organize the camp demonstrates the gradual growth of the Lubavitcher Yeshiva and of the new trend in education which the group has brought to Montreal. Although the Lubavitcher emphasize both the physical and spiritual development of the child, he is closely guarded so that he is not adversely influenced, G-d forbid, by worldly concerns and does not deviate from a Torah way of life.

17

The Lubavitcher Yeshiva was founded in Montreal ten months ago, and the pupil was to be exposed to an orthodox Jewish education by implanting in him piety and respect for the Torah, and instilling in him a desire to study Torah, to perform good deeds, and to have confidence and faith in G-d.

But with the arrival of the so-called summer vacation, the leaders of the Yeshiva became worried that the results of their efforts during the school year would be jeopardized . . . because whether the youngster was in the country or at a summer camp in which the religious atmosphere was lax, he might be jeered at because of his religious education and conduct. The outcome of the summer camp experience might, G-d forbid, uproot the youngster's feeling for Torah and Yiddishkayt. The result of such a summer camp vacation might be physically beneficial for the child but, at the same time, spiritually disastrous. (translated from Yiddish)

During their first year in Montreal, the nine Lubavitchers' main aim was to impress the relevance of orthodox Judaism upon the Jewish community. They reacted sharply against many Jews' slack attitude toward Sabbath observance and the laws pertaining to Kashruth and family purity. They were concerned that Jewish parents were neglecting their children's upbringing and not providing them with an orthodox Jewish education and to this end organized meetings to which the Jewish public was invited. At one such meeting a Lubavitcher maintained that parents preferred to supplement their income by urging their children to work part-time after school, rather than sending them to a Yeshiva. That meeting resulted in the following resolution:

1. Those present should urge their friends and acquaintances to observe the Sabbath, Kashruth, and laws pertaining to family purity.
2. Those in attendance should urge their friends to send their children to the Yeshiva. Those knowing the addresses of younger parents, who may not yet fully appreciate the importance of the Yeshiva should send the addresses to the Yeshiva and certain people would contact them and hopefully convince them to enrol their children in the Yeshiva.
3. To organize a Sabbath observers group which would propagandize the importance of Sabbath observance and do everything

possible to strengthen Sabbath observance in the Jewish community.

During 1942 and 1943 the Lubavitch Yeshiva continued to expand and used temporary quarters in various synagogues until it finally settled on Park Avenue in June, 1943 where it remained until 1962.

Within the first years of their arrival the Lubavitcher managed to attract a number of sympathetic supporters who assisted them in their activities.[4] The fact that there was already a Nusach Ari synagogue in Montreal helped as some members of the congregation had ancestors who had been connected with the Lubavitch movement in Europe, although by this time most of their descendants in Montreal had been assimilated and lost touch with the traditions and beliefs of the old country. Even with this support, disseminating traditional Judaism to the larger Jewish community was not an easy task. As one Lubavitcher recalls:

> . . . most probably you've heard that when the first Lubavitcher came over, people made bets how long it would be till they shaved off their beards. Some didn't even give them one week. Some said at most it would be a few months and then they would be like all the others. And, of course, to some of them, I suppose, they thought this was going to be detrimental to the Jewish community in Montreal because America or Canada or Montreal are not places for such kind of *Yiddishkayt*. . . . You know, even many well-meaning and well-wishing people said: "Well, you came over. Well, good, fine, very nice. But how are they going to settle? Who's going to marry such people?

Some of the difficulties the Lubavitcher encountered in settling in a new country were of a more practical nature. Even by 1947 kosher baking and dairy products were not readily available in the community. As a Lubavitch woman recalls:

> There were women who were baking at home, particularly a *challeh* for *Shabbess*, and if you didn't bake yourself you could purchase from these women. And there were also private people who brought in kosher dairy products and we bought from them.

Only in the late 1940s, with the arrival of other chassidic groups such as the Satmarer and Beltzer, whose members started commercial production of kosher food and dairy products, did these become available on a regular daily basis.

In 1943 several young men from the Canadian Government's internment camp at Isle Aux Nois, Quebec, joined the Lubavitch community. They were among the German and Austrian Jews who had been interned as prisoners of war in England after the German invasion of the Netherlands and had been shipped to Canada after the fall of France. About eighteen months later, a number of these Jews were released as a result of the Canadian Jewish Congress' appeal to the Canadian Government to allow the Jewish students to continue their studies. As a result of these efforts, fifteen young men eventually affiliated themselves with the Lubavitch community in Montreal. As they were already orthodox Jews, the friendship extended to them by Lubavitch in time encouraged them to become Lubavitcher chassidim. As one of them recalls:

> ... Many of us were very much impressed with Lubavitch. Lubavitch has something unique which you don't find anywhere else. As I told you last time, many of us felt that the Ahavas Yisroel and the selflessness that Lubavitch gave out was the right idea and connected ourselves with the Lubavitch *Rebbe* and, of course, later on we went to New York ... and all this helped to make us Lubavitcher chassidim.

By mid-1943 the community had grown to approximately twenty-five individuals. In addition, two of the original nine Lubavitcher had married which further increased the number of people affiliated with the community. As a Lubavitch woman explained:

> ... Now the families of the girls they married usually also became Lubavitcher. A good example would be Rabbi A. He married a girl whose maiden name was Z. Now her parents were very religious, but they weren't Lubavitcher. They met Rabbi A. and he came into the family and got the parents to feel the way he does and to be Lubavitcher too. Mrs. A. had two younger sisters who were growing up and it sort of became accepted that these two girls would probably marry Lubavitcher too, because the atmosphere at

home is already sort of Lubavitch oriented. And then Rabbi A's father-in-law had brothers who were religious but they weren't Lubavitcher. Now their children also became Lubavitcher and they had cousins and grandparents and everyone became Lubavitcher . . . .

In this way the Lubavitcher were able to increase their proselytizing activities in the city. In 1943, for example, an afternoon school on St. Dominique near Marie Anne was taken over by this chassidic group. Tuition fees were immediately eliminated and registration soon increased from thirty to approximately 200 students. The school flourished till the mid-fifties when the neighbourhood's Jewish population moved further west. In addition, by June, 1943 the Yeshiva had already organized *Messibbess Shabbess* (Sabbath gathering of Jewish youth) groups for Jewish children in the area. The groups met on Saturday afternoons and were led by older Yeshiva students who instructed Jewish children in the ways of traditional Judaism and instilled in them the desire to receive a religious education. A year later, the *Bays Rivkeh*—the Lubavitch girls' school—was organized, and in 1944-45 the Lubavitcher Yeshiva became a day school offering religious studies in the morning and secular subjects in the afternoon. In spite of these changes, the Yeshiva continued to offer afternoon classes for Jewish students attending Protestant schools.

The Yeshiva's location on Park Avenue became the focal point of Lubavitcher activities. It became increasingly important for Lubavitcher to reside in the vicinity of the Yeshiva for it was there that they congregated for prayer and community celebrations. Close proximity to the Yeshiva also meant frequent contact with one another so that the chassidic Jews could share experiences and remain closely informed about important events. The area bounded by Clark St. and Hutchison St. to the east and west, and St. Joseph's Blvd., and Bernard St. to the south and north, remained with only a few exceptions as the Lubavitch area of settlement until 1962-1965 when the Yeshiva moved further west.

During the next few years the community increased through a steady birthrate and also managed to attract some new individual supporters, but there was no further influx of Lubavitcher to

21

Montreal until 1947. In that year a group of about thirty Lubavitcher of Russian origin who had been stranded in Shanghai for the duration of World War II travelled to the United States, and a little later seven of the group settled in Montreal. About three years later, the final influx of Lubavitcher to the community started to arrive from Russia via Paris. Between 1950 and 1953 some seventy-seven Lubavitcher, including women and children, eventually reached Montreal and settled in the vicinity of the Yeshiva. With these new arrivals the Lubavitch community numbered around sixty families.

The Yeshiva's move in 1962 to Westbury and Plamondon in the Snowdon area of the city was prompted by two considerations. First, the facilities available to the Yeshiva on Park Avenue were inadequate to accommodate the relatively large student body. The Yeshiva had been looking for a new site for some time, and when it was offered land for a new building it immediately approved the new location. Second, most families whose children were enrolled in the Yeshiva had already moved further west into more expensive houses. It thus became practical to move the Yeshiva to a more central locale. The two considerations were, in fact, closely related. As a Lubavitcher put it:

> During the war years there was no thought of moving. Of course from 1941 till, let's say 47-48, till the war years wore off . . . everything was restricted and, of course, after the war years it took time. There was not enough materials . . . and there was no thought of moving. People stood fast in the places where they lived downtown. But in the beginning of the fifties when people started to move, the children were moved away. You must understand, people moved to much nicer homes. They didn't want their children to go to a school that was not up to date. I mean you lived in an up-to-date house, but to send the children back to Park Avenue was going to be difficult, to say the least. So there was the thought right there and then to build.

Within five or six years of its move to Westbury and Plamondon St., the majority of Lubavitcher lived within walking distance of the Yeshiva and approximately five years later the Lubavitch girls' school was established one block north of the Yeshiva. The move was not without its difficulties, however, for Lubavitcher encountered considerable opposition to their efforts to move to a new neighbourhood. A petition was circulated to those living in the vicinity of the proposed Yeshiva site to try to prevent the Lubavitch community obtaining the necessary building permit. Two Lubavitcher commented that:

> . . . people, nice people, at the time collected signatures not to give the Yeshiva a permit, because they were afraid. Again, they had just moved into a very nice neighbourhood, with very expensive homes, and they were afraid that as soon as the Yeshiva opened its doors the value of their property would fall by half.

> Opposition? Yes, there was. First of all, people felt that their homes would go down in value because a school isn't an asset to the neighbourhood. And there were synagogues that weren't very much in favour because they thought that the Yeshiva would probably have a big synagogue and would compete with their synagogue. . . .

The Community Today

It is difficult to estimate exactly the number of Lubavitch presently in the community for, as will be discussed in Chapter Two, there is no precise definition of a Lubavitcher. However, a number of Lubavitcher chassidim agreed that there are probably about one hundred families in the Montreal community at present which, counting the women and children, numbers about six hundred people.

The community is also supported by many non-orthodox and non-chassidic orthodox Jews who express varying degrees of loyalty both to the Lubavitch movement specifically and to orthodox Judaism in general. Many of these Jews offer little more than financial support, but others have been attracted to the point of participating in Lubavitch celebrations and other organized activities. As was the case when the first group of Lubavitcher arrived in 1941, the community is continually in touch with the Lubavitcher *Rebbe* and his headquarters in New York. The proselytizing zeal which characterized the community in the forties, fifties, and sixties appears to have made the Lubavitcher chassidim popular in the larger Jewish community, but, as was equally important from the very beginning, the community continues to guard against the larger society's potentially assimilative influences.

As will be shown in a later chapter, the Lubavitcher Yeshiva (school of religious study or rabbinical school) serves as both the religious and social centre of the community. It is administered by a Board of Directors whose responsibility involves raising and allocating funds. The day-to-day affairs of the Yeshiva are directed by two Lubavitch rabbis, one who serves as Director of the Yeshiva, and the other as his administrative assistant. Since many activities are organized in this building, a brief description of its physical appearance may be helpful. The building is situated on the corner of two streets in a mainly residential neighbourhood. It is a two-storey structure with a large basement and a main entrance leading immediately to an auditorium and to the administrative office on the first floor. There is also a side door that leads straight down to the basement and a third entrance from the school-yard leading to a flight of stairs between the upper floor and basement.

Virtually any part of the Yeshiva can be used for prayers, but they are usually conducted in an area of the basement sectioned off as the *shul* (synagogue). This area, which is divided from the rest of the basement by a moveable wooden wall, is where adults regularly come together for prayer and social gatherings. The remainder of the basement is used for a variety of activities including a play area used especially by younger boys during recess time, a prayer area for the women, and a dining area for wedding celebrations.

The Yeshiva is not reserved exclusively for the men in the community, but the women and girls use it less frequently and only on specific occasion such as religious ceremonies, weddings, circumcision ceremonies, prayer, lectures, and community-organized social activities.[5] On these occasions, Lubavitcher observe the strict community norm, which is the same for all orthodox Jews, and keep the sexes separated to minimize contact. When males and females are in attendance for prayer services or a wedding celebration, for example, a wooden screen or partition (*mecheetzeh*) separates them.[6]

Besides serving as the centre for community activities, the Yeshiva also contains classroom facilities for the boys' school and a rabbinical college (*Bays Medresh*) for students ranging from sixteen to twenty-two years of age. The classrooms for the elementary and high school students are on both floors of the Yeshiva, while a very large room on the second floor is reserved for the rabbinical students, who are called *bocherim*. This large room, known as the *Bays Medresh*, serves as a study centre for the students, and can be used for a wide variety of activities ranging from learning Torah, prayer, and meetings, to casual social gatherings. Although they are primarily intended for the *bocherim* of the Yeshiva, the facilities of the *Bays Medresh* including the library of religious books (*sforim*), are available for all adult men in the same way as the *bocherim* have free access to the *shul*.

The Lubavitcher Yeshiva, then, is used for a multiplicity of activities, several of which may be going on simultaneously. It is not unusual, for example, for prayer services to be conducted in the *shul* while a group of students are playing a soccer game in the adjoining part of the basement. Also, while some Lubavitcher may be engaged in prayer, those who have already prayed or intend to do so later, are engaged in conversations and move about the room as they please.

The majority of any Lubavitcher's time in the Yeshiva is spent in the synagogue section. Unlike most synagogues and churches that attempt to maintain a very formal atmosphere which may detract from participants' spontaneity, the Yeshiva, and the *shul* in particular, has an informal atmosphere in which individuals can take part in their choice of activities.

Even today the Lubavitcher are still immediately identifiable from other Jews, both orthodox and non-orthodox, by their appearance and manner of dress. This in part accounts for the generally negative attitude many Jews show towards all chassidic Jews. The men wear earlocks (*payess*) and a beard, with the rest of their hair usually cut close to the scalp. All men are expected to grow a beard but not to comb or trim it in the latest styles. Their dress consists of a long black coat (*kaftan*) or a dark-coloured, double-breasted suit and a wide-brimmed black hat. The women usually wear knee-length, loose-fitting, full-sleeved dresses, and as all married women must cover their hair when in public, they usually wear a wig (*shytl*) or kerchief.

Although the Lubavitcher have a distinctive style of dress, they are the least extreme of the chassidic groups and therefore tend to be more easily accepted in the larger community. However, all the chassidic groups arouse a variety of reactions from the Jewish community, ranging from mild curiosity to severe censure.

> They always stood out. I used to wonder about them; not why they dressed differently, but why they were old-fashioned. . . . I didn't really think about it too much, but I knew that's how they dressed and some people feel very strongly that they dressed differently. I don't think I felt too strongly about it. You sort of wonder, that's all.

> I just thought they were a bunch of queers, I don't know. I mean, after all, you see a man with a long coat and a big fur hat. I didn't know they were religious. I just thought they were a little queer because my uncle's religious too, but he looks like a normal man.

The chassidim's unusual clothing tends to encourage speculation about their way of life which has resulted in the misconceptions and usually inaccurate stereotypes that many Jews in the larger community harbour about them. While some are impressed with the chassidic lifestyle, the majority view them unfavourably and chassidim are frequently believed to be "dirty," "lazy," "intolerant," and "opposed to the State of Israel."

> Some of them are so dirty with *payess* (earlocks) flying all around, their flies open, torn stockings, one yellow stocking, the other green, a brown shoe, a black shoe, ripped laces. . . . Oh, what the hell. They are what you call pigs.

> I've seen them collecting money many times. I don't understand it. Don't they work for a living? Do they just walk from store to store collecting money all the time?

> They're fanatics and what disturbs me is that they're so closed-minded, They say their way is the right way and if you don't do it like they say, then you're not as good a Jew as they are. Friends of mine have been told by some of them that they're not Jews because they aren't observant.

... Anyhow they're the ones that don't recognize Israel, and stone buses and things like that.

The chassidic Jews are thus seen, in some respects, as a deviant subculture within the larger Jewish community, and as such, experience difficulties similar to those of other deviant subcultures. In spite of their proselytizing activities, their distinctive appearance and insulated way of life set them apart from other Jews many of whom, not fully understanding their underlying beliefs, view them with scepticism and suspicion.

Footnotes

[1] As I suggest in Chapter Three, the position of the *Rebbe* among chassidic Jews is not analogous to that of the rabbi in Judaism nor of the priest or minister in the Catholic or Protestant churches. Although all four are positions of leadership, the nature of this leadership is qualitatively different from the *Rebbe.*

[2] Although both terms, Torah education and Talmudic learning refer to the pursuit of knowledge of and familiarity with the tenets of orthodox Judaism, Talmudic learning refers specifically to the study of the Talmud, which is based upon and interprets the teachings of the Pentateuch. On the other hand, the notion of Torah education, though originally, perhaps, applied to the study of the Pentateuch, is now used as a general term to cover the learning of all kinds of Jewish laws, including the teachings in the Talmud.

[3] The practice of spelling God in this form is based on a prohibition of obliterating God's name. This would occur if, for example, the paper on which the word were written would be discarded or destroyed. The text upon which this prohibition is based can be found in *Mishneh Torah* by Miamonides, in the Book of Knowledge, subdivision "Laws Regarding Principles of the Torah", Chapter 6, paragraph two. For an English text, see the English translation of *Mishneh Torah* by Moses Hyamson, Boys Town Jerusalem Publishers, 1965, Jerusalem, p. 41b.

[4] While one element of the Jewish community welcomed the arrival of the Lubavitcher, some Jews were indifferent and others had no desire to see these orthodox Jews join the community. In fact, during the research, I heard several versions of a story that the Lubavitcher who arrived in 1941 were offered a sum of money to move to another city.

[5] In addition, being required by Jewish law to attend the ritual bath (*mikveh*) regularly, married women use the facilities in the basement of the Yeshiva.

[6] A cursory familiarity with this chassidic community leads one to believe that it is dominated by men. For the most part, the Yeshiva is frequented by men who try to meet there daily, whereas women are expected to remain in the home to raise the children and attend to the house. Outsiders to the community are often left with the impression that women are accorded a subordinate status in the community and that their main function is to cater to their husband's wishes. This, however, greatly distorts the importance and centrality of women to the community's way of life. The conclusion to an article "Is Woman's Role in Torah Law Secondary?", written by a Lubavitcher, reads:

> Lubavitcher *Rebbes* have, since the inception of *Chabad Chassidus*, emphasized in all their teachings, the vast potential of Jewish womanhood to continue the growth of *Yiddishkeit*. The dimensions of the woman's influence are immeasurable; in this role the Jewish woman is incomparably first. They have therefore directed and encouraged her to develop and use this vast potential and influence to the ultimate glory of *Torah* and G-d. (*Challenge*, 1970:220)

In a letter to the participants in the Annual Convention of the *Neshai U'bnos Chabad*, the Lubavitcher *Rebbe* remarked:

> We are living at a time when our people cannot move forward toward the Divinely promised "rest and inheritance" without the *active* participation of our Jewish women in the work of spreading the Torah and Mitzvoth in the daily life. In every branch of Jewish life, especially in the field of *Chinuch* (education) and *taharas-hakodesh* (sacred endeavours), Jewish women and daughters must fulfill the task which Divine Providence has bestowed upon them. This is the duty of *all* Jewish women and daughters, particularly of *Neshai U'bnos Chabad*, who have the *Zechus* (merit) of sharing in the illumination and inspiration of the teachings of Chabad . . . (*Teachers Programme*, Vol. 2:316-317)

Although it appears that women in the community have less importance and prestige than men (Gutwirth, 1970:323), the women do not feel themselves to be inferior. As in all matters, the Torah's guidelines both prescribing and proscribing patterns of conduct are unequivocally accepted by the community's followers.

Chapter Two

My Introduction to Lubavitch

The Background of the Study

My first contact with chassidim was during July, 1968, while I was working at a summer camp in the Laurentians. A group of chassidic families spent the summer months in an area near the camp, and I thought this would be a good opportunity to meet them informally. My strategy was to walk slowly by the chassidic area hoping that people would approach me and we could get into conversation.

During my first visit, on a weekday afternoon, the chassidic area appeared deserted. A few children were playing near a bridge opposite a synagogue and a few Yeshiva students were standing on the porch of the synagogue. I was not approached by anyone but the children stopped playing and stared at me as I walked by. I considered walking up to the porch of the synagogue, which also served as the *Bays Medresh* but thought this inadvisable on my first visit. Knowing that the chassidim, being orthodox Jews, prayed three times daily, I found out at what time the morning prayers began and returned the following morning at six o'clock to *davn shachress*, the morning service. Upon approaching the synagogue, I heard voices chanting loudly. From outside I saw mostly *bocherim* (older male students) who were pacing back and forth wearing Tefillin (phylacteries)[1] and reciting the morning prayers. What struck me immediately was the manner of their dress—long black coats, white shirts, and black hats. They all dressed alike. In my white jeans and multi-coloured sports jacket I realized that I was inappropriately dressed so I left without attending the service.

Although I was a practising Jew, my personal background in Judaism was remote from the chassidic way of life. I was familiar with many of the customs and laws that regulate and are practised by orthodox Jews, but my adherence to these customary and legal requirements was minimal. My upbringing and Jewish education, while never forcing me to become observant, did, however, instill in me a tolerance for others who were more religiously inclined than myself. Nonetheless, I knew little about chassidim and their way of life.[2] I mistakenly believed that chassidic Jews spoke only Yiddish among themselves and harboured an intense dislike for the State of Israel. Since I spoke, wrote, and read Yiddish fluently, I decided that studying the chassidic Jews would be both possible and fascinating.

It was only after my third visit to the chassidim that I prayed with them. Although I never expected to remain unnoticed, I had decided to modify my dress because I felt that it would create a better impression if I substituted a dark pair of slacks for my jeans. I realized it would be impossible to dress as they did and I learned to anticipate their stares, especially from the younger boys who would purposely stand very close to watch me put on *Tefillin* (phylacteries) and pray. My presence during the next few visits elicited little noticeable reaction. At best a few people, *ballebattim* (adults) and *bocherim*, nodded to me when I came and I was offered a place to sit. One morning after *davning*, as I was leaving the chassidic area a young boy informed me that someone wanted to see me. One of the adults, a rabbi, suspecting that my *Tefillin* were not in proper condition, asked me a few questions about them and about myself. He suggested that I put on another pair of *Tefillin* so that I would be certain of having properly fulfilled the precept of *Tefillin*. During this incident fifteen to twenty *bocherim* stood around and watched. One evening, prior to the *Myriv* (evening) service, for a reason unknown to me, most of the *bocherim* approached me, extending their hands to say: "*Sholem Alaychem*."

My first days in the field were a trying experience. Unlike Poll (1962), who studied chassidim in Williamsburg, Brooklyn, I had not attended a chassidic rabbinical school which, he claims, helped him "in comprehending the group norms and the significance of various Hasidic activities." (1962:267) Poll reports that he knew some of the chassidim from Hungary and that his difficulty was finding informants who would talk to him about the community. My initial difficulty was simply to meet chassidim.

During the summer I became friendly with a few *bocherim* who were followers of the Klausenburger *Rebbe*.[3] Toward the end of the summer, whenever I came to *davn*, one or two *bocherim* would offer to walk with me back to camp. These walks were excellent opportunities to learn about the chassidim. While I would sometimes ask specific questions, most of the information was volunteered. The *bocherim* were interested in telling me about themselves, the chassidic tradition, and the chassidic community.

I decided to speak to the chassidim in Yiddish, thinking they would be more comfortable conversing in that language than English as among themselves they spoke only Yiddish. Also, I reasoned, if they knew I spoke Yiddish they might be less hesitant about speaking to me, especially if their English was poor. While this was probably true for some of the chassidic Jews, others spoke to me only in English. It seemed that some approached me with the express intention of practising English, often apologizing at the outset for their poor command of the language.

The most valuable outcome of the summer's fieldwork was that I came into contact with, and spent some time among, chassidic Jews. By observing chassidim, talking and listening to them, I became familiar with some of their customs and mannerisms. For instance, I learned that a *chossid's* grip in a handshake was limp, not firm. I observed that both women and young girls were seldom seen near the *shul* and *Bays Medresh.* Except for one instance, I never saw a *bocher* together with a girl. I discovered that asking the *bocherim* questions about their relationship with girls resulted in a strained situation and that they were ill at ease and uncomfortable when asked to talk about the opposite sex. It is important to note that my contact during this period was primarily with the *bocherim* and only infrequently and sporadically with the adults. This was largely because I could only visit the chassidim on weekdays and adult males arrived from the city to join their families on Friday afternoon in time for the Sabbath, and returned early Monday morning.

When I returned to Montreal I decided to make a detailed study of one chassidic group rather than a more general study of several different groups. As Lubavitcher are a proselytizing group and therefore much easier to gain access to than the more insulated chassidic communities I decided to study this community.

My first contact with Lubavitch in Montreal was on a weekday morning after I had begun to visit the Yeshiva and spent some time wandering around the surrounding streets. On my first visit to the Yeshiva I saw some *bocherim* reciting the morning prayers and putting on *Tefillin*. Over the entrance to the Yeshiva was a large sign which read: "Join millions of Jews the World Over Who Have Begun to Put on Tefillin." As I stood at the entrance to the synagogue, which was in the basement, I was approached several times by *bocherim* who asked if I was waiting for anyone in particular or if I would want to go inside to pray. I told them that I had been invited to visit the Yeshiva by Rabbi _____ and asked if anyone would mind my presence. It was always made clear to me that I was very welcome. One *bocher* even offered to give me a tour of the Yeshiva, which I naturally accepted.

After a few visits to the Lubavitcher Yeshiva I learned that if I came in the morning I would be asked to put on *Tefillin*, as I was immediately informed that in 1967 the Lubavitcher *Rebbe* initiated a *Tefillin* campaign, to get as many Jews as possible to observe *Tefillin*.[4] I would always agree to put on *Tefillin* and ask the person beside me for assistance. Immediately afterwards, I would thank him, introduce myself and ask his name. Sometimes we would sit and talk. At other times I wandered about the Yeshiva prepared to strike up a conversation with anyone I could. It seemed that the mornings were not a suitable time to meet people. Those who came to pray at the Yeshiva appeared very preoccupied and immediately after *davning* either left for work or, in the case of the older Yeshiva students, ate breakfast and returned to their studies. I decided to start visiting the Yeshiva in the evenings.

During the first evening that I came a group of people were sitting around a table in the *shul*. I wandered back and forth in the passage-way hoping that someone would approach me to ask who I was. No one came over. Somewhat disappointed I decided to go upstairs to the *Bays Medresh* to see if any *bocherim* were there. On my way upstairs a *bocher* stopped and asked me if I was looking for someone in particular. I answered that I was interested in asking anyone some questions about Lubavitch and had been told by a Rabbi to go to the Lubavitcher Yeshiva. The *bocher* invited me inside and very formally said: "OK, what are your questions?" He soon apologized for having to leave but sent over another *bocher* who shook hands and introduced himself as follows: "Hello, I understand you're interested in talking to someone. I don't know if I can answer your questions but I'll try." We spoke for about an hour, and finally arranged to meet twice a week so that he could teach me more about Lubavitch. I set aside Tuesday and Wednesday evenings from 9:30 till 11:00 to study with my informant. He suggested that in order to understand the philosophy of Lubavitch I should study the *Alter Rebbe's Tanya* (book dealing with the philosophy of the Chabad movement). I proposed that we set aside some time during each session for a question-answer period and he readily agreed. My learning sessions with him were extremely useful for several reasons. First, he began to keep me posted on the coming events at the Yeshiva. If a *Farbrengen* (chassidic gathering) was scheduled, for example, he would encourage me to attend, or if the *Rebbe* spoke about a topic he felt might concern or interest me he would repeat the essence of the *Rebbe's* discourse. Second, through him I began meeting other Lubavitcher, *bocherim* and *ballebattim* (adults), and came to be identified as the person learning with one of the students. These brief encounters also provided opportunities to become better acquainted with other Lubavitcher. Finally, in the course of my conversation with him, I was introduced to the writings and *seechess* (discourses) of the Lubavitcher *Rebbe* and, as I soon realized, the *Rebbe* was the focal point of the Lubavitcher chassidim.

I realized that, at some point, I would be asked how and why I came to the Yeshiva. I was faced with the decision of whether or not to make my research intentions public. For some reason I felt that people would raise objections if they knew I was just working on a research project so I decided to explain that I was a student studying sociology at the university and that I would probably write a paper about the chassidim, but that, as a Jew, I was interested in what the chassidim, as Jews, had to offer. My feeling that Lubavitcher would be more ready to talk with me if they felt I was personally interested was later proved correct. Toward the end of a discussion at a Lubavitcher's I was asked:

He: May I ask you a personal question? Exactly why are you so interested in asking these questions? Is it for school or are you yourself interested?

Me: There are two reasons, both equally important. One is that as someone studying sociology I'm interested in gathering information on the chassidim and secondly, as a Jew, I have recently become interested in the ideas of chassidim.

He: I'll tell you why I ask. You see, if it is just for school then I can answer your questions without going into the reasons why I feel this way. Then I wouldn't have to let emotion come into the answers. But if you're also interested in this for yourself, then I would not only give you simple answers but I would also try to tell you why I feel the way I do.

During the first few months of the study it was necessary to inform only a few chassidim about my proposed research.

An important contact was made quite unexpectedly in October, 1969. During the holiday of *Simchess Toireh* I introduced myself to a Lubavitcher and asked if I could see him sometimes to talk about Lubavitch. He agreed and also introduced me to his wife who he thought would be interested in meeting me. His wife, as it turned out, was studying sociology as an undergraduate in one of the local universities. I told her about my research interests and she became interested in my work. I, in turn, helped her formulate some ideas for a sociology paper she decided to write on the chassidim. Mrs. Q. and I met quite regularly at her home on Thursday evenings. She was extremely helpful in giving me the names of Lubavitcher who she felt would be willing to help me. With her assistance, and that of her husband, I became familiar with some new and different aspects of Lubavitch. For example, our conversations sometimes centred on the kind of work Lubavitcher did, the difficulties facing certain families in disciplining their children, or the separation of boys and girls in the community. Mrs. Q. not only told me to try and meet certain Lubavitcher but usually briefed me about them in advance. She also cautioned me about topics that she felt others might consider too sensitive to discuss, or suggested the kinds of phrases I should use while discussing such topics. For example:

Me: I'd like to talk a little about sex which might be a sensitive area of discussion among Lubavitcher.

Mrs. Q.: Look, don't use the word sex, but say you would

> like to talk a little about the physical urge. That's
> a little more delicate. ... Wait, say you want to
> talk a little about the animal urge. In Lubavitch
> it's called the animal urge. ... You have to be very
> tactful because I think that you might upset quite
> a number of women.

Once contact with the Lubavitch community was established, and I had begun to collect data, I had to decide upon a theoretical approach in order both to analyse the data I had already collected and to organize my field work to collect more data in relevant areas.

The Study's Focus

From examination and review of the data I had already collected the theoretical focus of the study gradually developed. It became increasingly clear that one of the most interesting areas was the reasons for the Lubavitch community's persistence. More and more of the data I collected pointed to the recurrence of certain topics that Lubavitcher themselves brought up in the course of my discussions with them. My field notes included repeated references from Lubavitcher regarding the *Rebbe's* centrality in the Lubavitcher chossid's life, the importance of the Yeshiva as a social centre in the Lubavitch community, and the *bocherim's* enthusiastic pursuit of the *Tefillin* campaign and other activities intended to encourage non-observant Jews to fulfill the Torah's commandments. Gradually through discussions and conversations with Lubavitcher and others familiar with them, it became increasingly clear that these aspects of Lubavitch indicated features considered necessary for the community's persistence. The field notes on the Lubavitcher *Rebbe*, the Yeshiva, and Lubavitch's proselytizing activities were all concerned with the community's persistence.

From the outset certain individuals were pointed out to me as Lubavitcher whose background was other than Lubavitch. Initially I was not particularly interested in these people as a special group, so systematic data collection on recruits began only during the first summer of the study. From my reading about recruitment of newcomers into various institutions and religious-oriented groups I imagined that the process of becoming a Lubavitcher would be uniform for all and that recruits' entry into Lubavitch would begin with their immediate observance of basic religious precepts. My main hypothesis was that the community's strategy for processing newcomers was instantly to expect them to dissociate from their previous lifestyle while persuading them to practise the religious and cultural principles supporting an orthodox Lubavitch lifestyle. As I spoke to recruits (I interviewed fifteen—eight males and seven females) and to Lubavitcher who helped to socialize them, I discovered my hypotheses were incorrect.

The first recruit I interviewed informed me that he had begun to observe one *mitzveh* at a time and proceeded to an additional one when he mastered the first. When I inquired who decided which precept was to be observed first or when he ought to observe others he assured me that he decided when he was ready. By talking to other recruits I quickly realized that if their movement into this chassidic group were conceptualized as a status passage, the route of their passage was hardly uniform. The data from the first several interviews indicated that the direction and intensity of a person's movement into Lubavitch depended primarily on such matters as the individual's personal status, his interest in *Yiddishkayt* (Jewishness), and his level of *Yiddishkayt*. Thus, the categories or conceptual elements of the theory around which the data were integrated emerged from my discussions with the recruits themselves.

While certain hypotheses were reformulated only once, others were modified several times in the course of the study. Aspects of a recruit's case history that deviated sharply from what my hypotheses suggested, required me to revise my empirical generalizations in order to incorporate the deviant case. As a result, the final formulation of the process of becoming a Lubavitcher, described at the end of the study, is applicable, without exception, to all the newcomers contacted.

Because the data were shaping the theoretical framework rather than *vice versa*, I regularly retired from the field after a certain amount of data had been collected to appraise them and determine if and how they might be integrated with what was already available. The analysed data on hand served in turn as a guide for the kind of information to be sought next. This joint collection, coding, and analysis of the data allowed me to formulate a theory as it emerged from the data, in addition to providing support for the theory's credibility.

Gaining Access: Some Difficulties and Related Commitments

One of the distinguishing features that separates Lubavitch from other chassidic groups is its efforts to proselytize *Yiddishkayt* (Jewishness). An important outcome is that outsiders are made to feel welcome in Lubavitch. For example, if someone is interested in learning about *Yiddishkayt* he can quite easily find a Lubavitcher to assist him. As a newcomer I was always made to feel welcome.

To learn as much as possible about Lubavitch and the Lubavitch community in Montreal I began putting on *Tefillin* (phylacteries) at the Yeshiva and praying there in the afternoon and evening. I tried to make sure that, once in the Yeshiva, people would notice me. For this reason I would not, for example, sit in one place all the time but would wander about. I would try to say hello or at least nod to those people I already knew. I would also find out when certain functions were taking place and then hope to be invited or else invite myself. In short, I spent as much time as possible at the Lubavitcher Yeshiva.

Although some Lubavitcher knew I was doing research, I was identified primarily as a young man concerned about *Yiddishkayt* and interested in becoming more *frum* (observant). Although I continually reminded certain Lubavitcher about the research, I was told that people were interested in me as a Jew, not as a sociology student. In fact someone once said to me: "You know, the *Rebbe* doesn't mind people doing research on Lubavitch because this way they at least find out about *Yiddishkayt*." Lubavitcher who saw me regularly in the Yeshiva but did not know about my research interests thought of me as someone anxious to become a more observant Jew.

This image of me developed for several reasons. Firstly, when I began to visit the Yeshiva I wore a white *yarmlke* (skull cap), the kind often distributed at *Bar Mitzvehs*. As I was the only person in the Yeshiva to wear such a *yarmlke* and I had seen orthodox Jews wearing knitted *yarmlkess*, I bought one, partly because they looked more convenient to wear than the one I carried with me. When a Yeshiva friend saw me with a new *yarmlke* he said: "Ah, now this looks better than the white one. By the way, it really looks good on you. At least it shows that you're getting serious. That's good." To some, then, the new *yarmlke* indicated that henceforth my head would be covered at all times. Secondly, I sometimes travelled to New York to attend a Lubavitcher *Farbrengen* (chassidic gathering). Lubavitcher interpreted this gesture as reflecting my concern and interest in Lubavitch and *Yiddishkayt*. I would let it be known that I was planning to attend the *Farbrengen* and when I returned I saw to it that people knew I was there. On several occasions, upon seeing me at a *Farbrengen*, Lubavitcher from Montreal would remark: "Slowly, slowly, you're becoming a Lubavitcher." Finally, I sometimes reminded certain Lubavitcher that apart from the research I was doing, I was also interested in learning about *Yiddishkayt*. I was, in fact, telling the truth. In the beginning the *Yiddishkayt* aspect accompanying the research was the least important and almost incidental. As I continued, however, it began to assume increasing importance for me as a Jew.

On the basis of these observations it was assumed that, along with all orthodox Jews, my head was always covered, and, since I understood the importance of the *mitzveh* of *Tefillin*, I observed it regularly. For example, when I first started coming to the Yeshiva in the morning I was immediately asked if I had already observed *Tefillin*. After several months, however, I was no longer asked. It was taken for granted that I did.

While it may appear that Lubavitcher raised no objections to my research activity, such was not the case. I was never specifically told to stop my research, but I felt that several people were suspicious about my motives. As more Lubavitcher became aware of my research, some began to ask "what I was trying to show." Several were directly concerned that I might not portray Lubavitch favourably. At times some of my closer contacts would substantiate my suspicions:

> You know, I've noticed this about you just by watching you lately. You seem to be very reserved. ... It's as if you're not really yourself when you come here. When you talk to people, and by the way there are a few people who

say this, you watch your words very carefully. . . . What you're doing, and I'm telling you this for your own sake, is turning people off. People begin to ask what you are doing around here.

A Yeshiva student, talking about my research, said:

> . . . It's true that there are some people who don't know what you're doing and are afraid of what you might do. . . . It is possible that someone could write something bad about this place. So it isn't necessarily that people aren't interested in what you're doing. In some cases they're just afraid.

Once while I was interviewing a young Lubavitcher he was called to the telephone. I overheard him say that he was talking to Billy "who is writing something about Lubavitch." After a pause he said: "Look, what's the difference? He's going to find out all these things anyway. It's just a matter of time." On several occasions, after older Yeshiva students noticed me observing something in the Yeshiva, they would say: "Put that in your book," or "You know, things like this don't have to go into the paper you're writing." One of the Rabbis, once said, "Let me ask you something. Tell me, do you know that some of the information you get from people is not right?" He went on to explain that several people to whom I had spoken and interviewed were providing me with "false" information. Instead of providing me with the "truth," he claimed, they were telling me what they believed I wanted to hear, and what they hoped would impress me.[5]

Although some Lubavitcher may, at the outset, have provided me with false information, it is most unlikely that they could have pursued such a course for too long without being discovered. As Becker has noted:

> . . . to suppose that the subjects of field research are affected by the bias of the observer, and mold their acts and words to what they think he wants, supposes not only that they are willing to do so but that they are free to. It supposes that they are under no other constraints and so can follow their disposition to be pleasing, if they have such a disposition . . .

Consider . . . the people a field worker studies. They are enmeshed in social relationships important to them, at work, in community life, wherever. The events they participate in matter to them. The opinions and actions of the people they interact with must be taken into account, because they affect those events. All the constraints that affect them in their ordinary lives continue to operate while the observer observes. (1970:45-46)

As I continued the research I became increasingly familiar with those aspects of the Lubavitch community that were of particular interest to me, as well as other matters to which the participant observer is inevitably exposed. In time, Lubavitcher recognized that my understanding of the community's organization, its activities and the philosophy underlying them, its achievements and lack of them was becoming more detailed and complete. Consequently, it became progressively more difficult for these chassidim to mislead me with factually incorrect information. Certain explanations and phrases, used by Lubavitcher during conversation with me, served to indicate that this was the case:

If I didn't know you, then I could give one type of answer to your questions. But I know that you're familiar with the situation and so the answer wouldn't satisfy you. Okay. I'll tell you what I know but this should stay between us.

or:

Let me try to answer that very honestly. I mean, you spend a lot of time here (at the Yeshiva) and I know that you've spoken to other people about it, so I can't fool you.

The Interview Schedule

Along with participant observation I formally interviewed thirty-three Lubavitcher, mostly in their homes but also in the Yeshiva. The interviewing was unstructured and varied with each interviewee according to the difficulty encountered in overcoming his/her initial distrust and fear in speaking to me. One important outcome of the interviewing was that I was able to meet Lubavitch women. As it turned out, interviews were the only available means of approaching them.

Arrangements for an interview were usually made by telephone. I would call up the person, introduce myself as a student and say that I was doing "some research for school that has to do with Lubavitch." I would mention some names of Lubavitcher I had already spoken to and then ask if we might meet, during the day or evening, for about an hour. There were two typical responses: "If you've spoken to Mrs. _____ then I don't see how I can add more to what she said" or, "You're much better off speaking to someone like Rabbi _____ . He knows much more about this than I do." It was necessary to develop an approach to convince the person that meeting him would be more helpful than he imagined. In all but three cases those approached agreed to speak to me.

When conducting interviews I sometimes used a tape recorder. I decided to experiment with the tape recorder to find out if the interviewees would be distracted by its presence or hold back information if they saw that our conversation was recorded. For example, some people, when asked if I could use a tape recorder, said something like: "Well, I'll tell you, I'd probably speak more freely without the tape recorder." I found, however, or possibly rationalized, that a tape recorder did not really effect the nature of the conversation. I would tell the interviewee that the tape recorder could be shut off whenever he wished. Some people said during the interview: "If you turn off the machine for a second I'll tell you something else" or "You can leave the machine on but I don't want what I say now to be included in your report." Using the tape recorder, on the other hand, allowed me to record verbatim what the person said. In one case an interviewee regretted having been recorded. This person did not like "having everything I said on tape." In that case I suggested I bring the tape recorder and tape to her house where she could erase it. The interviewee became convinced the tape would be erased and declined the offer.

At the end of the interview I would close off the machine and say: "This research is really turning out to be interesting. Lubavitcher have a lot to say." Usually interviewees would then ask: "Which people have you already spoken to" and add: "You should speak to Rabbi_____ or Mrs. _____ . They can tell you more about_____than anyone." In this way I added to my list of potential interviewees.

The data for the study were collected over a period of about two and a half years. During this time I tried to visit the Yeshiva regularly and attend as many Yeshiva functions as possible. The interviews, however, were conducted over a period of about a year and a half. These were done, essentially, to supplement the data gathered through participant observation. Often, though, they directed me to certain features of the community of which I was unaware, while also yielding information different in kind from what I collected through observation.

The interviews did not all centre on a similar set of questions as certain Lubavitcher had access to specific information and the interview revolved around those areas they knew best. For example, when I interviewed a Camp Director the bulk of our conversation focused on the camp and its related activities. Another example were newcomers to Lubavitch. There was little to be gained by asking them about the history of the Lubavitch community in Montreal except to discover that they knew very little about it. My interest with them was to find out how they came to Lubavitch and the general process they underwent in becoming Lubavitcher chassidim. Consequently I did not have the same data from everyone I interviewed.

Aside from observing and interviewing Lubavitcher themselves I also used additional sources of data. The most important source was the literature published by the Lubavitch Kehot Publication Society which includes, among other things, books and pamphlets about the history of the Lubavitch movement and the diverse activities undertaken by the chassidim throughout the world. During my visits to 770,[6] the Lubavitch headquarters in New York, I bought as much of the literature as possible and also subscribed to certain weekly or quarterly publications. In addition I collected articles in newspapers which were written by Lubavitcher or were about Lubavitch. For example, I spent several weeks searching through *Der Keneder Odler,* a Yiddish newspaper, from 1941 to the present day for articles on the origins and development of the Lubavitch community in Montreal. Another source of data were individuals who had connections with Lubavitch but were not themselves Lubavitcher. For instance, I spoke to some of the teachers hired to teach secular subjects who provided me with information about the secular curriculum of the Yeshiva and their experiences implementing it.

Discontinuities in the Data

In any study relying primarily on participant observation the researcher will continually discover gaps in his data. Since he is studying a collectivity or individual over time it is almost impossible to avoid such missing links. Although the researcher usually tries to attend events which may be important to the study, there are times when, for various reasons, he cannot gain access to observe them. In the present study events and activities surrounding the women and girls in the community are a case in point.

Since Lubavitch enforces a social separation of the sexes, as is true of all chassidic groups, it is extremely difficult for the male researcher to gain first-hand information about females' involvement in the community. It is possible to discuss with parents their daughters' participation in Lubavitch organized activities. Such information, however, is second hand and does not include the girls' interpretations about their involvement in Lubavitch. It is impossible to observe the nature of the girls' discussions and conversations, the kinds of matter they consider important, their feelings toward their way of life and the wider Jewish community. Ideally it is best to observe people in their natural setting, but I was unable to do this with Lubavitch women and girls. I did , however, manage to collect data about their activities. These data were both quantitatively and qualitatively different from those on the men and older Yeshiva students.

A consequence of the above is that the analysis is less dense and rich than it might otherwise be. Although the available data suggest that females in Lubavitch engage in proselytizing activities, it appears that their encounters with non-orthodox Jews assume a different shape than the men's. For instance, in recent years the *Tefillin* campaign has become Lubavitch's central proselytizing activity to publicize *Yiddishkayt*, but, whereas the men can invite prospective recruits to the Yeshiva in order to maintain contact and develop a friendship, the women and girls must seek alternate means to make contact with interested newcomers. What these adaptations are and their degree of success are less than absolutely clear. Since the data on females is limited, it is difficult to provide a well-rounded analysis on such matters.

My closest and most intimate contacts were with a small group of older Yeshiva students. Through them I became quite friendly with many students in the *Bays Medresh*. Since many of these students active in proselytizing work, viewed me as a potential newcomer, and because of our closeness in age, it was perhaps inevitable that we would befriend each other. My intimate relationship with some allowed me to share with them problems relating to the research as well as certain other personal matters. They, in turn, shared their experiences with me, often using me as a sounding board for their ideas and reflections. Although we were still separated by different lifestyles, we were friends. As a result, my understanding and appreciation of these students' perspectives and their accompanying activities almost reached an intuitive level. It would be dishonest to claim that I was equally familiar with, and felt as comfortable in, the adult world. Much of the spontaneity that characterized my relationship with the students was absent here. With few exceptions, our contacts were more formally developed and acted out. I fully realized that a researcher some ten years older than myself could have obtained more informal access to the adults. On the other hand, his informal contact with the older students would probably have been qualitatively different from mine.

Although I collected data relating to the role of the family in the community through interviews, the discussion in Chapter Four about the significance of the family may be considered too brief and incomplete. My decision to limit discussion of the family, in fact, resulted from my conversations with Lubavitcher. While data were available on the tasks performed by the family in socializing the young[7], my respondents maintained that the significance of the family unit to Lubavitcher would be similar to that in any household where religion occupies a central place.

Despite the gaps in my data, I found that I had sufficient direct information from and experience of Lubavitcher to substantiate my theory on the persistence of the community. I felt that, from what I had learned from the interviews and from passing comments, although more data on the role of women in particular would be interesting, it would tend to substantiate

44

rather than contradict the first-hand data I had been able to collect.

Footnotes

[1] The law of *Tefillin* (phylacteries) is derived from the Biblical commandment: And thou shalt bind them for a sign upon thy hand, and they shall be as frontlets between thine eyes (Deut. 6:8). The *Tefillin* consist of two leather boxes containing a piece of parchment with passages from the Bible inscribed on it. These proclaim the existence and unity of God and serve as a reminder of the liberation of the Jews from Egypt.

> One of the boxes is placed upon the left arm (or right arm if one is right-handed) so as to rest against the heart—the seat of the emotions, the suspended leather thong being wound around the left hand, as well as around the middle finger of that hand, in accordance with ancient traditional practice. The other box is placed upon the head, *above* the forehead, so as to rest upon the cerebrum. In this manner our attention is directed to the *head, heart and hand*, and is to teach us to dedicate ourselves to the service of G-d in all that we *think, feel and do*. It is also to teach us not to be governed solely by the impulse of the heart, lest that lead us into error and superstition. Nor are we to be governed by reason alone, for that may lead to harsh materialism. (from a Lubavitch publication on *Tefillin*)

According to Jewish law, a Jewish boy, upon his thirteenth birthday, is regarded as a full-fledged Jew. He then becomes a "Bar Mitzvah." Every Jewish male having reached the age of Bar Mitzvah is commanded to wear *Tefillin* during the morning prayers on each weekday.

[2] I vividly recalled that when many of them lived around the Park Avenue area of Montreal, they were often referred to by younger Jews of my age as the "Park Avenue White Socks," referring to the white socks some of the men wore on the Sabbath and other Jewish holidays.

[3] As I mentioned earlier, the chassidic movement is comprised of a number of chassidic groups. One such group is the Klausenburger chassidim whose community in Montreal is relatively small when compared to the Lubavitch community.

[4] The significance of the *Tefillin* campaign, the reason for its initiation, and its organization, are discussed in detail in Chapter Six. At this point, a quotation from a Lubavitch publication on *Tefillin* will provide a brief

description of the significance of the campaign:

> The Tefillin Campaign was launched at the time of the tense situation preceding the Six-Day War. At the time it was particularly necessary to arouse the "fear of the nations" so that they would do no harm to the Jewish people, hence the choice of Tefillin as the subject of the Campaign. Moreover, the aim of the Campaign is not only to persuade Jews in the Holy Land to don Tefillin (although they are in singular need of the Tefillin's quality to strike terror into the hearts of their enemies), but also Jews the world over, for, since "All Jews are responsible for one another," the observance of the Mitzvah by any Jew, *wherever* he may be, has the capacity to benefit all Jews. ... each and every Mitzvah has its *own* peculiar characteristic of being beneficial in a particular way to the Jew performing the Mitzvah. Tefillin, too, have a special beneficial influence. The Torah states: "And all nations of the world shall see that you are called by the Name of the L-rd and they will fear you." Our Sages in the Talmud explain that the nations' fear is caused through fulfilling the precept of wearing Tefillin.

[5] For a discussion of subjects' response to the "demand characteristics" of the experiment and the alteration of their behaviour to confirm what the experimenter hopes to confirm, see M. T. Orne, "On the Social Psychology of the Psychological Experiment: With Particular Reference to Demand Characteristics and Their Implications." (American Psychologist 17, 1962; 776-783); R. Rosenthal and R. Rosnow, eds., *Sources of Artifact in Social Research* (New York: Academic Press, 1970); F. H. Blum, "Getting Individuals to Give Information to the Outsider." (Journal of Social Issues, 8:35-42).

[6] The Lubavitch headquarters are located in Crown Heights, Brooklyn, New York at 770 Eastern Parkway. The 770 address to Lubavitcher around the world represents the centre of Lubavitch activities. Not only is the main Lubavitch administrative office located there, but it is where the Lubavitcher *Rebbe* receives his chassidim and other guests. Anyone in contact with Lubavitcher soon discovers the significance that 770 holds for the chassidim of this group.

[7] For a discussion of the parental contribution to the religious education of the young, see Mintz, ibid.:64-71.

Chapter Three

Establishing A Distinctive Identity

Identity at the Individual and Community Levels

Anselm Strauss has argued that whatever else it may be, "identity is connected with the fateful appraisals made of oneself—by oneself and others." (1969:9) Identities, or self-conceptions are formed not so much by an individual's view of himself in isolation but rather by the interaction of people with one another. Each person develops some notion of himself from the way others view and treat him. This is what led Cooley to describe a person's sense of personal identity as a "looking-glass self." This idea has been described by various writers such as Shibutani who noted that a person "constructs the personification from the reactions imputed to other people." (1961:239)

G. H. Mead maintained that, in the course of his association with others, each person forms a conception of himself by evaluating his experiences from a generalized standpoint. Human beings, contended Mead, do not merely react to each other's actions but instead engage in a process of interpretation during which they impute meanings to others' behaviour believed to represent the standpoints common to the group. Therefore, a person's identity, reflects what he imagines others think of him; specifically those in the temporary group in which he participates. This may, of course, differ from what they actually do think.

An important contribution to a person's sense of identity is derived from the continuity of his experiences in time, consisting both of past memories and future aspirations. Shibutani has stated that "The consistency of all such experiences enables each person to integrate them into a unit, a whole which is also treated as a distinctive entity by other people." (1961:217) Identities are also reinforced by sustained social relationships which help others to recognize the person as an individual and to organize their actions toward him in a uniform manner. To conceive of oneself in a consistent way therefore helps to strengthen the sense of identity while allowing one to respond to others and to meet one's obligations toward them in an appropriate manner.

If we regard a community as consisting of those who, bounded by a specified territory, conceive of themselves as being alike by virtue of a set of common characteristics and are so regarded by others, we can consider the identity concept at the community level. At this level the term "consciousness of kind" rather than identity is used to refer to a feeling permeating those who are classified together and who conceive of themselves as being alike. This feeling of unity arises from a perception of resemblances among themselves and differences from outsiders. Shibutani and Kwan contend that "Any readily visible means of identification—similarity of physical attributes, distinctive modes of dress, or a common language—certainly facilitate the development of such awareness." (1965:42)

Consciousness of kind implies some degree of sympathetic identification or shared feelings and emotional reactions with others in the same category. Thus, when social distance between people is low they " ... can enter imaginatively into one another's minds and share their experiences; they are able to sympathize with one another's pains, joys, sorrows, hopes and fears. Those who feel close to each other are more relaxed and tend to be less defensive, for each feels that he can understand those around him." (Shibutani and Kwan, 1965:42-43) Concomitantly, those sharing a consciousness of kind have the conviction that outsiders are basically different from themselves and hence are to be treated differently.

Designated members of a community form the most important reference group and the sentiments and ideology underlying the community become the perspective around which they organize their frame of reference. Members of the community perceive certain aspects of the world from the community standpoint and, as many of the people they come into daily contact with also have this perspective, their self-images are largely defined by the collectivity. The community thus becomes an effective agency of social control, but the extent of its influence depends upon how closely the individual identifies himself with the community's practices and routines.

The central organizing feature of any religious community is its own distinctive identity, the cultivation of which is crucial for it effectively separates insiders (members) from outsiders. In addition, the inculcation of such an identity in the young helps ensure that the community will continue. Most important, however, is that the existence of a religious community necessarily implies the presence of a distinctive identity and that the very presence of such an identity allows us to recognize the entity as a community.

Techniques of Identity Maintenance in Religious Communities

One technique religious communities use in trying to preserve their identity is to channel their members' lives so that they conform to certain standards or sets of expectations intended to regulate their contact with outsiders. The identifying features that a community can use to make its members feel they belong to a distinct group can range from dress to insulation, language, and history.

Dress

Styles of dress are important identity symbols as they link the community with its past history and provide a visible distinction between community members and outsiders. Unlike certain chassidic groups such as the Satmarer who insist that their members dress as their ancestors did, Lubavitcher have adapted their clothes to Western customs. This is not to suggest, however, that Lubavitcher approve of their members wearing the latest fashions. Women and girls are continually reminded about the importance of a modest appearance, while the men's and boys' suits and jackets are expected to be dark coloured and simple. A young man in the community who began to wear the latest fashions was mildly criticized and at times even censured by some Lubavitcher. One of his peers once remarked to him:

> You see what happens when you leave the Yeshiva? (pointing to the wide tie and flared slacks). This is what happens and this is only the beginning. You know it, so what's going to be next? (translated from Yiddish).

However, as the Lubavitch community's attire is not sufficiently uniform always to allow the distinction between insider and out-

49

sider, dress is not considered an important identifying feature of the community under study.

Insulation: Physical, Cultural and Social

Many religious communities assign a high priority to insulation from the surrounding culture to prevent assimilation. Although insulation is sometimes spatial, it is more often social, aiming at minimal contact with individuals whose behaviour and ideas are contrary to those of the community members. Unnecessary contact with outside influences and technological advances are discouraged as they are considered potentially threatening to the community.

In the case of chassidic groups, the degree of insulation varies according to the concept the particular group has of outsiders and their estimate of the surrounding society's threat to the continuity of their way of life. Insulation ranges from actual removal from the city to a rural settlement, as exemplified by the Tasher and Squarer chassidim, to strictly enforced cultural and social separation from outsiders, as occurs among the Satmarer, to the Lubavitcher chassidim's more moderate social separation. In fact, the main distinguishing feature between Lubavitch and other chassidic groups is the former's efforts at contacting non-observant Jews and urging them to enter the orthodox fold. The Lubavitcher are thus more exposed to arguments and ideas directly opposed to their world view. While it may be argued that insulation serves to buttress a religious community's distinctive identity, the nature of Lubavitchers' relationship with outsiders suggests this is less the fact in their case than among other chassidim.

Language

Learning a new language is of considerable importance for it necessitates a reorganization of experiences and eventual acquaintance with a new world of objects. This is what Hostetler meant when he wrote about the Amish: "Roles and functions tend to organize around each language; thus when speaking English the Amishman tends to think and behave like the English-speaking person." (1968:139) As the ideas and perspectives of a

50

community are embodied in its language, the children will more easily comprehend and assume for themselves the community's conception of the world if the particular language of the community is their mother tongue. Successful instruction both to the young and newcomers adds to the community's distinctive identity and facilitates the development of shared understandings among the members.

Among chassidim, English will not, in general, be spoken unless the situation demands it. The language of everyday discourse is, for the most part, Yiddish and the Jewish curriculum in the Yeshiva is also in this language. The attitude toward learning an outside language, in this case English, is not uniform among the chassidic groups or even within the groups themselves. Lubavitcher, for example, are likely to be more fluent in English than are the Satmarer as greater attention is paid to secular education in the Lubavitcher Yeshiva.

In all chassidic groups some parents do not permit their children to study secular subjects until a certain age. As a result, it is not uncommon to find chassidic youth who, except at a most elementary level, neither understand nor speak English. A teacher in a Hungarian-Jewish Yeshiva remarked:

> ... first of all, half of the parents didn't approve of their children learning English at all. You have people who are born in Brooklyn, in X (name of city), who can't read and write English. They can't even sign their name. The only language they speak is Yiddish and the second language, if any, is Hungarian. Most of the parents consider it *goyish*, not English ...

The number of Lubavitch parents who refuse to allow their sons to study the Lubavitcher Yeshiva's secular curriculum is probably less than among parents in other chassidic groups.

History

The history of any group consists of collective memories of their ancestors' deeds, the difficulties encountered throughout its existence, and the events which have culminated in the group's present situation. (Shibutani and Kwan, 1965:43) However, " ... the way in which the history of the group is remembered is far more important than what it has actually been." (Ibid:43) As among other groups, historical events signifying major turning points for the group are recalled and celebrated by the Lubavitcher. These often centre on incidents relating to Lubavitcher *Rebbeim* and are celebrated at *Farbrengens*, or gatherings of Lubavitcher on days held sacred by them. At these gatherings the *Rebbe* delivers discourses ranging from Lubavitch philosophy to exhortations on how Jews ought to conduct their everyday lives.

Lubavitchers' identity is reinforced by their knowledge of the group's history, especially familiarity with its leaders. Kehot, the Lubavitch Publication Society, continually publishes collections of histories and anecdotes about the lives of previous Lubavitcher *Rebbeim* tracing the origin and development of the Lubavitch chassidic movement. The songs sung by previous generations of Lubavitcher have been carefully compiled and published. The central link uniting Lubavitcher since the founding of the movement is their study of the *Tanya*; written by the first Lubavitcher *Rebbe*, it outlines the principles of the Lubavitcher chassidim. It is this general awareness of the lives, work and teachings of the previous Lubavitcher *Rebbeim* rather than dress, insulation, or language that is the central and unifying feature of the Lubavitchers' self-conception and also the main distinction between them and other orthodox Jews.

The Organization of Judaism

Before distinguishing between Lubavitcher chassidim and other orthodox non-chassidic Jews, it is useful to provide the reader with a brief analysis of the organization of Judaism. Such an analysis will prove helpful in understanding the relationship of the Lubavitch movement to Judaism of which it is a part. The first question, however, is who can be considered to be a Jew, whether orthodox or not. According to Jewish law, a Jew is one who was born of a Jewish mother, or who formally adopts the Jewish religion according to the ritual prescribed by Jewish law.[1] Accordingly, the child of a Jewish father and a Catholic mother is not a Jew, according to the law.

The religious life of present-day Jews is begun with the eighteenth-century *Haskala* Movement (Enlightenment) with the Ashkenazim or Jews of central and eastern Europe. At this time, their contact with Western languages, manners, and lifestyles increased as new opportunities for trade arose. As a result, many wealthy Jews aspired to full acceptance in Gentile society, and a number of intellectuals started agitating for the end of the old ghetto lifestyle and for the emancipation of the Jews. The influence of the Enlightenment upon the Ashkenazic Jewish community cannot be underestimated. The altered economic and political conditions in the West stimulated the Jewish community to take a greater part in the world around them, and "many western Rabbis were now willing to build intellectual bridges spanning Jewish religious thought and the new knowledge spawned by scientific inquiry." (Rosenberg, 1966:54)

From this new interest in and awareness of Western society three movements or groups developed in modern Judaism— Orthodox, Conservative and Reform.[2] These groups can be seen as three intersecting circles each with different dimensions and distinctive philosophies, but all sharing some common beliefs.

Reform Judaism

The Reform movement began in the middle of the nineteenth century, mainly in Germany and America, and was the first of the modern interpretations of Judaism to emerge in response to the changed political and cultural conditions brought about by the Enlightenment. Although the different groups within Reform Judaism have undergone constant change over time, they all share the assertion of the legitimacy of change in Judaism and deny the biding authority of the Bible on questions of ceremonial and ritual law. The use of Hebrew in the Reformers' religious services was limited and practices such as the dietary laws, circumcision, and national messianism which gave the appearance of social segregation were omitted. "At the synagogue service, the organ was introduced to modernize and enhance the ritual, and the family pew, for men and women, took the place of the traditional segregation of the sexes at worship." (Rosenberg, ibid:56)

For many years, Reform congregations made some radical experiments in many spheres of religious practice. For example, for a time, some dispensed with the Jewish Sabbath and seriously considered introducing Sunday, the Christian Sabbath, in its place. Virtually all congregations gave up the belief in a Messiah as a physical redeemer, and for Reform Jews the notion of Messianism became transmuted into "active concern for social welfare in the present, and the Jewish role in history became Diaspora-centered, a mission to the Gentiles." (Encyclopedia Britannica, 1974, Vol. 10:323)

Orthodox Judaism

Orthodox Judaism considers itself the authentic bearer of the religious Jewish tradition and until the Enlightenment it held sway over almost the entire Jewish community. While the Jewish establishment in western and central Europe was affected by religious reform, the bulk of the Jewish population remained Orthodox—a term used by Reform leaders to designate their traditional opponents. Orthodoxy as a well-defined phenomenon within Jewry crystallized in response to the changes which occurred in Jewish society in the first half of the nineteenth century. The opponents of such changes, which were mainly concerned with greater secularization, insisted that both the written law of Moses and the oral law of the Rabbis, as codified in the *Shulchan Orech* (Code of Jewish Law) were divinely inspired and must be observed in practice according to the teachings and principles of the *Halachah* (Jewish Law). Adherents to Orthodox Judaism believe that every question and problem facing the individual can be answered according to these divine teachings. Attempts to adjust Judaism to the "spirit of the time" are rejected by Orthodox Jews who claim it is not the values of any given age but rather the revealed will of God that are the ultimate standards.

In contrast to Reform Judaism, Orthodox Judaism upholds the doctrines of the personal Messiah, the resurrection of the dead, and the restoration of the sacrificial service in the temple at Jerusalem. The followers of this branch of Judaism conduct their services entirely in Hebrew, men and women sit separately, there is no instrumental music, and head coverings and prayer shawls are worn by the men.

Although they are unanimous in their belief in the literal revelation of the Torah and their submission to the teachings of the Talmud, they do not agree on the interpretation of these laws. (Rosenberg, ibid.) Nevertheless:

All groups within Orthodoxy agree, ... that the only valid way to treat Jewish law and tradition is by applying the due process of its principles and precedents to the living situation. And this can be done only by means of learning: it is incumbent upon every Jew to study and to observe, and without the former, the tradition says, there is little significance to the latter. This explains why Orthodoxy places such strong emphasis upon education, and why it is that despite the many sacrifices it entails, thousands of Orthodox Jewish parents send their children to religious schools where traditional learning can be acquired, in addition to general, secular studies. (Rosenberg, ibid:59)

Of the three major camps in contemporary Judaism, Orthodoxy makes the greatest demands upon its adherents, demands which might have economic and social consequences. For example, Orthodox Jews must follow kosher food laws even if they live in a non-Jewish environment, and must not work on the Sabbath and other religious holidays.

Conservative Judaism

Conservative Judaism developed as a response to the Jews' efforts to become more emancipated. Those who identified themselves with Conservative Judaism supported the end of the ghettoization and the Westernization of Jewish lifestyles and education. Seeing the history of Judaism as a succession of changes, adherents of this philosophy proclaimed that changes could be validly made without sacrificing biblical and rabbinical law.

The renaissance of Jewish religious scholarship in the nineteenth century led both to the creation of the Reform movement and also to what became known as the Conservative movement. The Reform movement's emphasis on the universal elements in the Jewish past were felt by some scholars to be too one-sided and to neglect the distinctive Hebraic spirit of Judaism. Conservative Judaism maintained that the traditional forms and precepts of Judaism were valid and that changes in practice were to be introduced only with great reluctance.

In contrast to Reform, the Conservative emphasize the

distinctive elements in Judaism, asserting that the need to *preserve* the Jewish people as the vehicle of the tradition in no way contradicts the universalism of Judaism. In contrast to Orthodoxy, however, Conservative Judaism places high priority on the need to examine the *halaka* (Code of Jewish Law), and to change it wherever necessary, in accordance with its spirit, but based upon a desire to direct its growth. (Rosenberg, ibid:60)

In their belief that the essential spirit of Judaism rested on its adaptive capacity, the Conservatives experimented with certain changes in individual congregations in an effort to make biblical teachings more relevant to the times. These experiments involved the liturgy, and certain ritual practices, such as the introduction of the *Bat Mitzvah* for girls and the seating of men and women together at services. Conservative Judaism was, however, committed to the use of the Hebrew language in the liturgy, the observance of Dietary Laws (*Kashruth*), and the Sabbath, and on the whole came to traditional conclusions about religious observance.

A closer examination of these three major divisions within Judaism would show that, while there are differences among them, they are basically unified by common elements. As Rosenberg has noted: " ... all three names—Reform, Orthodox and Conservative—are borrowed from the world of Christian denominationalism, and are, in effect, adjectives that have come into vogue only in modern times. Modern Judaism to be sure, ... is divided into three aspects. Essentially, however, it is the noun "Judaism" that is more important to all three groups, than the new-found adjectives, "Reform", "Orthodox". or "Conservative." (ibid:63)

A figure common to all three divisions of modern Judaism is the rabbi. Originally the rabbi did not hold a religious position, but was rather a communal official responsible for attending to all the needs of the Jewish community. Since the Enlightenment, particularly in Western countries, the functions of the rabbi have undergone a radical change. In modern times the Rabbinate became, for the most part, a religious rather than a communal agency, as the civic life of Jews increasingly came under national states in which they lived.

The education of rabbis is carried out in seminaries or Yeshivas where the candidates complete a course of religious studies at the post-graduate level. Reform and Conservative seminaries require a Bachelor's degree before accepting freshman students. Four or five years of graduate studies are the minimum requirement for ordination. In addition to his religious training, the rabbinical student must equip himself in the social sciences, particularly in psychology, sociology, and general history. In contrast, the modern Orthodox seminary is less exacting in its demands for secular education; studies are concentrated on the fields of Talmudic learning and Jewish law.

The majority of graduates from these seminaries serve as congregational rabbis. Their role is similar to that of a minister or priest in Christian denominations, but they have some additional functions because of the particular nature of the Jewish community. The modern rabbi, whose role is essentially the same in Reform, Orthodox, and Conservative Judaism, is expected to devote much of his time to pastoral guidance, assuming responsibility for the ceremonies surrounding birth, confirmation, marriage, and death and attending to such other matters as religious education, synagogue worship, and preaching. These duties roughly parallel those of his Protestant colleagues. The rabbi's wife, called the *rebbetzin*, assumes a place in synagogue life comparable to that of the vicar's or minister's wife who presides over the home in a Protestant parish.

Although modern Judaism can be subdivided into three major components, each is, in turn, comprised of a number of subgroups. What marks the various bodies in the Jewish community is their differences in ritual practices, but the ritual variations shade from one group into the other. Thus within Orthodoxy there is a continuum ranging from strict observance to leniency, with Chassidism being at the pole of total adherence to the laws. Within the chassidic movement, however, can be found numerous groups, including, for example, the Lubavitcher or Chabad chassidim, the Belzer, Satmarer, and Tasher chassidim. Thus Lubavitcher chassidim are a division of the general chassidic movement, which in turn is a subgroup of Orthodoxy, a component of contemporary Judaism. This may be schematically shown as follows:

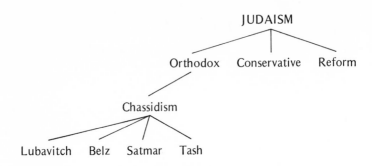

The Distinction Between Lubavitcher and Other Orthodox Jews

While all Lubavitcher chassidim adhere to the precepts underlying the Jewish religion, the majority of orthodox Jews are not Lubavitcher chassidim. As we have seen, the basic difference between Lubavitcher and orthodox Jews not affiliated with Lubavitch centres on the former's relationship with their *Rebbe*, the nature of which defines one as a Lubavitcher. The source and nature of the Lubavitcher *Rebbe's* authority is unlike that of a Rabbi who is ordained only to decide on questions of ritual law. While usually respected for his learning and scholarship, the Rabbi is not regarded by his congregants as possessing unique powers which may be exercised for their benefit. To his followers, on the other hand, the *Rebbe* is believed to be endowed with extraordinary powers of perception and wisdom. None will engage in any important event without his consent. As Mintz suggests: " . . . in his relationship to his followers the *Rebbe* functions in the uncertain areas of life rather than in the clearly defined domain of the law." (1968:89)

This difference was expressed by one Lubavitcher in this manner:

> They don't have a *Rebbe* . . . Today, truthfully, there are no *misnagdim* (opponents of chassidim) because even if they don't have a *Rebbe*, they listen to their *mashgiech* (kashruth supervisor), or to the Rabbi of the Rosh Yeshiva. Now, they'll ask many of the same things that we ask the *Rebbe*, except he's not a *Rebbe*, so they have a way out. . . . If you want to ask, you ask. If you don't want to ask, you don't ask. You listen. If you don't want to, you don't

listen . . . But a *Rebbe* is a different thing altogether. The *Rebbe* is like your soul; you feel he wishes the well-being of your soul. . . . So you listen to him differently.

When Lubavitcher are asked to comment on what characterizes a Lubavitcher *chossid*, all emphasize recognition of the *Rebbe* as the central figure in one's life and a willingness to practise and accept his views and their consequences. As the following comments show, a Lubavitcher is expected to pattern his life as closely as possible on the *Rebbe's* teaching and instruction:

Well, I would say, that you're asking the same kind of question as what constitutes a Jew. What makes a Jew? Now if I tell you that man's a good Jew you might have a different picture in your mind of what a good Jew is, than what I have in mind. Being a good Jew is so vast that to pin down being Jewish would be very hard because there's so much . . . to being a Jew. By the same token I'd say this about Lubavitch. . . . There's so much that it takes to be a Lubavitcher, but nevertheless there are some essentials so when you ask me: "What's a good Jew?" you and I would probably see alike on many points by saying that a good Jew is one who's trying to observe a large part of the commandments. We'll probably agree that it's someone who keeps *Shabbess*, who keeps *Tefillin* and a few other essentials. We would say that even if he bypassed a lot of others, if he did these essentials, he would probably be considered a good Jew. . . . By the same token, I would call a Lubavitcher someone who starts along any of these paths, who believes and wants to get there. Not someone who has got there. A good Jew is someone who tries to be observant . . . someone who believes and has the feeling about the *Rebbe* and has a sort of understanding of what *chassidess* is and would like to live his life this way. Even though he's at step number one, along each of these lines, to me he's a Lubavitcher.

It's hard . . . what makes a person a Lubavitcher. It's simply someone who decides that the *Rebbe* is someone he will look up to and he will follow his advice and his directions, and he tries to take on *minhogim* (customs) of Lubavitch as much as he can. It doesn't necessarily mean that he does everything in one day. . . . The main idea is, I would say, following the *Rebbe*.

Closely connected to Lubavitchers' ties to their *Rebbe* is their specific heritage, encompassing the history of the Lubavitch movement principally in terms of the previous *Rebbeim's* work. The Lubavitch movement, founded almost two hundred years ago, with its specific heroes and unique line of historical development, provides the fundamental basis for Lubavitchers' distinctive identity. When these chassidim reflect upon the course of Jewish history over the last two hundred years, they necessarily include the accomplishments of their *Rebbeim*. In contrast, the affiliation of non-chassidic Jews with the past does not centre on a specific group of individuals.

A less important but relevant distinction between Lubavitcher chassidim and non-Lubavitch orthodox Jews revolves about their attitude and behaviour toward non-observing Jews. Lubavitch's emphasis of *Ahavas Yisroel* urges these chassidim to initiate and sustain contact with Jews of varying degrees of religious observance to encourage them to fulfil the traditional requirements of Judaism. The Lubavitch philosophy teaches that "A Jew can be whole only when he has attained the true fulfilment of the *mitzvah* of *Ahavas Yisroel*—of loving each and every Jew without exception as he loves himself." (Challenge, 1970:176) As a result, though it is possible to be a very good Jew simply by observing the precepts of traditional Judaism, Lubavitcher are not content merely to fulfil these requirements. Unlike the majority of orthodox Jews and most other chassidic groups which, while organizing their lives around the Torah, display little if any concern for non-observing Jews, Lubavitcher encourage and assist them to reorganize their lives around *Yiddishkayt* (orthodox Judaism). Lubavitchers' pursuit of this activity was once well illustrated at a *Farbrengen* by the present Lubavitcher *Rebbe* when he said:

> I was privileged to hear from my father-in-law of saintly memory the following story . . . :
>
> His father, of saintly memory, was once asked, "What is a Chossid?" and he replied, "A chossid is a 'street-lamp lighter.'" The lamps were there in readiness but they needed to be lit. Sometimes the lamps are not as easily accessible as lamps on street corners; there are lamps in forsaken places, or at sea, but there must be someone to light even those lamps, so that they should not be wasted, but light up the path of others. (Teachers Programme, 1969:334)

Lubavitcher and their Rebbe

As the Yeshiva plays an important role in reinforcing the individuals' self-conception as a Lubavitcher chassid, it can be regarded in many ways as the nucleus of the Lubavitch community. Yet the essence of this community, and of the Lubavitcher chassidim everywhere, is the Lubavitcher *Rebbe*. As one Lubavitcher said:

> 770 (the world headquarters of Lubavitch from where the *Rebbe* carries out his work) spiritually is more important than the Yeshiva. 770 is the heart and soul of every Lubavitcher because the *Rebbe Shleete* (he shall live good long years, Amen) is what Lubavitch is and therefore 770 means very much to every Lubavitcher.

An older Yeshiva student expressed his feelings regarding the *Rebbe* in this manner:

> The *Rebbe* is the head of our generation. The *Rebbe* is the head of *Yiddishkayt* now. As Yeshiva students we have more opportunity of absorbing the *Rebbe* than we will when we are out of the Yeshiva. We don't want to miss any bit of that. We came here to Montreal because it's away from home, but we don't want to be away from the *Rebbe*. And the *Rebbe's Farbrengen* is worth so much to us that we will give up three days of learning to go.

Writing about the Lubavitcher *Rebbeim*, an emissary of the previous Lubavitcher *Rebbe* claimed:

> In his personal greatness and in the greatness of his leadership, every Lubavitcher *Rebbe* in the chain of their descendance has personified those ideas and ideals which Chabad Chassidus presents to mankind. They brought to perfection the ability to instill in the hearts and the conduct of their disciples, chassidim and students, each according to his abilities and devotion to the study of chassidus, that path which is within the reach of everyone, from the highest chossid to the furthest. (*Di Yiddishe Heim*, Vol. 12, No. 4:9)

The *Rebbe's* centrality to the Lubavitch community is immediately striking to anyone familair with these chassidim. Evidence of his importance can be gleaned from the frequency with which

Lubavitcher refer to him in their everyday conversation, especially with visitors and newcomers. When I first visited the Yeshiva a young man spoke to me about the *Rebbe*:

> He's a tremendous man. I think that as you go on you will understand what the *Rebbe* means to us and why we believe in him so much. I mean, how that one man does so much is beyond understanding. The correspondence he carries on is just fantastic. It has been said, I don't know by whom but I believe it, that the postmaster general has said that the *Rebbe* has the second largest correspondence in the United States. ... He has a few secretaries but he should really have a dozen because there is so much work to do. It has been said that sometimes the *Rebbe* is in the Yeshiva till three or four in the morning. It's also said, and I can believe it, that sometimes he's even up till six o'clock because he has so much to do. I know. I've seen it. There's a story about the *Rebbe* that when a summer camp opened in New York they asked the *Rebbe* to come and give his blessings. Five years later after they made new improvements in the camp they asked the *Rebbe* to come and see the camp again, and they had a letter from him saying that he still had to catch up on the five hours of work which he lost on his first visit. ... This just goes to show how busy the man is. It is said that the *Rebbe* has left New York only twice except for his visits to his father-in-law's grave, and there also seems to be more to his visits than meets the eye because it's said that after the *Rebbe* returns different things happen at the places he has been.[3]

I soon discovered that all Lubavitcher display the same high esteem and reverence toward the *Rebbe*. The miraculous stories related about his activities, the efforts made by Lubavitcher to be in New York during Lubavitch celebrations, and the kinds of advice sought from him all testify to his dominating influence among his followers.

Rabbi Menachem Mendel Schneerson, the present Lubavitcher *Rebbe*, is the seventh *Rebbe* in the line of Chabad chassidim founded by Rabbi Schneur Zalman (1745-1812). He is reported by Mintz as being a quiet intense man with a kindly expression, and gives the impression of "a man restraining a well of emotion." (1968:152) Born in 1902, he was a student of mathematics and science at the Sorbonne in Paris and trained in electrical engineering. He assumed the position of *Rebbe* after the previous Lubavitcher *Rebbe*, Rabbi Joseph Isaac Schneerson, his father-in-law, passed away. The position of *Rebbe* is usually inherited, often transmitted from father to son through several generations, but the previous *Rebbe's* family included two married daughters but no sons. Under such circumstances the selection of a new *Rebbe* is determined by following the instructions in the previous *Rebbe's* will, and if such information is unavailable the elders of the movement decide. The most likely candidates to assume the position in this instance were the previous *Rebbe's* two sons-in-law. Menachem Mendel Schneerson was chosen to be the new leader of the Lubavitch movement, while his brother-in-law remained head of the network of Lubavitcher Yeshivas. A newspaper account claimed: "There was no election, but he was the natural candidate on dynastic grounds and on the basis of scholarship and personal qualities." While never officially confirmed, it is often reported that Menachem Mendel only assumed his new position with some reluctance. As Weiner reports:

> For his part Menachem Mendel was genuinely reluctant to assume the leadership. He had taken courses in electrical engineering in Paris, while his wife was studying architecture, and they had planned to earn their living in these professions. It required two years to persuade him to accept the position of rebbe. (1969:151)

From his office situated to the left of the entrance to the Lubavitch headquarters on 770 Eastern Parkway, the *Rebbe*, with the assistance of his small office staff, directs the affairs of the Lubavitch movement throughout the world. In addition to meeting regularly with his followers and answering their inquiries, Lubavitcher claim that all correspondence issued from the *Rebbe's* office is carefully checked by him and must receive his approval. The *Rebbe's* work load is often so heavy that his office hours sometimes last into the early hours of the morning.

Although he has been married since 1929, the *Rebbe* and his wife are childless—a fact of great concern to his followers. Reluctant to discuss the practical implications of this situation for the Lubavitch movement, the *Rebbe's* followers often suggest that a very possible solution to this dilemma will be the Messiah's arrival. When the *Rebbe* was asked who was to be the eighth

Lubavitcher Rebbe he replied: "The Messiah will come and he will take all these troubles and doubts. He could come while I am here. Why postpone his coming?"

When asked by college students "What is the function of the *Rebbe*?" the *Rebbe* replied: " . . . to find the right switch in every Jew to connect him to the powerhouse" and referred them to a reply he had previously given to the same question:

> We can realize what the Baal Shem Tov did by noticing the relationship of an electric powerhouse with a switch that is connected to its wire. In order to connect oneself to a powerhouse, one must find the right switch or push the correct button. The soul of every Jew is connected to the powerhouse, but in order to employ the benefits of the powerhouse, the correct switch must be found or the right button pushed. It was the Baal Shem Tov's merit that he was able to discover the right switch in every Jew, so that through their connection to the powerhouse their lives were transformed from their dark despair to one of harmony and happiness. (Discussion of Princeton Students with the Lubavitch *Rebbe*—5720 [1960])

Due to the tremendous demand on the *Rebbe's* time, each Lubavitcher is granted a private audience with him only once a year, usually around the time of his birthdate. During this personal audience the *Rebbe* may be asked for advice or a *brocheh* (blessing). Although restricted to one personal audience Lubavitcher can ask the *Rebbe* for advice or for his blessing at any time by "writing in."

As Lubavitcher should strive to listen to and follow the *Rebbe's* personal advice as well as his general teachings and directions to all his followers it is essential that the Lubavitcher is aware of these teachings and directives and understands the *Rebbe's* perspective on particular matters. This may be accomplished in several ways, the most desirable of which is by attending as many as possible of the *Rebbe's Farbrengens* which are celebrated in Crown Heights, New York. Although the Lubavitch community may listen to the *Rebbe's Farbrengen*, all Lubavitcher agree that it is far preferrable to attend personally. An older student remarked:

Come on, you've been there. You know what it is. When

you're there you see the *Rebbe* and you can actually feel what he's saying. You can see how holy the man is. Alright, here in the Yeshiva you can listen, but it's not the same thing as seeing, my friend.

As expected, Lubavitcher eagerly take advantage of the hook-up and willingly contribute toward the financial cost. This institutionalized means of binding the chassidim to their *Rebbe* is more effective than the previous technique whereby someone present at the *Farbrengen* would, upon his return, report on the proceedings. Lubavitcher claim that is is more rewarding and spiritually satisfying to listen to the *Rebbe's* voice and hear the manner and tone in which he addresses his audience. The shared experience of listening to the *Rebbe's* discourses is believed to have a profound impact on those assembled in the Yeshiva's auditorium:

> Look, everyone here (in the Yeshiva) would rather be in New York with the *Rebbe*. There's no question about it. It's not always so easy to get away. So we have a *Farbrengen* here. And what better way is there than to be able to listen to the *Rebbe*. I can't tell you how important the *Rebbe* is. I mean everything in Lubavitch involves the *Rebbe*. You name it and the *Rebbe* is involved. You want to know how concerned the *Rebbe* is about Jews—I mean all Jews, not only Lubavitcher—listen to his voice. That tells it all. You see, this is what we all have in common here—the *Rebbe*. Believe me, no one here would miss the chance of using this hook-up.

The opportunity to listen to a *Farbrengen* holds additional advantages for the community. As Lubavitcher continually aim to disseminate the *Rebbe's* teachings to the larger Jewish community, they can freely invite the Jewish public to share in the experience of listening to the *Rebbe*, and their presence in the Yeshiva affords Lubavitcher the opportunity to discuss with them matters related to Judaism. In addition, these hook-ups permit the chassidim to impress upon their children the reverence and respect to be accorded to the *Rebbe*. On these occasions rows of tables and chairs are arranged in the Yeshiva's auditorium and, as on all occasions when men and women are present, a partition (*mecheetzeh*) separates the sexes. If the *Farbrengen* is celebrated on the Sabbath or a holy day when Sabbath restrictions forbid broadcasting, Lubavitcher present at the *Farbrengen* attempt to memorize the *Rebbe's* words so that they can relate them to others when they return. The sight of men huddled around a table in the Yeshiva listening to a Lubavitcher recount the substance of the *Rebbe's* remarks is very common.

The *Rebbe's* discourses, activities, and published letters are Lubavitchers' basis for discussion and argument during their proselytizing activities. Lubavitcher re-listen to and re-read the discourses and other published material and try to memorize their *Rebbe's* words. It is not surprising, then, that their reasoning and discussion with less observant Jews are drawn mainly from them. The accuracy and manner with which the Lubavitcher successfully reiterates the *Rebbe's* message varies from person to person, but the act itself helps root its truths firmly in the individual's mind and to reinforce his self-conception as a Lubavitcher. For example, I once overheard a Yeshiva student stressing the following point to a university graduate:

What do you think has kept the Jews together throughout history? If you're going to tell me that it was the State of Israel, then I think that you're wrong. I'll tell you what it was. What has united the Jewish people is the Torah and its commandments. This is what the Jews had in common regardless of where they were.

Compare these remarks with those of the *Rebbe*:

The essential element which unites our "dispersed and scattered people" and makes it "one people" throughout its dispersion and regardless of time, is the Torah and Mitzvoth, the Jewish way of life which has remained basically the same throughout the ages and in all places. The conclusion is clear and beyond doubt: It is the Torah and Mitzvoth which make our people indestructible on the world scene in the face of massacres and pogroms aiming at our physical destruction and in the face of ideological onslaughts of foreign cultures aiming at our spiritual destruction.

On another occasion, a Lubavitcher, discussing Jewish youth with a college student, argued that the older generation compromised their religion, leaving their children to believe that in today's society traditional Judaism is outdated and hence irrelevant—a point frequently presented by the *Rebbe*.

Along with arguments drawn from the *Rebbe's* discourses, stories reflecting the *Rebbe's* foresight and miraculous powers are sometimes offered as sufficient reason for observing a particular precept. The following story is widely circulated in Lubavitch circles:

> ... (An) American soldier in Korea ... one day wandered off from his squad looking for a stream in which to wash his hands before opening his can of C rations. A shell struck the squad's position, killing every one of his comrades. Today the young veteran vows he owes his life to a visit he had made, just before he shipped out to Korea, to the rebbe of the Lubavitcher movement. The latter had counselled the young man to observe, even while in combat, as much as he could of the Jewish law, including the commandment to wash one's hands before eating. (Weiner, 1969:141)

Another example of the influence of the *Rebbe's* teaching on all Lubavitcher occurred when a young man, in the Yeshiva for the first time for the morning prayers, was asked when his phylacteries (*Tefillin*) were last inspected. When he replied that they had never been inspected, the Lubavitcher welcoming him stressed the importance of having *Tefillin* inspected by a scribe:

> You know, this is a true story just to show you what I'm talking about. This person was very sick and wrote to the *Rebbe* asking him to wish him a *refooeh shlaimeh* (complete recovery) so he would get better. The *Rebbe* answered that he should have his *Tefillin* checked by a *soifer* (scribe) and that's all. So this guy figures "Well, if the *Rebbe* says so ... " So it was found that in the saying, "You should love God with all your soul and serve Him with all your heart," the word heart was scratched away. And it turned out what was wrong with this guy? Heart trouble. So, you see, it's really important to have the *Tefillin* checked.

Socializing Lubavitch Children

Since the *Rebbe* is so highly regarded by his followers, it is to be expected that they will try to implant their reverence for him in their children. While the community's educational institutions, including the schools, summer camps, and other organized activities, reflect the *Rebbe's* teaching, the way in which children are socialized in their homes to become aware of and appreciate his presence and authority is, in many ways, more important.

There is no prescribed sequence of steps by which the family educates its young about the *Rebbe*. Instead, it is expected that the child will be generally influenced by the ever-present Lubavitch atmosphere encountered in the home. In fact, the child's relationship to the *Rebbe* is considered so vital that as soon as the child is born the father will phone the *Rebbe*. References are made so frequently to the *Rebbe's* teachings and activities that his presence directly affects all aspects of family life. As Lubavitcher suggest, through the family's relationship with the *Rebbe* the young child inevitably becomes aware of his presence and importance:

> ... You only have to enter into a Lubavitcher household to see what I mean. I'm not talking about pictures hanging on the wall, but about *sforim* (religious books), letters, collections of what the *Rebbe* said, of what the *Rebbe* is giving out. ... I think it's experiences that really matter to a child. There is a lot of things that you experience within Lubavitch almost on a daily basis; that's really where a child is going to take it from. ... I don't think there are many days that go by in the house when the *Rebbe* isn't mentioned. ... There are any problems? The *Rebbe*. Any *simcheh* (celebration)? The *Rebbe*.

In addition to the chassidic atmosphere encountered in the home, the young child accompanies his family to *Farbrengens* in New York and is taken to personal audiences with the *Rebbe*. Such experiences, claim Lubavitcher parents, inevitably leave an indelible impression in the child's mind.

> Take my three-year-old as an example and I don't think this is an isolated instance. You ask who the *Rebbe* is. He'll tell you: "He lives in 770. He gave me wine when I went up, and he gave me a blessing." He'll tell you exactly what the room looked like and he'll tell you what the *Rebbe* looks like. ... Already at three years old when we bring him, he

can relate. (Does the child go to New York?) Yes, when he's old enough to understand, the whole family goes. There's no doubt, they take him along. And on special occasions when the family as a group has a particular audience with the *Rebbe*, then the family takes advantage of having everyone come in. Now my married daughter . . . had an audience with the *Rebbe*. . . . Her child is only 7 or 8 months old, and she and her husband and the baby all went in. Now I'm sure that the baby doesn't understand anything at the moment, but if she goes in now, and she'll go in a year from now, it will become a tradition.

As young children mature they are continually brought into contact with events and experiences relating directly or indirectly with the *Rebbe*. Through his upbringing, then, the young Lubavitcher is taught and learns to recognize the *Rebbe* as a special kind of person whom his parents and others around him both trust and revere.

Belief in the Rebbe's Advice

There is a wide range of subjects on which the Lubavitcher may seek the *Rebbe's* advice: moving to a new house, taking a new job, seeking solutions to health problems, or planning a summer vacation. Typically, the *Rebbe* is called on to offer advice whenever the issue is uncertain, for his power is believed to consist not only of foreseeing the outcome but being able to influence future events. One need not be faced with a critical situation to write to the *Rebbe*, and it has become customary to write in to ask for a blessing (*brocheh*) on the occasion of any celebration such as a birthday of wedding anniversary.

No firm guidelines regulate the kinds of problems the *Rebbe* will consider, and each person decides on which matters to seek the *Rebbe's* counsel. Convinced of the *Rebbe's* special powers, which are believed to penetrate to the essence of every matter, Lubavitcher expect his blessing to help ensure the success of an undertaking. For example, when I mentioned to some Yeshiva students that I was preparing for an important examination, one suggested: "Why don't you write in to the *Rebbe* for a *brocheh* (blessing)? It can only help." A newcomer to Lubavitch consulted with the *Rebbe* about whether he should go back to school although he now had a wife and family to support. In another case, a woman asked the *Rebbe* for the kind of advice usually received from a pediatrician. She was nervous about her new baby who was not sleeping or eating well. Although the *Rebbe* only told her to relax more, which is what any pediatrician would have told her, because the advice came from the *Rebbe* she had more confidence in following it.

The above remarks suggest two important features of the *Rebbe's* relationship with his followers. First, it is left to the individual's own discretion to decide on which matters to seek the *Rebbe's* counsel; second, since he is a righteous man, a *Tzaddic*, Lubavitcher believe that he can offer only helpful advice. It is, in fact, the Lubavitchers' belief that the *Rebbe's* advice can only be helpful that is important, rather than the advice itself. This is what a newcomer, not yet totally sharing Lubavitchers' reverence for the *Rebbe*, referred to when he said: "I mean the *brochess* (blessings) have a certain effect and you wonder to what extent the person reads into the situation, rather than the *brocheh* objectively producing something." This attitude reflects W. I. Thomas' dictum: If men define situations as real, they are real in their consequences. (Volkart, 1951) Because the *Rebbe* is perceived by his followers as unable to do wrong, they are willing to claim to have misinterpreted and not "really understood" his advice if it should prove objectively false. Consequently, it is impossible to have a disconfirmation of the *Rebbe's* teachings.[4]

A Threat to Identity Maintenance in Religious Communities—Assimilation

Although the Lubavitch community's effort to maintain a distinctive identity is mainly reached through its relationship with the *Rebbe*, internal unity is not enough. If any religious community is to persist, it must also resist the threat of assimilation into the larger society. Certain common conditions threaten and compromise any community's efforts to maintain its identity, and many of the same features that help to create the identity may also be used to resist assimilative influences from the surrounding society.

Such features as dress and insulation seem to be becoming

decreasingly effective as the larger society's assimilative influences begin to penetrate the community's barriers, resulting in a blurring of the boundary between member and outsider. The group's distinctive garb gradually becomes modified by the fashions regulating dress on the outside, especially by the young who are sometimes embarrassed by their parents' old-fashioned clothes. Hostetler reports that among the New Order Amish, distinctive dress and hair styles show a marked modification. These Amish trim their hair and beards shorter and shorter and "with the dwindling of the beard an Amishman may no longer identify himself as an Amish person . . . Secularization in apparel appears to be greater among men than women, and more advanced among the young than the old." (1968:329)

The same trends can be seen in varying degrees in the chassidic communities. A young man, raised in a chassidic milieu, once told me:

> A lot of the older guys wear these baggy pants and the suits they get for their kids don't look too good on them either. But you'll see the younger guys, those who can afford it, buying suits that are in style. OK, they won't be the real fancy stuff, but the suit will be made well, at a good place. All they do is give the guy the material.

It is also becoming increasingly difficult to resist the outside influences penetrating the community's lifestyle and to maintain physical, cultural, and social insulation. In an urban setting, community members are inevitably exposed, both visually and aurally, to influences considered detrimental to the community's special lifestyle, and the elders are especially concerned about the effect on the young. Conversations with the young from different chassidic groups indicate they are aware of the styles and fads in the outside world as well as their elders' concern about this awareness. A Yeshiva student said: "They (teachers and elders) realize it's impossible or very impractical to keep us from seeing things which the *Yaytzer Ho'Ro* (Evil Inclination) puts in our way. It worries some of them a great deal."

One way in which religious communities try to maintain their distinctive identity is to set up strict criteria to distinguish between who is really inside and who is outside. This distinction can only be maintained effectively when the community insulates itself from those conditions in the outside world which are contradictory to its lifestyle. But it is both impractical and in many ways undesirable for a community to isolate itself completely from the influences of outsiders.

Outsiders' Effect on the Community's Identity

Unlike other chassidic groups which attempt to minimize contact with non-orthodox Jews, the Lubavitch philosophy teaches, and the Lubavitcher *Rebbe* continually reminds his followers, that all Jews must be brought into the orthodox fold and that it is their duty to help accomplish this goal:

> However the Jew must not think only of himself. The commandment "Love thy fellow as thyself" demands the same attitude towards the fellow-Jew. No Jew should ever be given up. It is necessary to kindle in him that pure and holy light, even if it appears to be good only for no more than one day; for even that in itself is worthwhile, and more,—it will steadily grow from day to day, and gradually illuminate his whole life. (Teachers Programme:97)

To this end, Lubavitcher organize a series of activities designed especially to be attractive to Jews of varying degrees of religious observance. Outsiders are invited and encouraged to come to the Lubavitchers' Yeshiva, their homes, and other social and religious functions. The Lubavitch aim is to extend a warm welcome to these Jews in the hope of drawing them progressively closer to observing the practices of traditional Judaism. Since outsiders are invited to mingle with Lubavitcher, the boundaries guarding against outside influences are less effective than among, for example, the Satmarer chassidim. Lubavitcher should, therefore, experience difficulty in maintaining their distinctive identity, since the boundaries separating insider from outsider are less clearly demarcated. In fact, however, Lubavitcher are successful at maintaining their identity and, paradoxically, outsiders contribute toward that effort as Lubavitchers' proselytizing serves to reinforce their own beliefs and clarify their definition of themselves as Lubavitcher.

Conclusion

For the Lubavitch community to persist it must cultivate and maintain a distinctive identity. To belong to this community Lubavitcher should both consider themselves as members of the group and also be seen by other Lubavitcher as belonging to the group. A schematic classification of the Lubavitch community can thus be constructed along these two dimensions. When the two dimensions are cross-classified they produce four cells or different categories of Lubavitcher. (see Table 1)

Table 1

		Do other Lubavitcher regard this person as one of them?	
		Yes	No
Does this person regard him/her-self as a Lubavitcher?	Yes	Lubavitcher 1	2 (deviants)*
	No	3 shtikl	4 affiliates

*Parentheses indicate this category is logically possible but no such persons were encountered.

Cell 1 includes those who think of themselves as Lubavitcher and are so regarded by other Lubavitcher. The majority of the individuals in this category stem from a Lubavitch background although some *tzugekumenne* (recruits) are also found there. Some of those in this category are what Lubavitcher label as "hard-core" or "right-wing" Lubavitcher. This group is best characterized by its resistance to secularizing influences within the community. The boys of these parents typically do not receive a formal secular education but study religious subjects the entire day.

Cell 2 consists of those who may be called deviants. These would be persons who regarded themselves as Lubavitcher chassidim but whose self-definition was not shared by other Lubavitcher. Although this category is logically possible, I have not encountered any such individuals.

In Cell 3 we find those called *shtikl* (partly) Lubavitcher. Their chief characteristic is that while other Lubavitcher are prepared to consider them as Lubavitcher, they are either unwilling or unprepared to regard themselves as such. For example:

> There's a popular word in our community that's cropping up—*shtikl* Lubavitcher—and it's probably because there are some people . . . like our neighbour across the street. He wouldn't do any business without asking the *Rebbe* and if the *Rebbe's* answer contradicts his own, he'll still do it because the *Rebbe* said so. Yet he doesn't study any of the *Rebbe's* chassidic discourses. He doesn't keep a lot of the laws that chassidim would want him to . . . and I don't know whether if somebody asked him: "Are you a Lubavitcher?" he would like to be called one . . . but he hasn't reached the stage of considering himself as one.

Some of these *shtikl* Lubavitcher are recruits (*baal tshuvess*) who, with Lubavitchers' assistance, are being processed into orthodox Judaism and Lubavitch. Since there are no clearly marked stages in becoming a Lubavitcher these individuals often face the dilemma of whether or not to regard themselves as Lubavitcher chassidim:

> There's a X (type of occupation) in our community. . . . Well, . . . he probably told you how long he's been in Lubavitch. This dates back to about a year or two ago and he told us of his problem when someone asked him all of a sudden . . . : "Are you a Lubavitcher?" And it was the first time he was confronted with the fact, is he yet or isn't he yet? And he had to do a lot of analysis to come to a positive answer. He just worked along those lines and he wasn't quite sure that he's hit them. . . . And he realized that sooner or later he'd have to give such an answer and because he had spent so many years learning and at the *Farbrengen*, he wasn't ashamed to be called Lubavitch whereas a year before he might have been ashamed to be

called one because he felt that he hadn't been accepted or would even like to be tied down by the name.

Cell 4 incorporates those who are affiliated with the Lubavitcher and their activities, but do not consider themselves nor are they judged by Lubavitcher to be chassidim of this group. There are various degrees of affiliation ranging from those whose contact ends with their financial contribution, to those who pray at the Lubavitcher Yeshiva and send their children to the Lubavitch schools. For example, I once asked a Lubavitcher about a specific individual and he replied, "He *davns* in the Yeshiva. . . . He's not a Lubavitcher but he has strong feelings for the Yeshiva." About another person he said: "Mr. _____ *davns* in Lubavitch. . . . We're going to call some of them semi-Lubavitcher, sort of tied to Lubavitch." On one occasion I asked a person if he considered himself a Lubavitcher. He replied: "Me, no, I'm not a Lubavitcher and these people sitting here (pointing to six people who sat at the same table) are also not Lubavitcher."

A major distinction between those in cells 1, 3, and 4 lies in the nature of their relationship with the Lubavitcher *Rebbe*. Those in cell 1 experience the closest relationship, whereas for those in cells 3 and 4 the relationship typically becomes progressively weaker. It is, however, possible to move from one cell to another and, since the Lubavitch movement remains open to anyone wishing to enter, such movements occur continually. Individuals can either transfer themselves or be transferred from one cell to the other, usually from cell 1 to cell 3, or from cell 3 to cell 1. Passage out of cell 1 is, however, fairly rare and any movement from the first to the fourth cell usually includes the second cell as a transition point.

Footnotes

[1] "In the Orthodox ritual the convert appears before a rabbi, in the presence of two other learned men or rabbis, and makes the following declaration: 1) that he knows and accepts the duties and obligations of Jewish law and sincerely intends to fulfill them; 2) that he rejects those tenets of his former faith that are out of keeping with Judaism; 3) that he has been baptized in the traditional ritual bath; and 4) that he has been circumcised.

The Reform ritual is not so elaborate. The candidate for conversion is required to answer seven questions: 1) that he enters Judaism of his own free will; 2) that he is willing to renounce his former faith; 3) that he will pledge his loyalty to Judaism; 4) that he promises "to cast his lot with the people of Israel amid all circumstances and conditions"; 5) that he will lead a Jewish life; 6) that he will rear his children in the Jewish faith; and 7) that he will have his male children circumcised. The candidate then makes a formal pledge and repeats, in English and in Hebrew, the prayer: 'Hear O Israel, the Lord our God, the Lord is One.'

Before he can be accepted in Judaism the candidate must prove that he is familiar with the faith which he has chosen. He must have completed an intensive course of studies, including the Bible, the prayer book, customs and rituals, holiday and Sabbath observances, and Jewish history. The modern convert to Judaism often knows more about his faith than one who is born a Jew and takes his religion for granted.

The Orthodox ritual calls for the new initiate to attend the synagogue on the Sabbath following his conversion. He is called to the reading of the *Torah*, and a special blessing is recited. . . . He is then given a Hebrew name for use in all ritual acts." (Kertzer, 1960:178-179)

[2] It would be fallacious to believe that all Jews could be neatly classified as being either Orthodox, Conservative, or Reform. There are many Jews who may be referred to as secular Jews, who follow many of the traditions handed down through generations, but do not adhere to the laws.

[3] Some recent studies about the chassidim deal with the *Rebbe's* importance to his followers. Mintz (1968), for example, tells us that one aspect of the *Rebbe's* role is that he serves as a mediator between his followers and God. Mintz presents an analysis of the *Rebbe's* functions regarding his followers and the interrelationship resulting between the two. Weiner (1969) in his chapter on "The Lubavitcher Movement" describes his personal audience with the Lubavitcher *Rebbe*. For a discussion of the Satmarer *Rebbe*, see Rubin (1972), pp. 56-62. Gutwirth's study (1970) of the Belzer chassidim includes discussion of the Belzer *Rebbe*.

[4] A similar point is suggested by Rubin in his discussion of the Satmarer *Rebbe*:

. . . what is important is the way he is perceived by the members of the community, rather than the way he might score on some objective value scale. (1972:59)

Lubavitcher Rebbe, Menachem M. Schneerson. *Photo courtesy of the Lubavitch Foundation. Used by special permission.*

A Lubavitcher Farbrengen. *Photo courtesy of the Lubavitch Foundation. Used by special permission.*

The Tefillin Campaign. *Photo courtesy of the Lubavitch Foundation. Used by special permission.*

The Sukkehmobile. *Photo courtesy of the Lubavitch Foundation. Used by special permission.*

The Tefillin Campaign. *Photo courtesy of the Lubavitch Foundation. Used by special permission.*

The Lubavitch Bookmobile. *Photo courtesy of the Lubavitch Foundation. Used by special permission.*

Study Classes in the Yeshiva.

Study Classes in the Yeshiva

The Lubavitcher Bocherim

Bocherim in the Bays Medresh

Chapter Four

Maintaining A Tenable Way of Life

In the previous chapter it was argued that for a religious community to persist it must cultivate a distinctive identity for itself and for its members. This chapter will deal with the closely related point that not only must the community have an identity but it must also create a way of life that is tenable. "Way of life" is used here to mean an ideology that is collectively maintained and supported by the community members and that involves them in a set of activities which reinforce their loyalty to the community's rules and sanctions. "Tenable" refers to conditions which allow for the maintenance and support of the community's way of life. It is first necessary to establish those characteristics present in the community which makes its way of life tenable, and then to identify that part of the community's ideology that helps to insulate members from those cultural features of urban life which conflict with their conduct as orthodox Jews and Lubavitcher chassidim. The community's ideology also reinforces Lubavitchers' determination and desire to organize their lives around the Torah's teachings and abide by the practical consequences as interpreted by their *Rebbe*.

Features Contributing to the Community's Tenability

The features of the community discussed here are not intended to be an exhaustive list, but will focus on three of the community's distinctive characteristics which help advance its institutional completeness and hence its tenability: the Yeshiva; the distance from the Lubavitcher *Rebbe's* headquarters; and the nature of Lubavitcher's occupations.

The Lubavitcher Yeshiva: Its Centrality in the Community

In the course of a casual conversation with a non-Lubavitch Jew

82

the Lubavitcher Yeshiva was mentioned and I asked him if he had ever heard of it. He quickly replied:

> Don't tell *me* about them. I once went there just out of curiosity. Downstairs they have the *shul* where they hold their services. Really, I mean it was just dirty and messy— that's all I could say. Tables were pushed around and so were benches. Drinks were spilled on the floor. Prayer books were all over the place. Cigarette butts were on the floor. And some people were sitting there and they just couldn't seem to care less about the mess. It's like they were used to it. I mean I've gone to synagogues and I've never seen one like this . . .

A few weeks later I was sitting in the Yeshiva waiting for the service to begin. The *shul* (synagogue) was filled and in the next room younger Yeshiva students were preoccupied with their soccer games. A Lubavitcher sat down beside me and said:

> This place is really something. I mean, can you imagine if someone from the outside who didn't know about this place came in? I mean, just imagine. If he has been to *shul*, he's going to compare this place with his *shul*. Here there's no carpets, the benches aren't so comfortable, tables are pushed together. . . . There's only one or two ash trays so people use the floor. And by *Olaynoo* they spit. I mean, what does such a person think about this place? I'll tell you this, if he doesn't understand this place, he'll leave with a bad impression.

I once asked the *shul's* beadle what was most difficult about the work he did. He answered: "Everyone thinks he is the owner. Everyone thinks he is the boss. How can I be expected to keep this place orderly if nobody wants to listen?" (translated from Yiddish) On another occasion an older Yeshiva student, talking about the possible reasons for the apparent disinterest in synagogue attendance in general among young Jews, referred to the Yeshiva:

> If you go into a synagogue you'll notice how quiet it is, how formal everything is. And that's very simple—it's like most of the people are guests in the synagogue because they go there so little and, you know, guests have to act properly. But here, because people spend so much time here, they feel at home.

Since men and boys spend as much time as they can in the Yeshiva (approximately thirty-five hours a week for the men) they learn to be comfortable and relaxed there. Unlike those Jews who attend services at a synagogue and promptly leave as soon as the service ends, Lubavitcher remain in *shul* and "just sit around and talk." As Lubavitcher insist, this is important since the topics of conversation are mostly related to *Yiddishkayt*. A Lubavitcher who spends at least part of each day in the Yeshiva feels himself to be part of it. He considers the Yeshiva to be his, just as it belongs to other Lubavitcher. If, for some reason, he decides to move some tables and benches together, he feels free to do so. If he feels inclined to study from one of the *sforim* (holy books) he does not request permission to open the cabinet where they are kept, but simply helps himself. The *chossid* feels himself at home in the Yeshiva and from an early age his sons are taught to respond likewise.

The Yeshiva serves not only as a spiritual centre where Lubavitcher come to pray (*davn*) but also as a social or community centre where various community functions such as weddings, *Bar Mitzvess*, and circumcision ceremonies are regularly held. A person can continue to be a Lubavitcher primarily by attending the Yeshiva, for it is there that he encounters other Lubavitcher, *davns* and studies with them, and becomes familiar with the most recent events related to the *Rebbe*. In the course of a conversation about Lubavitch, a *chossid* told me:

> ... you see, this marks the real Lubavitcher. ... The real Lubavitcher can go to a *chassenneh* (wedding), or a *Bar Mitzveh* somewhere else, but he's not at home. He's at home in Lubavitch, in the Yeshiva. If for a time, for one reason or another, he's not in the Yeshiva, if he's from X (name of city), and he's not in the X Yeshiva or in another Lubavitcher Yeshiva, he is not himself because the Yeshiva is part of himself.

In his chapter, "Court Life," Mintz (1968) claims that the *Bays Medresh*, which corresponds fairly closely to the *shul* in the Lubavitcher Yeshiva, is the central point for the activities of a chassidic group: "It serves not only as the place of study and prayer but is also the hub of hasidic social life—a place of rest, meditation, conversation, politicizing, children's play and story—

telling." (1968:48) The spiritual and social activities in the *shul* and other parts of the Yeshiva are the source of Lubavitchers' "spiritual nourishment," their tie with God. Coming to the Yeshiva is not, therefore, relegated to specific times of the week but instead occurs as often as Lubavitchers' work schedule and other commitments allow. The Yeshiva's centrality to the community is illustrated well in the following comment by a Lubavitcher:

It is the centre, it is the life, the Yeshiva *is* the life of the Lubavitcher. It is the nucleus, the source of their existence, their spiritual nourishment, it's their tie with G-d, in fact ... to some people, that's life. The Yeshiva is life ... *that* is life. Actually the home and the house is a necessity. You have to live in a certain place, you have to be married, you have to have children. You have to lead a physical life, but the spiritual life—that is the Yeshiva. And at certain times for a spiritual uplifting you go to the *Rebbe*, for a higher spiritual uplifting and for guidance and for moral fiber. The Yeshiva fulfils many functions. You *davn* (pray) in the Yeshiva. Reb _____, ... said that when he came to the Yeshiva in Russia, all they knew was that the Yeshiva is their life. You studied in the Yeshiva as a boy. If you came there before *Bar Mitzveh*, you got *Bar Mitzveh* in the Yeshiva. You got married in the Yeshiva. You had children while being in the Yeshiva. You brought up your children in the Yeshiva. It was your life, from when you came to the Yeshiva, from the cradle to the grave. ... The Yeshiva is the most realistic way of life because to Lubavitcher the world is to be enlightened because the *Alter Rebbe* says in the *Tanya* that as the days go by the world is getting darker and darker. That means that wickedness gets stronger all the time. So one needs, one is interested in moral values, one needs moral support all the time and one needs to go out in the world to purify the air. ... So we get this stimulus and the moral fiber from the *sheeur* (study session) we just had and after the *sheeur* we have *Tanya*.

The Yeshiva Building

Some of the main features of the Yeshiva are the *shul* in the basement, the auditorium, and the schoolyard which together provide virtually all the services needed by the community. The *shul's* architectural and decorative simplicity are its most striking features and stand in marked contrast to the more stylish design of an orthodox synagogue directly across the street. While used primarily for prayer, it also serves as the centre for various other activities including study classes and *Farbrengens*. The interior is roughly furnished with benches and tables which can be moved about to suit any occasion. Its frequently disorderly appearance shows clearly that it is much used both by adult males and younger boys attending the Lubavitch school located in the Yeshiva. In contrast to worshippers in modern synagogues who sit on pews arranged in rows, Lubavitcher face one another seated on benches around tables. This seating arrangement allows for intimate social contact and thus helps to maintain the spirit of unanimity underlying this chassidic community. Normally the *shul* is separated from the rest of the basement by a sliding wooden wall, but during the Sabbath and religious holidays when females attend the services this is replaced by a *mecheetzeh* or special partition to separate the men from the women. The relatively large basement is used, when necessary, to accommodate the female guests at a wedding or *Bar Mitzveh*. It is also sometimes used for services, but usually it is where *Bays Medresh* students eat breakfast and lunch, Lubavitcher and other Jews assemble for study classes, and Yeshiva students spend their recess period, lunch hour and other spare time.

The main floor of the Yeshiva consists of administrative offices, an auditorium with a seating capacity for approximately five hundred, and a corridor lined with classrooms for the elementary grades. As they have a large auditorium, Lubavitcher can organize their celebrations, primarily weddings, in the Yeshiva. The kitchen, equipped with kitchenware and electrical appliances, is adjacent to the auditorium and is supervised by Lubavitcher so there are no problems about *Kashruth* (the dietary laws) which might arise if they were forced to rent an auditorium elsewhere. The auditorium is also used for the Lubavitchers' proselytizing activities, such as Encounter with Chabad, the *Chanekkeh*[1], and *Purim*[2] rallies, and rehearsals for the Lubavitch women's drama group. Finally, functions such as money-raising rallies, testimonial dinners, and graduation exercises are also held there.

One other part of the Yeshiva's facilities bears mention—the schoolyard. As with all schoolyards, Yeshiva students use theirs for whatever recreational activities are popular at the time. The Yeshiva's schoolyard, however, serves additional purposes. As driving is prohibited by Jewish law on holidays which occur on weekdays, many Lubavitcher use the schoolyard instead of the street for parking their cars to avoid parking violations. Finally, the schoolyard is used for wedding ceremonies as it is customary among chassidic and non-chassidic orthodox Jews to perform the marriage ceremony outdoors.

The Yeshiva as a Spiritual Centre

The Yeshiva serves as the inspirational source through which the Lubavitcher arm themselves for what is regarded as a war against the *Yaytzer Ho'Ro* (Evil Inclination). The Yeshiva is both a place for prayer and also the meeting place for those who come to learn and study.

Like all practising orthodox Jews, those Lubavitcher who can, meet in the *shul* three times daily for services; at any time from dawn until noon for the morning prayer (*Shachris*); and at dusk for the afternoon and evening prayers (*Mincheh* and *Myriv*). Some Lubavitcher begin to arrive in the *shul* as early as seven o'clock in the morning to prepare themselves for the morning service. As only ten men are required to begin the service, several services begin at different times and sometimes overlap. Those who can, return to the Yeshiva later in the day for the *Mincheh* and *Myriv* services. Since the times for these vary with the hour of sunset, some people's work prevents them from coming to the Yeshiva in time to pray with the rest. They must, therefore, pray alone. As with the morning service, there are usually several after- noon and evening services, some of which again overlap. Even if they are unable to be at *shul* during the week, all Lubavitcher attend the Sabbath services if at all possible.

The Lubavitch philosophy stresses that at any particular mo- ment each Jew is at his own individual level in *Yiddishkayt*, and their objective is to raise themselves to the next higher level. A Jew must not, therefore, become complacent with his degree of religious observance but must continually strive to achieve even more. A Lubavitcher once put it like this:

... Actually, it is a chassidic philosophy that you recognize that every person is on a level and his job is to get to the next level. Not to get ten levels ahead, and not to get on someone else's level, but it's his particular level. So when you're with a person, you try to get him to take the next step, to go to the next level. For a person who doesn't keep *Shabbess* at all, maybe for that person to give up smoking puts him on a different level.

Studying the Torah's laws is the most effective way to advance as this familiarizes one with the Torah's precepts and increases one's understanding of their significance and relevance. The Yeshiva serves as the central place to fulfil the *mitzveh* of learning Torah since, for the majority of Lubavitcher, it is the most convenient place to meet.

The Lubavitcher *Rebbe* continually emphasizes the importance of studying Torah. Lubavitcher share their *Rebbe's* concern but work and family obligations often make it difficult to devote as much time to this as they would like. To facilitate matters, study classes are organized to meet during the time between the afternoon and evening services. One such class studies the *Alter Rebbe's* (the first Lubavitcher *Rebbe*) Code of Jewish Law (*Shulchn Orech*). The number of participants varies between seven and ten and the class usually lasts half an hour. As the different Jewish holidays approach, the relevant sections of the Code of Jewish Law explaining the specific *mitzvess* pertaining to the holiday are studied. Another class, meeting later in the evening, studies *Gemoreh* (the portion of the Talmud discussing the laws of the *Mishneh*—mainly the interpretation of the Biblical law). As one Lubavitcher said: "These are people who because of press of business and working, wouldn't learn anything if there was no *Daf Yoymee* (daily portion of Talmudic learning). This class meets every single day except when it is practically impossible as, for example, *Yom Kipper*. The usual number of participants is approximately twenty."

Although they stress the importance of learning[3], more Lubavitcher do not participate in these classes for a variety of reasons. First, some meet as a group and study on their own. One group of approximately five people meets three times weekly and studies *Gemoreh*. Second, some people learn together secretly because, as a Lubavitcher explained:

Now at certain times there are some people learning together that not many people know about because there's a
brocheh (blessing) in it when not everybody knows about it,
and they learn *Chassidess* and they learn *Gemoreh*.

Third, since the various study classes are intended to attract
people at one level of knowledge of *Yiddishkayt,* they do not
draw those at different levels. A Lubavitcher reported the following about the class studying the Code of Jewish Law:

> . . . well, usually you won't find at the *Shulchn Orech* very
> learned people because the very learned people tend to
> learn something deeper, because *Shulchn Orech* they can
> learn by themselves or they have learned it and they can
> learn it at home.

The study classes organized in the Yeshiva are accessible to every
Lubavitcher, but it is expected that people will only join the class
that is at the most suitable level for them at that time. For
example, it is considered less beneficial for a recent recruit to
attend the *Gemoreh* class than to meet privately with a Lubavitcher and concentrate on such basic *mitzvess* as *Kashruth* and
Tefillin. A Lubavitcher once pointed to a small group learning in
a corner of the *shul* and said: "That is an elite class." When I
inquired whether anyone could attend that class he replied:

> If I'm interested in going to such a *scheeur* (class), I would
> speak to one of the participants and OK it with him. . . . I
> sometimes thought of sitting down there but that class is
> really above my speed and I don't know how much I
> would get out of it.

On the other hand, it is not unusual for someone at a more
advanced level of *Yiddishkayt* to participate in a more basic class.
Such participation is simply intended to fulfil the *mitzveh* of
learning:

> Tonight you had different people (attending the class). X
> can learn. And Rabbi_____ can learn. And I can
> learn *Shulchn Orech.* But it's a *sheeur* and it's between
> *Mincheh-Myriv* and there's a *mitzveh* of learning, so one
> learns.

In some instances Lubavitcher meet in someone's home and learn there. This is the case especially for those who live some distance from the Yeshiva and must go there on foot, but they usually prefer to meet in the Yeshiva as it is more than just the spiritual centre of the Lubavitch community.

The Yeshiva as a Social Centre

The Yeshiva also serves as the focal point in the Lubavitch community's social life, but this does not imply that there is a definite break between the spiritual and the social life. Lubavitcher continually emphasize that *Yiddishkayt* must be regarded as a way of life to be lived twenty-four hours a day, rather than a series of commandments to be performed at certain prearranged hours. What may, therefore, appear as a purely social gathering to an outsider is, in fact, infused with religious activity and significance.

One often finds pairs or groups of people in the Yeshiva who appear to be just sitting around and talking for the Yeshiva is the place where information can be exchanged. As a Lubavitcher told me:

> ... but you'll also have a lot of people just sitting around and talking. It's a curious thing. ... In a sense among *Misnagdim* (opponents of chassidim) that would be a horrendous thing. How can you just sit around and talk? And yet, that's a very important thing, just sitting around. It's learning, but in a sense it's, it's ... what is a *Farbrengen*? One of the claims of *Misnagdim* ... (is) what do the chassidim do? They get together ... and they sit and talk. ... And yet that's a type of friendship. It means a lot, and that's as much a community activity as a bazaar is and perhaps even more.

"Just sitting around," is not just time wasted for the conversations might, for example, centre on a recent *Farbrengen* or the *Rebbe's* discourse about a particular issue, or it might focus on laws (*deenim*) and their practical implications. In some way or other most conversations are linked to *Yiddishkayt* but topics ranging from sports to politics and business are not uncommon. While not regarded as study in the traditional sense, it is informal learning. A Lubavitcher's account best illustrates this:

... Here, for instance I wasn't home today at all. I went away in the morning, it was *Shabbess Mevorchim* (first Sabbath in a new month), I had to start saying *Tillim* (Psalms). I just managed to come home for *Havdolleh* (the prayer separating the Sabbath or holiday from the coming week) and that was it. Why? I came in the morning to *shul*, I started saying *Tillim*. There came up a question whether you're allowed to open a container on *Shabbess*. I mean it's a result of talking, it's true, but meanwhile I found out with ... a whole group of people a couple of *deenim* (laws) whether you're allowed to do so and so on *Shabbess* or not. It's called, you know, doing something against *Shabbess*. Now it went from opening a container to ... opening a can, to opening those cans that you zip open, to opening these no deposit no return bottles, if you're allowed to use a hot plate, for instance, ... Before you know it, it must have been three hours shooting off. I didn't waste any time. I can't say I wasted time. I can't call it learning definitely, although it is. We didn't have any books. Now take a person who just walked into the *Bays Medresh* upstairs. He sees a whole bunch of guys just sitting down and just chatting away. He doesn't know exactly what. He would say: "Ah, these guys are just fooling around." Actually these guys are learning. Alright, you can learn from the book and you can learn from question leading to question, one thing to another. For instance, whether you're allowed to turn on the hot water on Friday night and let it run throughout the *Shabbess*. You're only allowed to turn it on on *Shabbess*. But to turn it on on Friday and let it run straight through, are you allowed or not? Let's say "Yes." If I'm allowed to, am I allowed to turn on the cold water? If I turn on the cold water while the hot water is running through the sink, I'm warming up the cold water. Am I allowed to do that? One thing leads to another thing. Before you knew it two hours had gone and there were a lot of things you still hadn't come up with. Then you have *davening*. ... Now if you want to look at it from the outside ... it surely looked like we were sitting and talking, just nothing. But it was constructive. So here you have a *Shabbess* where no one went home, I mean of this crowd anyway, and you have some constructive things that came out of it.

The Yeshiva also serves as a social centre for the younger students of the Yeshiva. They often use the basement to play soccer, football, hockey, and other games. In fact, it is not unusual for such games to be played while (older) Lubavitcher chassidim are praying in the *shul*. Lubavitchers' attitude is that if the students spend their free time in the Yeshiva rather than elsewhere, they are less likely to be exposed to undesirable influences.

The previous chapter briefly referred to the importance of the family in socializing the young. While emphasizing the centrality of the Yeshiva, the family's role in helping to preserve the community's tenability should also be mentioned. In many ways it is difficult to pinpoint this role as the effects of Lubavitcher's beliefs pervade all aspects of family life, and conversely the tightly knit family unit that this tends to create in turn effects and is reflected in the community. However, some of the ways in which the family contributes to the community's persistence can be related both to the *Rebbe's* influence on Lubavitcher and to the way the Yeshiva is used as the centre of all social activities.

As the religious education of the young is of primary importance to the community, and as such education starts when the child is very young, the family's role is of considerable importance. Lubavitcher emphasize that the closeness and cohesiveness of the family are directly related to the *Rebbe* and it is his influence that creates the atmosphere of *Yiddishkayt* in the home.

The significance of the home and family is frequently stressed in Lubavitch publications. For example, an article in *Di Yiddishe Heim* states:

> In this troubled and afflicted world, the Jewish home is the last bastion of reality and strength—reality in recognizing the malady and strength in not submitting to social trends.
> ... The truly Jewish home suffers least from all the deviant behaviour of our day. ... Let us continue to demonstrate that the answer to the world's dilemma, the ounce of prevention, begins, like charity, in the home. (Vol. 10, No. 1:24)

But, as Lubavitcher recognize, their families are like any family in which respect for higher authority governs their way of life. One Lubavitcher remarked that "children do come out different in that home, more stable, than children in families where everybody is just doing their thing." The following quotation from a conversation with a Lubavitcher underlines the view that the quality of life in their homes is different only in degree, and not in kind, from other homes in which the importance of the family unit is stressed and respect for a higher authority is present:

> Firstly, you must be impressed that in most orthodox homes the family is still a very important unit, in contrast to what we see in the world at large. So in any orthodox home, whether it is chassidic or not, the family plays a very important role. And if it's orthodox, then the holidays and the special red-letter days on the calendar play a very important part, and that again is where the family gets together to participate in whatever ceremony or occasion is the order of the day. I remember reading an article a few years ago, when juvenile delinquency became a new problem to cope with, where some psychologist said that the dinner table was a very good remedy against juvenile delinquency, and I immediately attached it to our lifestyle and began to understand why the general consensus of opinion is that you'll find a much smaller percentage of juvenile delinquency in orthodox homes than other homes. To ask why or how a Lubavitch Jewish family and home differ from any religious home—I don't think it's so much the home as the general view of things. Assuming that all agree that the family is important, and there's respect for elders and respect for religion and customs and traditions in the family—all these things are, more or less, equal. Differences do come in on the basis of the *Weltanschauung* of these different groups.

Because there are such strong family ties there is relatively little intergenerational conflict in the community. The community is unified by a common allegiance to both the Torah's teachings and to the *Rebbe* for guidance and leadership. As a Lubavitcher remarked: "It's true the generation gap isn't big because you all adhere to one principle—the Torah and its teachings. Also, the same *Rebbe* who asks things from the parents asks the same things from the child." The demands and expectations regulating the various age groups are quantitatively rather than qualitatively differentiated on a practical basis:

... That there is less (of a generation gap) in an orthodox home is due, I think, to the fact that since we are told that the best method by which we can teach our children is by example, in orthodox homes the children see their parents obeying a superior power or being that is not present. In other words, we are living by some commandments and directions for which possibly we don't even have an answer or a reason, or at least there's no one to say why or challenge that or to say "I don't want to." It's given to us and we accept it and we obey. Consequently, they (children) don't have any ground for arguing against their parents when they are told to do something. ... On the whole, in orthodox households there is much less of a generation gap than in general, if there is any at all. Because we have the same basic truths and those basic truths refer to anyone and everyone, regardless of age, ... and these truths relate to all of us, so there's no challenging it, there's no getting away from it, and that makes for much less difference. We have too much in common for there to be a gap.

Lubavitch youth are in continual contact with adults whether at home or in the Yeshiva. One of the major incentives for many of the student's activities, ranging from *davening* to organizing the *Tefillin* campaign, is that it encourages them to enter the same world as their parents and become concerned with similar goals. Although the various age groups do not always agree on how best to achieve certain goals, the bases of the Lubavitch way of life—observance of the Torah's precepts and affiliation with the *Rebbe*—are not challenged. As an older Yeshiva student remarked.

... Now, of course, the world has gone through a generation gap, a big one. Lubavitcher take this generation gap and use it for the good. My father ... was asked a question: "Did the generation gap affect the Lubavitcher?" He said: "Yes." "Was a division created between the young and old?" "Yes." "Did the young stop putting on *Tefillin*?" "No." "Did the young stop feeling close to the *Rebbe*?" "No." "What happened?" "On the contrary, the young became better chassidim. The young cling to the *Rebbe* more than the older do." In other words, the generation gap came out for the better. ... Whereas the generation gap has taken society and is trying to break society, ... in

Lubavitch this is not the case. They (the young) did not try to break society. They did not form a society of their own—they bettered Lubavitcher's society.

The Community's Proximity to 770

I have already stressed the significance of the Lubavitcher's relationship to the *Rebbe* and argued that the nature of this link identifies the person as a Lubavitcher. It is difficult to over emphasize the *Rebbe's* centrality to his chassidim for as one *chossid* said: "The *Rebbe* is the centre of Lubavitch. Whatever Lubavitcher do as Lubavitcher is because of the *Rebbe*." The author of an article in *Di Yiddishe Heim* put it like this:

> We must admit, however, that Lubavitch hardly has a monopoly on spiritual devotion; many others have it too. Yet the performance of the Lubavitcher chassidim is unmatched. Why? What is their secret? Any of them will be only to glad to reveal it—*THE REBBE* .... Should you try to praise any Lubavitcher chasid or group for their marvelous work, you are bound to hear the same reply: "It's not really my own credit," Australia, Europe, Eretz Yisroel, across the North American continent, everywhere you will inevitably hear it sooner or later in the conversation, "It is the *Rebbe's* achievement, not ours." (*Di Yiddishe Heim*, Vol. 13, No. 4:7)

Since the *Rebbe* is the leader and spiritual guide of his chassidim, they are naturally eager to see and hear him whenever possible.

In the previous chapter, two occasions when the *Rebbe* and his chassidim come together were mentioned, *yecheedess* (private audiences) and *Farbrengens*. Lubavitcher have only one *yecheedess* a year, but the *Farbrengens* occur regularly throughout the year and are the best opportunities for the chassidim to see and hear their *Rebbe*. Lubavitcher attend *Farbrengens* as frequently as possible for, as many claim, seeing the *Rebbe* leaves them spiritually rejuvenated and encourages them to carry out the *Rebbe's* requests to diffuse *Yiddishkayt*. One Lubavitcher said:

> If I lived in New York I would be at all the *Farbrengens*, so here I make sure to go (to the Yeshiva) whenever there's a

hook-up. That's the least I could do. But whenever I can, I go to the *Rebbe's Farbrengen.* I don't have to tell you that the hook-up and being there are not the same thing. You know, as much as you can, you help the *Rebbe* carry out his work to spread *Yiddishkayt* but every once in a while you get a little lazy or maybe you do it, but your heart isn't in it so much. But when you're in New York and you see the *Rebbe* and you can tell from the way the *Rebbe* talks how important all this work is to him, you come back and it's like you're a new man.

Lubavitcher are obviously restricted in the number of *Farbrengens* they can attend for some of them live as far from New York as London, Australia, or Israel. Lubavitcher chassidim in those communities usually settle for a telephone hook-up with 770 (the Lubavitch headquarters) or a written report summarizing the contents of the *Rebbe's* discourses. The Lubavitch community in Montreal, however, is only seven hours from New York by bus and only one hour by plane. As the community often charters a bus, the Montreal Lubavitcher are able to attend *Farbrengens* on a regular basis.

Since the Montreal community is one of the larger Lubavitch communities in North America, Lubavitcher from smaller communities often come to Montreal to find suitable spouses for their children. Although the community cannot always produce a sufficient number of males and females of marriageable age, its proximity to New York greatly reduces the possibility of Lubavitcher's out-group marriage and helps to ensure that the children will marry either into families with a Lubavitch ancestry or strictly orthodox families that are attracted to the *Rebbe.*

Lubavitcher and Their Work

As with all other activities, employment is balanced on a scale of religious values. Lubavitcher, as is true of other chassidim and non-chassidic orthodox Jews, are mainly concerned to earn a living in a manner that will not interfere with their religious observance. For example, a Lubavitcher, or indeed any orthodox Jew, will not work on the Sabbath, which begins at sunset on Friday. As greeting the Sabbath involves certain preparations and travelling on the Sabbath is forbidden, the Lubavitcher must leave work early Friday afternoon. In addition, the fact that orthodox Jews may not work on the various Jewish holidays imposes further restrictions on the type of employment they can take:

> I would have to say that if you're from a religious home then this makes it difficult. First of all, because of *Shabbess*. But you also have Friday afternoon. When I left high school I found it difficult to get employment because the office was open five and a half days a week. There was no work on *Shabbess* but there was office work which had to be done.

or:

> No hospital will employ her with her needs for religious observance. The Torah says that a doctor must care for the sick, not that he may work on *Shabbess* but that he must. It is written. But there is no such dispensation for any other group.

In several studies of chassidic communities there are accounts of the kind of work in which chassidim are employed. Mintz (1968), for instance, reported that most chassidim in New York belong to the ranks of the skilled workers and are employed in the diamond centre as cutters, polishers, and dealers; they hold jobs as linotype operators, electricians, carpenters, upholsterers, sewing-machine operators, pattern cutters, and other such trades. Poll (1962) wrote that other chassidim have responded to the particular needs of the chassidic community and have established enterprises concerned with the production and processing of meat, milk, cheese, bread, noodles, salt, etc. Still others are connected with the supply of religious books, *Tefillin*, *yarmlkess* (skull caps), wigs, and candles. Finally, others enter religious-oriented occupations and become ritual slaughterers, Rabbis, teachers, *Kashruth* supervisors, and fund raisers. In his discussion of the economic behaviour of the Williamsburg chassidic community, Poll notes that " ... The occupational mobility most desired is from dependent to independent labor situations." (1962:94) In other words, most chassidim aim at becoming self-employed. Being occupationally independent is generally preferred to earning a large salary in a subordinate position.

The occupational breakdown of the Lubavitch community

Table 2

Occupational Breakdown of the Lubavitcher Chassidim in
the Lubavitch Community

Religious-oriented work	41
Company employee	4
Businessman	15
Jeweller	3
Dry-cleaning store	1
High school teacher	2
Real-estate agent	1
Professor	3
Teacher	1
Electrician	1
Electrical contractor	1
Pharmacist	1
Printer	1
Total	75

(Table 2) indicates that over 54 per cent are involved in religious-oriented occupations including those of Rabbi, teacher, ritual slaughterer (*shoichet*), fund raiser, and *Kashruth* supervisor (*mashgiech*). Due to the nature of their work, these individuals never have difficulty in leaving their work to observe the Sabbath and other Jewish holidays. The 20 per cent categorized as businessmen are owners of stores, companies, or factories and can therefore determine their own working hours. As the four per cent of wage earners work in companies owned by Lubavitcher, the establishments are closed on all Jewish holidays. Two of the jewellers are self-employed, while the third works for an orthodox Jew. The remainder, the owner of the dry-cleaning store, the real-estate agent, electrician, pharmacist, and electrical contractor are self-employed, while the teachers' and professors' schedules are sufficiently flexible to allow for the rescheduling of classes when necessary. If we examine the occupations of those who

Table 3

Occupational Breakdown of Congregants in the Lubavitcher Yeshiva

Religious-oriented work	41
Butcher	2
Company employee	9
Businessman	29
Jeweller	3
Dry-cleaning store	1
Manufacturing	6
High school teacher	3
Real-estate agent	2
Wholesaler	2
Professor	4
Insurance salesman	1
Teacher	1
Electrician	2
Printing business	2
Electrical contractor	1
Locksmith	2
Pharmacist	1
Total	112

pray at the Lubavitcher Yeshiva (see Table 3), we find that an overwhelmingly large proportion are either self-employed or work at jobs which allow them to observe the religious holidays.

Since Lubavitcher chassidim maintain a network of *Yeshivess* and girls' schools, most of the *Bays Medresh* graduates become teachers in their own *Yeshivess* or in other schools. For instance, the entire Jewish curriculum staff at the *Bays Rivkeh*, the Lubavitch girls' school, are graduates of the *Bays Rivkeh* schools. The Yeshiva also encourages its graduates to enter religious-oriented occupations such as those mentioned above. In the Lubavitch community under study we find that not all Lubavitcher are Yeshiva graduates and that all Yeshiva graduates do not necessarily enter religious-oriented occupations. We do find, however, that in all instances these people engage in work which allows them to regulate their everyday life according to the Torah's precepts.

A Lubavitcher and I once spoke about the difficulties an orthodox Jew might experience in observing the Torah as an employee of a non-orthodox Jew. I mentioned that a young man affiliated with Lubavitch was not permitted to wear a skull-cap while employed at one of the universities. He replied:

> . . . it depends what situation they're in. . . . You see, the thing is, people who are Lubavitcher will generally direct themselves to professions where they don't have that problem. Like certainly if they work for the Yeshiva they won't have that problem. Teaching, or if they go into their own business. . . . I know one person who had a job as electrician and, you know, he had that problem. He changed his job . . .

Another Lubavitcher, a businessman, once spoke to me about the advantages of being one's own boss:

> . . . and, you know, I've had the chance to make more money. I've been offered a partnership with two other people. But I don't want it and it's very simple, my friend. This is where I belong, here in the Yeshiva. If I want to stop working an hour earlier to come here, no one stops me. When you're not your own boss you can't do that, you know. Some people work and work and work. . . . They think that the more they work the more money they earn. It's not like that, my friend. You get what's coming to you and no more. It doesn't matter how much you work. But I have to be here when I want because this is the place to be, my friend.

Within the Lubavitch community work is viewed as a means to an end. The end, however, does not revolve primarily around material acquisition but upon the pursuit of a way of life guided by Torah. One's work, then, must not lead to disobeying or disregarding the Torah. The nature of work is, therefore, conditioned by one's religious attitudes and beliefs rather than *vice versa*.

100

The tenability of the Lubavitch community's way of life is also to a considerable extent dependant upon the chassidim's attitude to the surrounding society. The community can collectively select which features of the society's culture and technology to incorporate into its everyday life and, by defining various fads and fashions of urban society which are threatening to its distinctive lifestyle, can develop a set of beliefs to support their disapproval. For example, they discourage watching movies or television, taking drugs, wearing mini skirts, and the pleasurable reading of newspapers. Their discouragement of these pursuits is supported by two main arguments which will be examined in the following section.

Lubavitch Ideology and Their Disengagement of Popular Fads and Fashions

Lubavitcher consider that modern society is degenerate and point to such phenomena as drugs, crime, lust for material possession, and sex as evidence for their argument. Although many of these phenomena are common to all segments of society, Lubavitcher are mainly concerned with their consequences for Jews. As such, the Lubavitcher *Rebbe* continues to urge his chassidim to befriend all Jews whose observance of orthodox Judaism is minimal, and to make special efforts to make Lubavitch accessible to Jewish youth alienated from religious observance. These chassidim contend that while many Jews are searching for something more meaningful in life, they, Lubavitcher, possess the answer. As a Lubavitcher put it:

> Some people think this might be the answer and others turn to this religion to find something missing. We have the answer and we want to share it. When you have something that's proven and priceless, you want to share it with others.

Based on conversations and discussions with Jewish students, and on their reading of the printed media, Lubavitcher conclude that the course of modern society is misguided. Standards of morality, as they see it, are continually in flux, the majority of campus youth experiment with drugs and indulge freely in sex, and people's disenchantment with their accomplishments in life results in divorce, separations, and crime. Addressing himself to

101

"the alienation of certain segments of Jewish youth," the *Rebbe*
remarked:

> ... today's problem is to be attributed in great measure to
> the distortion of values among parents who are more
> concerned with external appearances and superficialities,
> and with making a favourable impression upon the "next
> door neighbour," than with raising their children in accord-
> ance with the tenets of their faith. ... The lack of self-
> discipline and moral principles on the part of the parents,
> and their laxity in matters of religion, are easily discernible
> to their children. Children seek firm direction; they long for
> sincere and solicitous parental authority. But the atmos-
> phere in the home is one of permissiveness—after all, we live
> in a free society. ("An Encounter With Chabad," 1971:12)

The first paragraph of "On College," an article in *Di Yiddishe
Heim*, reads:

> This is the second introduction I have written for this
> article. The first simply describes the obscene posters,
> photographs, drawings and diagrams to be seen in the
> corridors and classrooms of most colleges and universities.
> But it was evident that by their very nature they were
> unsuited for "Di Yiddishe Heim." My own feeling at first
> was that this milieu needed to be described to be believed,
> since imagination could never by itself conjure up images to
> match the reality. But it may be that the very fact that they
> cannot be described for publication here, surely indicates
> how outrageously they violate our whole way of existence.
> (*Di Yiddishe Heim*, Vol. 13, No. 3:3)

Lubavitchers' discussions about modern society's goals and
priorities are always related to their emphasis on traditional
Jewish practice as a guide to everyday life. These chassidim's
encounters with non-observant Jews of various ages are specifically geared to impress upon them that orthodox Judaism must, in
time, become the basis of their lives. It is precisely this gradual
commitment to and practice of orthodox Judaism that Lubavitcher offer as the solution to those Jews concerned with the
purpose and meaning of life. As a Lubavitcher said:

> Take a look at what's happening, my friend. Doesn't it

make you think? The kids in college today care about drugs, sex and protests. But what about Judaism? Where does *Yiddishkayt* come in? For most of them it doesn't. And a lot of those students are unhappy, they've got problems, they don't know what they want to do, they don't know why they're there. They've got no purpose. But take a look at the kids here, my friend. You won't find one in the *Bays Medresh* who's confused about life, why he does things. I'm not saying they don't have problems, I'm not saying that. But they know there's a purpose in life, that they're Jews and as Jews they have to do certain things. If these college students realized this, I'm telling you, they wouldn't have their problems with drugs and everything. They wouldn't need it.

Referring to Jewish youth, the Lubavitcher *Rebbe* declared:

Our youth must be imbued with the truth, free of compromise and personal bias. Only the unadulterated truth of Torah can make an everlasting impression upon our youth. This is not only the proper, but the only, approach, and anything less would be a continuation of the compromise which led to their alienation in the first place. ("An Encounter With Chabad," 1971:13)

Convinced that the popular fads and fashions of modern society directly contribute to its negative features, Lubavitcher predictably insulate themselves from these influences.

Two mainstays of Lubavitcher's negative views toward certain popular fads and fashions are the belief that they are conducive to unproductive use of time and that they do not contribute positively toward shaping the individual into a better person who organizes his life around the Torah's precepts. While analytically separable, these arguments are closely interlinked in discussions or arguments with outsiders. They are strongly supported by the *Rebbe* who has often addressed himself to the potentially harmful consequences resulting from seemingly attractive features of North American society.

As do many people, Lubavitcher regard time as a precious commodity and efforts must consequently be made to spend it productively. Certain popular pastimes are considered overly time-consuming and are therefore replaced by approved alternatives. The following remarks help illustrate Lubavitcher's belief that a person's time ought to be used in the pursuit of specific objectives:

> ... it is just that a boy's time should be taken up with studying.... The outside world thinks that Lubavitch is trying to shut everything out, whereas in Lubavitch you don't have the time for other things. ... There is nothing wrong with reading a newspaper except for the fact that in the time that you are reading the newspaper, you could have studied the *Gemoreh*.

> I like to read a lot. I know that if I get my hands on a newspaper I read it from beginning to end and that would take about three hours, and I don't think it's worth three hours of my time to read the *Star* or to read any sort of newspaper. I think I would much rather spend my time reading a *sayfer* (a book of religious content) where I know I would be learning something.

> Do you really get anything out of watching television? I mean can you actually learn something from watching something stupid like Westerns? What I am asking is what is added to yourself by watching other people on TV? Now I can pick up this *sayfer* and begin to read it and know that I am getting something out of it.

Another facet of their argument is concerned with the potential danger of exposure to ideas contrary to the Torah's teaching:

> The contents of many TV programs consist of either some type of sexual connotation, it's usually overloaded with sexual activity, or many aspects of violence. And I feel a lot of it has to do with other religions, other forms of religious observances, the worship of the Church and other religious ways. ... I don't feel it's to their (the children's) benefit to see all the programs on television.

> What does it mean to have an education? You see, when you say that you want to educate someone, what this means is that you want him to be a good Jew, a good human being. You want them to have *Yeerass Shomayim* (fear of God), you want them to have respect. I mean watching television, going to movies, spending hours reading news-

papers—you read and see things that the Torah says to do the opposite. The Torah says you should not steal, you should not kill, and movies and newspapers deal with stealing and killing. A young person can think that what he sees is real. Why should he see this?

Lubavitchers' negative attitude toward some of the activities popular in today's urban society mirror the views expressed by the *Rebbe* at *Farbrengens* and in his published letters. The *Rebbe* has addressed himself, on several occasions, to the disenchantment with established religious values which he claims "inevitably follows permissiveness and compromise." He said that:

> The lack of self-discipline and moral principles on the part of parents, and their laxity in matters of religion, are easily discernible to their children. Children seek firm direction; they long for sincere and solicitous parental authority. But the atmosphere in the home is one of permissiveness—after all, we live in a free society. ("An Encounter With Chabad," 1971:12)

In this respect, the *Rebbe* repeatedly reminds Jewish women not to be swayed by the most recent fashions but, instead, to abide by the laws relating to modesty (*Tzneeus*). Referring to the growing lack of modesty in dress, especially during the summer months, the *Rebbe* wrote to a group of women:

> I particularly urge you to continue your good efforts in this area of *Tznius*, which, although basically reflected in the manner of attire also concerns general conduct and conversation.

An article in *Di Yiddishe Heim* reiterated the *Rebbe's* stress on modesty in appearance:

> In a society that is so free that there are virtually no moral standards whatsoever, Chabad (Lubavitch) women above all can demonstrate ideals and principles of *Tznius*, modesty, that a woman or girl dress and speak and conduct herself with an awareness of her true worth. She will be free because she will not be "the servant of servants," a slave to every insane immoral whim of fashion designers and the entertainment world. (Vol. 10, No. 1:4)

The *Rebbe* continually reminds his chassidim, including Jews in general, of the importance of patterning their lives on the Torah's teaching. On one occasion, while underlining the Torah's significance and the importance of observing its precepts, the *Rebbe* said:

> The one and only common factor which has been present with Jews throughout the ages, in all lands, and under all circumstances, is the Torah *Mitzvoth*, which Jews have observed tenaciously in their daily life. ... The essential factor of our existence and survival is our adherence to the Torah and the practice of its precepts in our everyday life. Let no one delude himself by taking the easier way out, nor be bribed by any temporary advantages and illusory gains. (*Di Yiddishe Heim*, Vol. 4, No. 2:2-3)

Lubavitchers' development of this ideology contributes to the community's tenability, for the community must provide individual Lubavitcher with sound reason why popular recreational attractions such as television, bowling, or movies ought to be avoided. The two main arguments accepted by Lubavitcher as justifications for their behaviour are based on the observance of the Torah's precepts (*mitzvess*). A consideration of *mitzvess* in Lubavitch will help to show how they provide the necessary substitute for the recreational activities popular in the wider society.

The Centrality of Mitzvess

A *mitzveh*[4] may be defined as a religious obligation incumbent upon all Jewish adults. *Mitzvess* are the life-blood of the Lubavitcher chassidim, as they are expected to be among all orthodox Jews. The most characteristic feature of the Lubavitch community is their strict observance of the Torah's religious obligations, their continual emphasis on their importance in everyday life, and their *Rebbe's* constant reminders underlining their significance to all Jews. As the *Rebbe* once said: "The Jew must observe the *Mitzvoth* whether or not he understands their deeper significance; his experience of the *Mitzvoth* eventually will develop the faculties of his understanding, and in this he has Divine Providence." (*Di Yiddishe Heim*, Vol. 10, No. 4:1) On another occasion, replying to a letter, the *Rebbe* wrote:

> The Torah and *Mitzvoth* are the channels to receive G-d's blessings also in one's material needs, as the Torah declares: "If you will walk in My statutes"—the G-d will send all blessings mentioned in that portion. This is, therefore, the way to ensure one's lasting happiness, materially as well as spiritually. (Teachers Programme, Vol. 2:355)

The *mitzvess* cover all the circumstances an orthodox Jew may meet in his daily life, including prescriptions and proscriptions concerning marriage, charity, care of the sick, business practices, sexual relations, property law, and a number of other subjects. (Mintz, 1968:Chapter 6) An orthodox Jew believes that God has decreed the *mitzvess* and that they therefore represent the complete code of the Jew's moral conduct.

I suggested in the previous section that Lubavitchers' rejection of much of modern life makes it necessary for them to provide a suitable substitute. Since sensual, indulgent fun is rejected as a goal or system of reward, they must create their own medium of exchange. The basic unit of this system of rewards in the community is the fulfillment of *mitzvess*. Analogously speaking, *mitzvess* are to religious life what money is to commercial life, and as money, *mitzvess* can be collected in various ways all of which focus on observance of the Torah. Such activities as prayer, eating only kosher food, observing the Sabbath prohibitions, learning Torah, or helping others thus add to the individual's accumulation of *mitzvess*. The extent of the person's observance and collection of *mitzvess* is believed to have a bearing on his soul both in this world and in the afterlife, on the welfare of his family, and on innumerable other contingencies in his everyday life. (Mintz, 1968:122-131) It is not surprising, therefore, that parents regard the religious education of their children as one of the most important considerations.

Since observance of *mitzvess* is a central feature of the Lubavitch community's persistence, special activities are organized to ensure that *mitzvess* are fulfilled. Lubavitcher's proselytizing ventures, including the *Tefillin* campaign and the *Sukkehmobile*, exemplify this concern. The *Sukkehmobile* is best described as a *Sukkeh*, or temporary booth for the Feast of Tabernacles, on wheels. During this holiday, all male adults are required to recite the appropriate blessings over the symbolic palm branch and citrus fruit connected with the *Sukkess* holiday. To guarantee that as many Jews as possible will observe this precept, Lubavitcher construct a *Sukkeh* on a truck and drive about the Jewish sections of the city inviting all Jews to recite the blessings. Although proselytizing activities serve to reinforce the distinctive identity of the Lubavitcher, they can also be viewed as examples of *mitzvess* in action, culminating in non-religious Jews' observance of Torah commandments.

While *mitzvess* constitute the medium of reward in the Lubavitch community and Lubavitcher are impressed with and impress upon others their importance, these chassidim feel obliged to account for the majority of Jews' neglect of these religious obligations. If the observance of *mitzvess* is as crucial as Lubavitcher claim, why do more Jews not attend to their requirements? The concept of *Yaytzer Ho'Ro* (Evil Inclination) helps Lubavitcher, and other orthodox Jews, to account for this situation. The reason many fail to observe the commandments (*mitzvess*) is that the *Yaytzer Ho'Ro* " . . . leads one to commit acts of passion, to have sceptical thoughts of God and His works, and to rebel against God's decrees." (Mintz, 1968:126) "A Torah Thought Of The Week," in *Di Yiddishe Heim*, states that:

> We possess a *Yetzer Hora* (Evil Inclination) whose entire purpose and raison d'etre is to cause us to do the opposite of G-d's will. He may clothe and camouflage his aim in claims that the precept is too difficult, etc., etc., but his *real* intention is to persuade us to go against G-d's will. Hence, the more vital a certain precept is for a particular person, the more effort the Yetzer will invest to dissuade the individual from performing the commandment. Even though the injunction may, in fact, be a very easy one to observe, it will *seem* extremely difficult, due to the devious cunning arguments employed by the *Yetzer*—who knows how important it is that the individual perform this *Mitzvah*—(precept).
>
> . . . There are many who argue that Jews would become more observant—if only the "burden" of the Torah's laws would be lightened. If there were only just a few simple laws to observe, they claim, all Jews would devoutly adhere to them. These people show an unfortunate misunderstanding of the basic "spiritual make-up" of the Jew, and

the aim of the *Yetzer*. For even when there was but one simple solitary commandment—and *that* for only three hours, it nevertheless seemed impossibly difficult to fulfill. (*Di Yiddishe Heim*, Vol. 9, No. 2:inside cover)

Lubavitchers' philosophy of the *Yaytzer Ho'Ro's* intentions and powers helps them rationalize the unconcern and disinterest many Jews show toward the Torah's *mitzvess*, while simultaneously offering an explanation for their own deviations. Their belief that these non-observant Jews "possess the self-determination and inner strength to conquer the Yetzer and implement G-d's will" (*Di Yiddishe Heim*, Vol. 9, No. 2:16) helps to explain their proselytizing zeal.

Footnotes

[1] Chanekkeh—A Jewish festival, known also as the Feast of Lights, which begins on the twenty-fifth day of the Hebrew month of Kislev (occurring in November or December), which lasts for eight days. The holiday commemorates the victory of the Maccabees over the Syrian Greeks in 165 B.C. The holiday is celebrated, in part, by the lighting of candles, beginning with one on the first day and increasing the number until eight are lit on the last day.

[2] Purim—A Jewish festival occurring on the fourteenth day of the Hebrew month of Adar (February or March). It commemorates the events narrated in the Book of Esther in which the Jews were saved from Haman's plot to kill them. It is called the Feast of Lots after the lots cast by Haman to determine the month in which the slaughter was to take place.

[3] The reference to learning must be understood in a religious context and relates to the acquisition of sacred knowledge by study and instruction. The prerequisite for status in the community under study, and in chassidic communities in general, are piety and Torah studying. For a discussion on learning among chassidic Jews, see Gutwirth, ibid:186-193, and Mintz, ibid:52-54.

[4] The Old Testament includes 613 *mitzvess* composed of 365 negative commandments and 248 positive ones. As Mintz indicates: "As elaborate by the talmudic writers and their successors . . . the mitsves comprise a vast compendium of custom, ordinance, and law encompassing all the activities of life, and they represent the legal and social needs of diverse ages" (1968:122).

Chapter Five

The Schools

Religious communities typically view public education as a threat to their distinctive lifestyle and seek to offset its potential influences. (Gutwirth, 1970; Hostetler, 1968; Poll, 1962; Redekop, 1969; Rubin, 1972) This is generally accomplished by arranging the secular curriculum to ensure that it does not conflict radically with the contents of the children's religious studies. The nature and degree of the manipulation of the secular curriculum is determined by how disruptive assimilative contacts might be to the community and especially to the young. Since the public school is the most powerful agent for equalizing the differences between children from varying backgrounds, it has traditionally served as the battleground between the school authorities and leaders of the religious community. This chapter includes an examination of the Lubavitcher's efforts to minimize the impact of the secular curriculum on students attending the two Lubavitch schools. As the reader will notice, the *Rebbe's* views on secular education are presented in considerable detail. It is important to stress that Lubavitchers' views on this topic and also on the actual secular curricula followed in Lubavitch schools are shaped directly by the *Rebbe's* ideas and beliefs.

Although the Lubavitcher Yeshiva serves as a spiritual and social centre, it is mainly used as the boys' school. Since education among the Lubavitcher, as among other orthodox Jewish groups, is not co-educational, the girls' school, the *Bays Rivkeh* Academy, is two city blocks from the Yeshiva. Both schools include a nursery, kindergarten, and Grades 1 through 11, thus matching the organizational framework of other public schools in the city. Whereas the Yeshiva maintains a *Bays Medresh*—Rabbinical College—which provides further education to the high school graduates and from which ordained Rabbis, ritual slaughterers, and teachers are graduated, the *Bays Rivkeh's* program finishes with Grade 11 and graduates must leave for New York or Paris if they wish to pursue more advanced studies at a Lubavitch Teacher's Seminary.

In accordance with the Lubavitch philosophy of exposing Jews of all ages to orthodox Judaism, the Lubavitch schools are not restricted to Lubavitchers' children, but seek to attract students from all segments of the larger Jewish community. As a result, when organizing the schools' secular curricula, non-Lubavitcher's expectations must be considered. A Lubavitch educator alluded to this when he remarked:

> You see, we have to be realistic. When Lubavitch builds schools we are not building the schools for people who give their children a Yeshiva education anyway. We are not neglecting them, but we want to give it to the general public as well. . . . You see, there is a difference in outlook between Lubavitch and the other chassidim. The other chassidic groups want to look after their own group. We're the opposite. We want to go out and reach the general public. Without the secular studies, we wouldn't reach them and they wouldn't come to us. So we have to give (secular studies) so that they send their children.

Although the highly organized secular curriculum is related to encouraging outsiders to send their children to Lubavitch schools, this does not imply that all Lubavitcher strongly resist secular studies. While, for reasons that will become clear, a segment of the community refrains from enrolling their sons in the Yeshiva's secular program, other Lubavitcher do not regard the secular curriculum as particularly dangerous and consider it an important element in their sons' education.[1] As one Lubavitch woman, speaking for a minority, observed:

> We, for ourselves, had we been able to get together a group of parents who only wanted this type of thing (religious studies), we would have been so much happier. . . . But even within the Lubavitch community there are certain parents who wouldn't settle for that, who would definitely want their child to be able to go out into the world with a good secular background.

Although the emphasis on secular education is not the same in the two schools, Lubavitcher claim that they do not regard secular studies as of secondary importance and attempt to impart this to the students. This attitude was best summed up in the following remark from a teacher: "The *Rebbe* has said this many times: if you give secular studies it shouldn't be a waste of time. It should be taught in the right manner. If not, you're cheating yourself and it's a waste of time."

The two schools in the Montreal Lubavitch community comprise approximately 550 students. In the Yeshiva, attended by nearly 350 students ranging from nursery to Grade 11, only 30 per cent are from Lubavitch families. The remainder come from Sphardic and Ashkenazic[2] homes—33 and 37 per cent respectively. We find a roughly similar breakdown in the *Bays Rivkeh*. Of the 200 students, 75 per cent are from non-Lubavitch backgrounds, equally divided between students of Morrocan and Canadian origin. At most, this school includes from thirty-five to forty girls from Lubavitch families. In both schools, then, Lubavitcher comprise approximately 25 per cent of the student population. The problems and advantages of having non-Lubavitch students in Lubavitch schools will be dealt with in more detail later, but it is important to note that their recruitment and presence is strongly approved of and supported by the *Rebbe.* Referring to the *Rebbe's* views about attracting newcomers to the Lubavitch schools, a Lubavitcher remarked:

> . . . I remember a number of years ago I was taking this class. . . . There are two views on what method of education one should undertake: whether to popularize education and expose everyone to it and let each one accept whatever he can, or have a select few whom you know are capable of absorbing what you have to give them, and then you know that your efforts aren't wasted. And, of course, Lubavitch follows the first method. The question was raised about what sort of guarantee we have that we will not be influenced by outsiders before we accomplish anything with them, and the answer was "the *Rebbe's brocheh*" (blessing). The *Rebbe's* blessing is our protection.

Both the administrators at the two schools, and parents sending their children there, see themselves as providing the students with a certain kind of Jewish education. Although the Jewish curriculum in the Lubavitcher schools and several other non-Lubavitch schools is similar, Lubavitcher regard their schools as being qualitatively different. The major difference lies in the manner in which Jewish studies are presented. Whereas they are taught in the Yeshiva as a way of life grounded in Torah, they are approached in many other Jewish day schools as part of the Jewish culture and tradition—principally as a series of facts to be recalled. The principal of one of the Lubavitch schools described the difference this way:

> You see, X (a Jewish day school) is a very good school. They have good quality teachers, their methods are good. . . and they achieve results. But where we differ, I would say is that we have polarized philosophies of living. They are an expressly secular school and even the Jewish studies, Hebrew studies, are presented in a secular way. They do not stress the religious part. Religion is only treated in the best case as culture or as part of tradition— take it or leave it as much as you please. It's not a religious school. They might teach *Sidder*, they might teach how to *davn*, but it's a way of social life. It's important to learn how to say the *Maftir* because one might be in a *shul* where one would have to know how to do it before the congregation. It's entirely different. In our school it is taught as a way of life.

One of the adults argued as follows:

> Here in the Yeshiva, in the *Bays Rivkeh*, the student finds out what *Yiddishkayt* is. I mean it's explained to them that *Yiddishkayt* is a way of life and they can actually see *Yiddishkayt* in practice by watching their teachers. I mean when someone looks at Rav _____ , you know what I mean. But take the _____ (a Jewish school), the kid learns *Sidder*, but who's teaching him? I'd bet you that it's someone who's not *frum*, does not keep *Shabbess* or *kashress*, and I could go on. So sure, the kid is influenced by his teachers, but in this case he's influenced in the wrong way.

The Rebbe's Views on Secular Education

Lubavitcher consider that the Jewish curricula in many Jewish schools does not influence the students in the way that a Torah education should. In fact, a main selling point of the two Luba-vitch schools is that the students will be exposed to *Yiddishkayt* in its traditional sense and that any compromise of the Torah's precepts will neither be practised nor encouraged.

The Lubavitcher *Rebbe* has addressed himself on several occasions to the importance of a Torah education. A number of the *Rebbe's sichess*, as well as articles in *Di Yiddishe Heim* have urged parents to fulfil their obligation by providing their children with a thorough Jewish education. "It is ludicrous to begin thinking of a child's education six months before his *Bar Mitzveh*," the *Rebbe* once delcared at a *Farbrengen*, "it must begin in earliest childhood." At that same *Farbrengen* the *Rebbe* said:

> The physical necessities and desires of the child must be filled in a manner congruous to its spiritual drives. The soul of a Jew is actually a Divine part of G-d and it therefore has an inherent longing for its source. Expression of this natural tendency can be found only through a life in accordance with the Torah, as prescribed for a Jew by his Creator. Consciously or subconsciously the soul's craving prevails. If only the child's physiological needs are cared for, and his education is not compatible with the uplifting characteristics of his soul, opposing gravitations are apt to create a split personality.
>
> We witness much too often . . . the Jewish child, whose Torah education has been neglected, when becoming aware of what has happened, pleading helplessly with his parents over the irretrievable past, crying "why have you done this to me." (Teachers Programme, 1969:396-397)

On a separate occasion the *Rebbe* stated:

> One of the greatest frailties in contemporary Jewish life is the complacency toward the true Torah education of our youth. . . . In our generation we have become the unfortun-ate witnesses of the tragic fruits of this complacency—intermarriage and assimilation. Parents who neglected the Torah education of their children thinking that matters would somehow take their proper course without it, or that it just wasn't that important—without realizing the conse-quences—have become victims of devastated homes and disgraced families because of their children's behavior.

Elements foreign to Torah way of life beckon the Jew to come and share their society. But the Jew can never acquiesce to this society, for a Jew cannot survive in a life devoid of Torah, just as a fish cannot live without water. (Teachers Programme, 1969:392)

Since a Torah education is considered vital, Lubavitcher are likely to stress its significance whenever possible. The Lubavitch summer camps, as well as other activities through which Lubavitcher come into contact with non-orthodox Jews, serve as occasions when the significance of orthodox Judaism can be stressed. It is, therefore, to be expected that *Di Yiddishe Heim* will periodically contain articles focussing on Jewish education. These articles emphasize that religious education is "the very basis of our life and survival." (Vol. 2, No. 2:15) The following two excerpts from articles exemplify this:

One of the fundamental fallacies of the present day thinking on the question of Jewish education is based on a basic misconception of Judaism. While many parents will readily admit that Jewish values are very important and useful, they believe that the modern child should be allowed to find his own way towards G-d when he is older and maturer; as if Torah is something purely rational, and would come of its own accord to the intelligent person. The truth of the matter is that religion is basically an EXPERI-ENCE. It is only when the child is given an opportunity to experience it at an early age, when he is more receptive and responsive to emotional experience, that such experience will leave an indelible impression on him . . .

This child should be taught *Yiddishkayt* everywhere—in the home, at Hebrew school, in the synagogue, and in all his social activities as well. This ideal can be realized in a Yeshiva Day School. (Vol. 2, No. 2:16)

. . . Today too, Pharaoh the King of Egypt still exists in the guise of the mores and norms of the country, in the guise of the demands that Jewish children should be cast into the mould of the behavior patterns and customs of the land. Our children, says the modern Pharaoh, should immerse themselves and be submerged in the river, in whatever will ostensibly provide them with economic sustenance. Jewish children should be placed within the walls of Pithom and

Ramses, the treasure cities of Egypt; they should be wholly involved in those matters which symbolize the economic power and most intensive pre-occupation of the land. . . . Consequently we must stand with the greatest fortitude against his decrees and educate our children in the spirit of Eternal Israel.

Practically, this means that at the time when we are involved with the education of Jewish children it is not only unnecessary, but actually forbidden to immerse them in the paganism of the land. It is prohibited to overwhelm children with concern about the pursuit of adult economic and occupational goals. The sole way of life is a complete and thorough Torah education—with the "Torah of Life." (Vol. 10, No. 4:15)

The present Lubavitcher *Rebbe's* emphasis on Torah education together with a similar emphasis by previous Lubavitcher *Rebbeim* has led some Lubavitcher to expose their children only to a Torah education. While some of these Lubavitcher admit the possible benefits of a secular education, they are also quick to point to its potential dangers. These dangers centre on exposure to ideas which conflict with a religious interpretation of the creation and development of the universe. A *bocher* once told me:

> I mean some people might call these people, these parents, fanatics because their views are so extreme. But I can understand their point of view. These parents are afraid that some wrong ideas might get into their kids' minds and they just don't want to take a chance on it. And why should they?

Although the *Rebbe* continually emphasizes the importance of a religious education, he does not specifically discourage secular learning for all of his followers. I have been told by Lubavitcher, however, that the *Rebbe* is opposed to secular education "where it is not needed." On the other hand, the *Rebbe* has adopted a definite negative attitude toward a Yeshiva *bocher's* pursuit of a college education. As one examines the *Rebbe's* argument, it is possible to understand how certain Lubavitcher have extended his views to refer to secular learning even at the primary school level.

From a copy of a letter written by the *Rebbe*, we are told:

... There is a well-known parable for this, about the boy who strayed from the road and later found himself in the midst of the woods. He got there by making a small false step off the road, which led to another, and yet another.

The conditions and environment in a country such as this call, therefore, for an even greater spiritual reinforcement of the Jewish boy and girl than even before and elsewhere. This reinforcement must be of such strength and duration that the Jewish child will always be conscious of the fact that no matter what the environment is, he is the bearer of the sacred tradition of the Divine Torah and Mitzvoth, and belongs to a people that is holy and different. For this, it is essential that right from earliest childhood to adolescence the Jewish child should receive the fullest possible Jewish education, throughout his formative years.

Hence when a Jewish boy completes his compulsory education, it is an absolute must that for a couple of years, at least, he should dedicate himself to the exclusive study of the Torah and sacred subjects, in a most conducive atmosphere of a Yeshivah, without distraction of secular studies, all the more so as the teen-age years are crucial and formative and of lasting effect, in the crystallization of the character.

This would have been my opinion even if the college entailed no more than the distraction of secular studies. Actually there is much more involved. Theoretically a college and its faculty should not try to impose any particular views, much less a way of life, on the students. Actually, however, the student cannot help being impressed, on the conscious and subconscious level, by the views, outlook and way of life of his professors. These, as well as the whole atmosphere of a college are unfortunately not compatible with the Jewish way of life, and frequently if not always quite contradictory to it. This is so even in colleges which are theological, or having so-called religious studies. Needless to say, the whole atmosphere of college is in violent conflict with the Shulchan Aruch way of life— whereby the Jew is totally committed—in every detail and aspect of his personal daily life—to the Torah and Mitzvoth and the service of G-d, as is written "You shall know Him in all your ways", ...

In other words, the Jewish boy (or girl) entering college,

yet desiring to retain the Jewish way of life in accordance with the Torah, finds himself tossed about in the raging waves of conflict between two contradictory worlds.

He is at a further disadvantage in finding himself in a minority camp, since those sharing his views and convictions are few on the college campus, while the forces pulling in the opposite direction are overwhelming; forces he must confront at every turn—among the student body, faculty members, textbooks, newspapers and periodicals. It is very doubtful whether even an adult and mature person who is subjected to such "shock treatment" day after day, would not be shaken; how much more so a teenager.

... Some people ask, is there really such a conflict between attending college and remaining an observant Jew. I can speak from experience and personal knowledge, having attended various colleges and seen the painful inner upheavals of Jewish students, and having for many years been the confidant of Jewish students who are otherwise reluctant or ashamed to open their hearts, I can therefore state with the fullest measure of conviction and responsibility that he who sends his child to college during the formative years subjects him to shock and profound conflicts and trials and invites quite unforseen consequences.

In view of all the above, it is my definite and considered opinion that all Jewish children, upon completing their compulsory secular education, should devote at least several years to the exclusive study of the Torah, without the interference of other studies, not even training for a trade, in order to obtain the maximum insurance against all risks and dangers that their future life may hold, when they attain adulthood and settle down to a family life. (Teachers Programme, Vol. 1: 173-174)

When Weiner, during a personal audience with the *Rebbe*, asked: "But you too have studied in two worlds, and your Hasidim are rather proud of the fact that you once attended the Sorbonne. Why then do you discourage them from studying in the 'other world'?" The reply was:

Precisely because I have studied, and I know what the value of the study is, I recognized its usefulness. If there are people who think they can help God sustain the world, I have no objection. We need engineers and chemists, but engineering and chemistry are not the most important things. Besides, to study does not mean only to learn facts. It means exposure to certain circles and activities which conflict with a believer's values and faith. It's like taking a person from a warm environment and throwing him into a cold water shock treatment several times a day. How long can he stand it? In addition, studies in college take place at an age when a man's character is not yet crystallized, usually before the age of thirty. Exposure then is dangerous. (1969:174)

The *Rebbe's* attitude toward secular education is characterized by two underlying thoughts: first, that secular studies inevitably expose the person to secular ideas which may be in conflict with his religious upbringing; second, that attention to secular studies detracts from the most important task, that of acquiring knowledge of the Torah. For example, the *Rebbe*, urging someone to continue learning in the Yeshiva, made this analogy: "Just imagine if someone were offered the chance to invest one franc in order to earn a thousand francs in return, he would not regret the one franc investment, but on the contrary, would wish to invest even more and more." (Teachers Programme, 1969:357)

The Schools and Their Curricula

The curriculum in both the *Bays Rivkeh* and the Yeshiva are structurally similar in that approximately three and a half hours each are officially devoted to religious and secular studies. The Hebrew curriculum is studied in the morning. This is not because secular teachers are not available in the morning, but rather reflects the greater importance attached to the *Limudai Kodesh*—the Hebrew studies. As one teacher remarked: "Hebrew studies are always in the morning. It's more important and the child is more impressionable then and he's more alert." Another teacher viewed this scheduling as closely linked to the community's religious philosophy:

... this is a religious outlook, the same as we say prayers in the morning. It is something like the life span of the person—the young years, the middle years, and the old years. So education is given to the young years. You don't train a child to make money and then when he gets in his thirties to get his education. First comes the foundation.

119

It's the same with the day. First comes the prayer, then the study and then go out to work. We would like the children to follow the same pattern when they grow up, to know that first comes the *Aibishter* (Almighty), and then you can attend to your other needs. In the morning first comes the *davening* (prayer), then the Hebrew studies, and then the secular studies for making a living.

Those enrolled in the secular program in both schools follow the curriculum outlined by the Protestant School Board of Greater Montreal with which the schools have gained affiliate status. In return for following the provincial regulations governing the administration of secular education, the school receives a subsidy from the government for each child attending secular classes.

While a secular curriculum is readily available in both schools, one finds that norms governing attendance of the classes for boys and girls differ. Such norms reflect the different expectations concerning both the amount and kinds of religious knowledge males and females must acquire in order to fulfil their respective religious obligations. The males are expected to be familiar with many more religious precepts than females and consequently must concentrate more on religious studies. A boy's curriculum schedule must, therefore, be more closely and carefully organized than a girl's to ensure he makes adequate progress in religious studies. As a result, while all girls attend the secular studies program in the *Bays Rivkeh*, two educational streams are pursued concurrently at the Yeshiva. Along with the large majority of students that attend both religious and secular study classes, a minority of students from so called "hard-core" Lubavitch families refrain from learning secular subjects and tend to assume negative feelings for those who do.[3]

Those Lubavitcher who fear that a formal secular education will interfere with their son's religious upbringing and consequently do not enroll him in the secular program are firmly convinced that they are pursuing the proper course of action. When one woman was asked whether her son would attend the secular program, she replied: "I firmly believe that the only way to educate boys is to give them the best possible Jewish education. They won't learn any English subjects." When asked if her sons studied religious subjects all day, another woman explained: "Of course, the only way to educate a Jewish boy is to give him a thorough Jewish education." Finally, a Lubavitcher defended her action by referring to what she believes to be the *Rebbe's* expectations.

> For our children, with the standards that the *Rebbe* has and what he expects of them, it's a waste of time to sit through the classes and do what they do. I mean, it's enjoyable. I understand that from the education that I've had. But for boys who are capable and should be putting their efforts to better things, it's a waste of time.

Parents whose sons begin school by only receiving a Jewish education are not necessarily opposed to every form of secular learning. In certain instances their sons might begin to attend the secular program at a later date:

> My son who is thirteen and a half went to Grade 1 at nine years old, he skipped Grade 2 because I helped him with his phonetic sounds at home. My second son went straight into Grade 3, skipped out Grade 4, and then continued 5 as normal. My youngest who is eight is still going to Jewish full-time.

In other cases, a tutor is hired to instruct the boy in certain secular subjects that it is thought will be important to him later on. One woman admitted that her boys had private lessons when they were "in the higher grades." Another said: " . . . when they are about thirteen to sixteen they may get lessons in arithmetic, reading, and writing." As these parents argue, their main responsibility is to ensure that their son becomes a *mentsh* (a person whom they can be proud of). Anything which might interfere or conflict with this goal is of lesser importance. For example:

> Let me put it to you this way. I'd say that this really proves a certain amount of subservience to the movement of Lubavitch on the part of a *chossid*. After all, a *chossid* realizes that his child will have to come up in the world and one day will have to make his own living. And it takes a lot of belief, so to speak, . . . to say: "God will help if I make him a *mentsh* first, and I feel that secular training will prevent him from becoming a *mentsh*, . . . " Then I don't really care what will happen to his livelihood. I do, but I'm not going

to spoil any of his chances to become a *mentsh*, even if it is at the cost of his livelihood or how he is going to do. ... The *Rebbe* many times stresses that if you go on the right path, there can be only blessing, because good can only bring good and we know that . . . this is the right *derech* (approach), this is the right path, therefore it can only bring blessing and bounty with it.

Except for those who do not attend secular classes, students both at the Yeshiva and *Bays Rivkeh* find the school day divided between religious and secular studies. While the practical emphasis between the two is balanced, greater philosophical importance is attached to the religious curriculum. One of the principals explains:

Let's say, I insist and I try to see to it that all girls take the Provincial exams and we are trying to equip them to pass. High marks on the one hand. On the other hand, I am definitely not promoting college entrance. I definitely think that every girl who finishes high school should rather go to teacher's seminary, if she has some flair for it, and get more knowledge in Hebrew studies, and also get professional instruction on psychology and methods of teaching. ... And besides, what's going on on campus now, who would dare to direct any of his kids to this environment?

It is precisely the religious curriculum, in which students are taught the importance of practising and living the traditions of Judaism, that sets the Lubavitch schools apart from other Jewish parochial schools in Montreal. While the schools' secular program is patterned on the one outlined for public schools, the religious curricula are intended to help mould the students' character and attitudes. One way this is accomplished can be seen by briefly examining the Hebrew department's curriculum content in the first few grades in both schools at the elementary level.

Yeshiva
Grade 1: Students begin with the *aleph bays* (alphabet) and are expected both to read and write Hebrew; they learn about the Jewish holidays and cover, in an elementary way, the history of the first book of the Pentateuch; and begin to learn some prayers. *Grade 2:* They continue learning *Siddur* (prayer book) to

become more fluent in reading the daily prayers; learn more prayers; begin to study various Jewish laws and learn about the Sabbath; they continue to study the Pentateuch, and begin to learn to write Yiddish.

Grade 3: Students' study of the Pentateuch becomes more advanced; they start to study a little *Mishnayess* (Code of Jewish Law), and are introduced to the study of *Rashi.*

Grade 4: Students start to study *Gemoreh,* pursue their study of *Rashi,* and advance in the study of the Pentateuch.

Bays Rivkeh

Grade 1: There is a concentrated effort to teach students to read and write Hebrew, and learn some prayers; students have discussions relating to the Sabbath and other Jewish holidays and the accompanying customs; Lubavitch holidays are touched on briefly and they begin to study the Pentateuch.

Grade 2: Students concentrate more on Pentateuch, and begin to read and write Yiddish.

Grade 3: They continue to study the Pentateuch.

Grade 4: Study of the Pentateuch is continued and they begin to study the Prophets.

As one can see, the males' religious studies are more intensive than the females'. Both sexes, however, are introduced to religious content in the earliest grades and, while the same basic subject matter is emphasized, it becomes increasingly more concentrated.

The curriculum is intended to instruct the student in matters relating to Judaism, but neither school specifically concentrates its efforts on converting the non-Lubavitch students to Lubavitch. As one of the principals remarked:

> In general, we don't sell too much *chassidess* (Lubavitch chassidic philosophy). There's not too much stress on the *Rebbe.* We don't even have pictures of the *Rebbe* in the classroom. We don't feel that this should be made into propaganda. We feel more that it should come in a natural way.

At the same time, however, the Lubavitch philosophy is both formally and informally introduced in the schools. At one extreme, teachers become the embodiment of this chassidic philosophy serving as examples to all students, and are instrumental in drawing Lubavitch holidays and events surrounding the *Rebbe* to the students' attention. A *Bays Rivkeh* administrator observed that:

> ... every Lubavitcher holiday is brought to their attention. And every letter that the *Rebbe* sends is read to them, as is the wine that the *Rebbe* distributes and the cake and the dollars that the *Rebbe* gives to all the children.

At the other extreme, the Lubavitch atmosphere in the schools is expected to germinate naturally without outside interference. One of the Yeshiva administrators expressed this view when he observed:

> You see, the feeling is done by itself. The teacher practises it and is a living example. It's in the air. It's not a programme, you know. It comes naturally. As we would say, parents don't have a programme to educate their children. They act naturally and it rubs off on the children. This is the same thing as living. It is not artificially made.

Unlike many public educational institutions which emphasize the relationship between level of educational achievement and occupational role in adulthood, Lubavitcher do not regard their schools in this way. (Rubin, 1972:40) While they do recognize the advantages to be gained from secular schooling, they are quick to emphasize that a university education is hardly a guarantee for successful occupational placement and performance. For instance:

> I can give you an example of myself. ... I never started Grade 1 (secular) and I think I'm finding my way around life. I'm not stuck. I never started Grade 1 because when I was supposed to start the *Rebbe* came out with the big campaign ... no English whatsoever. ... And no one of my age group got any English education. One picked it up by hanging around in the community, and the other picked it up by looking in books himself ... but everyone ended up knowing English one way or another. And no one can say that any became a *shlemazel* or a *goilem* and couldn't get a

job because of this. Success in work doesn't have to do with how long you study English subjects.

It is generally believed that success in one's work or occupation is forthcoming regardless of college and university attendance. As a Lubavitcher emphasizes, the critical variable to be considered is whether or not the person "has a head on his shoulders":

> . . . There was once an article in the Reader's Digest about the proportion of jobs, whether college actually adds anything to the job or not, and they came to the conclusion that college really does nothing for a job. But if we look at it statistically, we find very simple that 90 per cent of the people that go to college end up with fantastic jobs and the *shlemazolim* that don't go to college end up with nothing. So it must be college, right? But the answer is not true. Who goes to college? Someone who has a head on his shoulders. A guy that has no head doesn't go. That's it. Now this same *shlemazel*, if he has a head, and did not go to college, would find the same job. On the other hand, the *shlemazel* who goes to college without a head wouldn't find a job. So it is not college that is doing it, it's actually the head.

In summary, Lubavitchers' interest in attracting non-orthodox students to their school has been largely responsible for the organization and maintenance of well-developed secular departments. While recognized as necessary, the secular curriculum is not intended to whet the student's intellectual appetite to pursue secular studies at a more advanced level. Instead, the main emphasis in both schools is on inculcating the young with a desire to accept the significance and centrality of orthodox Judaism as a guide to everyday life. In line with other religious minorities, Lubavitcher expect their schools to serve as a bastion against undesirable acculturation. As such, special attention must be devoted to hiring the secular staff and screening the curriculum.

Hiring Teachers and Screening the Curriculum

Finding teachers to fill the positions in the schools' Jewish departments should, theoretically, present little difficulty as the community is able to train its own teachers. Those presently teaching in the Yeshiva are ordained Rabbis, the majority of whom are Lubavitcher and have taught there for many years. If younger teachers are desired, the graduates of the *Bays Medresh* are considered to have the necessary background knowledge to teach. The recruitment of younger teachers to the Yeshiva is, however, problematic. The Lubavitch philosophy, emphasizing the dissemination of orthodox Judaism, has always held a special attraction and appeal to young married couples. Many, consequently, prefer to seek positions in less well-established Jewish communities in which their "success" is more noticeable. A Lubavitcher expressed the problem this way:

> There is in Lubavitch, the *Rebbe* stresses this very much, the desire to go out and create something. So, it's strange to say, but a boy would rather go to the other *ek* (corner) of the *velt* (world) and start from scratch than to come to an established school and feel like the fifth wheel to the wagon. The capable boys . . . would rather work somewhere in a Chabad house with students than to come here.

As for the *Bays Rivkeh*, high school graduates are encouraged to attend a Lubavitch teacher's seminary and return to join the school's Jewish department. The school has, apparently, succeeded in its efforts as the entire Jewish department's staff is comprised of *Bays Rivkeh* graduates.

Although the community does experience some difficulty in recruiting staff for the Jewish departments, it has, in fact, been able to produce enough of its own teachers. Such, however, is not the case with staffing the secular departments as graduates of both schools are discouraged from pursuing their secular studies. The following comments illustrate that while Lubavitcher recognize the many benefits of having their own kind staff the secular departments, the risks involved in Lubavitcher students continuing their secular education to the necessary level are believed to offset any such advantages:

> You see, I feel that you have no right to expose somebody to danger. You never know what will be the outcome if somebody goes to college. It would be very nice (if secular teachers came from within the community). But, then again, you're going into the conflict that we don't want to expose our girls to the university and that makes it very

hard. You just can't do it. You can't have teachers if they're not going to go to university. And the university is a dangerous place, especially, I think, for our children who have been so cloistered all their life. To let them out like that, they have to be very strong-minded not to get pushed around and not to be pushed onto the wrong paths.

The formal qualifications of the teachers are likely to vary; some have both a university degree and a certified teacher's diploma whereas others may have only one or the other. All teachers are hired on a part-time basis, which again creates problems in finding sufficient suitable staff.

While some of the other chassidic groups, for example the Satmarer and Tasher, consider a person's religious observance as an important criterion for hiring secular staff, the Lubavitch approach to this matter is more tolerant. As a Yeshiva administrator said: "In Lubavitch when we want someone to teach mathematics, we're first concerned with his mathematical capabilities." A teacher in the Yeshiva, supporting this view, remarked:

> ... if you could get secular teachers that were observant, it would be much better. But we can't get this. We don't have it. When we are looking for teachers, we are looking for the best quality teachers. We prefer they should be male teachers.

Yet, on the basis of discussion with teachers and administrators of both schools, it appears that in addition to formal qualifications, less formal considerations are also important:

> ... I don't know if it's a policy of the school, but I know there's a tendency to engage Gentile teachers so that if she should teach or say anything that is not appropriate, well the explanation is: *"Zeez a goiyeh, zee vayst nisht"* (She's a Gentile, she doesn't know), rather than to have an irreligious Jewish teacher.

Commenting on the potential problems of hiring non-religious Jewish teachers, a *Bays Rivkeh* administrator states:

> ... sometimes it's even worse than a Gentile. Their not being religious sometimes makes more conflict. A Gentile

woman comes in and she knows she's not allowed to say anything, do anything, and that's it, because it's two different worlds, while a Jewish girl thinks "Well, I'm religious enough, I can tell these kids anything," and that's where all the trouble starts.

The above comments point to what may be regarded as the ideal appointment to the secular staff: a Jew with a teacher's diploma who not only attended a religious school but also practises the tenets of traditional Judaism. For such a teacher, remarked one of the principals:

> ... it would be easier to control the material which she is presenting. I mean, let's not kid ourselves. Even in a secular department we have to watch our steps. In the textbooks there are things that are contradictory. ... so, therefore, it is my duty to see that the teachers should remember not to get into controversial problems at a certain stage where the kids are not yet ready to digest them properly.

As such teachers are difficult to recruit, secular staff are expected to remain strictly within the limits of their subject and not influence the children unnecessarily. (Poll, 1962:173)

A striking feature of secular education among the chassidim is the degree to which the subject matter is screened. The rationale for this is succinctly expressed by Rubin:

> What concerns community leaders most is the possibility that the exposure of the youngsters to strange people and materials may be an avenue for undesirable acculturation, a gap in the isolating wall they try to build around the young until they grow up and are ready to deal with the environment from the more favorable vantage point of adulthood and full-fledged incorporation in the community. (1972:150)

One way this screening is done is by issuing a handbook containing instructions to teachers informing them of proscribed areas of discussion with students. A teacher at an orthodox girls' school, which included girls from chassidic families, remarked:

> ... at the beginning of the year the Rabbi made up a manual for all the teachers. A section of this manual was

devoted to explaining to teachers what we must not teach.
. . . It said something to the effect of: everything contrary
to Jewish religion must not be taught . . . such as evolution.
Anything philosophical and contrary to Judaism must not
be taught. Sex is absolutely out. If a teacher feels a serious
need to communitcate these ideas to the students, then she
is to consult the Rabbi first, but under no circumstances is
free discussion to be allowed in the classroom.

In some cases explicit verbal instructions are given by the principal. For example, a university graduate who was teaching
chassidic boys from various *shteeblech* (chassidic groups) had this
to say:

He (the principal) told me a few things that I shouldn't be
discussing with the kids. Things that would conflict with
their religious beliefs. . . . Don't talk in terms of time, long
periods of time, because they just won't believe you. They
all just sort of block it out or they'll challenge you . . . because the earth has been in existence for a certain amount
of time for them and if you talk in terms of millions of
years . . .

Along with such instructions, the reading material is inspected to
ensure that both the written and pictorial content of books will
not suggest or imply anything contrary to what orthodox Jews
are expected to know. Thus, for example, certain areas of discussion are not only intentionally avoided, but all references to them
are forbidden. A secular teacher at a Hungarian chassidic Yeshiva
recalled:

Now, when . . . the _____*Rebbe* wanted them to
learn English, even in the higher classes, they had to learn
from certain books that were approved by them. For
instance, if there was a picture of a woman, even a cartoon
picture, anything, it didn't matter whether she had a long
skirt on or not, it had to be marked in black. And I told the
_____*Rebbe* that if I mark it in black the boys will
be more curious, but this had nothing to do with it. It had
to be marked off. All the *Rabonim* (Rabbis) saw that, even
for the youngsters, every single illustration was taken out
and all references to women were taken out.

Writing about the Satmarer, Rubin notes:

> For example, one of the tasks imposed on the principal is a continuous combing of the textbooks for potentially subversive content (e.g., love stories or pictures), a task to which he devotes a great deal of his available time. (1972:151)

In addition, some chassidic schools limit the secular educational experience to the classroom. While school assignments may extend secular studies to the home, organized extra-curricular activities are discouraged. The following was recounted by a teacher in a Hungarian chassidic school:

> I wanted to take my kids to the museum and to the Redpath (museum) and it had to go through the Council and it was refused just like that—they just wouldn't allow it. Also I wanted to start a library. It was refused, ostensibly, you know, on technical grounds that there wasn't enough room in the school. ...They didn't know which books I would bring in and they thought the threat was too great and it would be too much trouble anyway, so they said to forget it. ...Their list of priorities didn't include their kids reading anything like Hardy Boys mysteries, or anything to get them interested in reading.

In contrast to the secular departments in other chassidic schools in Montreal, Lubavitch schools' secular curricula closely follow the guidelines outlined for all public schools. As such guidelines permit flexibility, in that certain subjects are mandatory and others are optional, the Lubavitch schools' curricula do not include biology which is believed to contain views that are contradictory to an orthodox Jewish conception of the nature of the universe. The following incident illustrates this:

> It happens that I was teaching . . . at the time and we were studying personal health, and I was just surprised how little girls knew about the human body. This was in high school. And I was discussing this with the principal and I just mentioned to him that for science I was surprised that the girls didn't study biology instead of chemistry. It certainly would interest them more and it's certainly more directly applicable to them. And the answer was: chemistry is more objective and it's more specific, whereas with biology you could get into various views and various theories, and the easiest way was to stay away from it.

Nonetheless, the schools' administrators recognize the need to screen the subject matter and to be fully aware of the discussions and arguments that teachers wish to enter with their students. This, they claim, is to avoid situations in which material contradictory to the students' religious beliefs is brought into the open. As a Lubavitch administrator emphasized: "Teachers are told in the beginning two things they are not supposed to discuss—one is religion and the other is politics." Another administrator remarked:

> We told them that anything that has to do with religion, they should leave up to the Hebrew teacher. Last year we had a problem. ... the girls in one of the classes were discussing with their teacher things about their body and the discussion seemed to have gone quite well. But one of the little girls went home and told her mother "Oh boy, what we had in school today" and it bounced back. And the teacher was told: "Look, anything except your spelling and arithmetic don't touch, that's all. If the children want to know anything, let them go and ask their mothers. The discussion might be perfectly healthy and normal, but these children are brought up differently ...

When asked if his staff was presented with instructions proscribing consideration of certain topics, one of the principals replied:

> I don't make it so formal, but while talking to a teacher I give the teacher to understand, and, besides, as she has three hours in the afternoon to cover English language, composition, spelling, arithmetic, geography, there's so much to do before coming to these problems. And let's say that you take a kid and you'll tell him in Grade 5 or 6 how dinosaurs lived ten million years ago, his concept of time is so limited that it actually wouldn't enlighten him. It might mix him all up. I see no educational purpose in it even from a secular point of view. ... I just say: "Don't get involved in problems that clash with religious beliefs ... " On the contrary, I do believe that kids should not even be involved in these abstract discussions at all because their concept of time and numbers at this age is so limited and they only take it religiously. They believe because the teacher told them so.

While material considered openly contradictory to orthodox Judaism can easily be avoided or deleted from the curriculum, there is greater concern about students' exposure to subtle contradictory influences that may sway them against their religious upbringing. A Lubavitch woman remarked that:

> Today you can't help but head into it (evolution) wherever you are. Thank G-d, for our children it's not disastrous, because they feel G-d created the world. OK, there's a problem, so the problem exists, but G-d created the world. I mean no one's arguing that. So really, the problems aren't too great for our children. Their belief, by the time they reach it, is strong enough. I'm much more afraid of the things that are not strongly contradictory to *Yiddishkayt* that would endanger the child. (For example) things like, talking about physical enjoyments in life in a book that makes it sound so good and cushions it up so well. You know, romanticized. This is what I would be much more afraid of as influencing my child than anything else. I think that in any scientific beliefs a child, by that time, has enough Torah within him to keep him well-rooted.

The readers children use are also inspected to ensure that stories or passages in novels either related to other religions or in direct conflict with traditional Jewish beliefs are not studied in class. For example:

> The literature books today are just impossible. Well, at least Shakespeare, half of it is not understood, so they don't know what's coming off. But Mordecai Richler, or any of the others, I mean their books are just impossible for girls to read. _____ tries to censor them as much as possible and to bring in only material that's both acceptable to the Quebec Board and also to us. It's very difficult to find.

Whereas in some chassidic schools such negatively defined content is deleted with a black pen, it is simply replaced with another story in the two Lubavitch schools:

> The reader series, if they are from the Protestant School Board, are oriented to the Protestant School Board's way of

thinking. So, therefore, sometimes, when they plan that a book should be finished in Grade 1 or in Grade 2, right in the middle of the book where they consider the children will be three months after school begins, there'll be stories about Christmas and about Père Noel. We just replace it by something else. I don't replace the pages. I just tell the teacher: "Don't get into these stories, leave this story, take another one." So the children can still read it. You cannot close the child. Anyway the child goes out in the street and he sees this Père Noel. On the other hand, in the Hebrew department, the child gets this: this is not for me, this has nothing to do with me.

Although the secular curriculum is closely supervised, Lubavitcher realize the difficulties inherent in shielding the students from all potentially dangerous secular influences. Thus, while such influences are viewed as the inevitable accompaniments of a secular curriculum, it is expected that they will be offset by the schools' Hebrew departments. For instance:

... There is a direct influence and an indirect influence. The direct influence, for instance, evolution, doesn't bother the children because we discuss it with them and it has no influence. But there is an indirect influence and you can't help it; for instance, a way of life described in a book. You can take (secular studies) or leave it. There's no way you can avoid (secular influences). It's impossible. ... You see, the child is exposed to it in the street, in the newspapers, everywhere. ... We must help the child understand the situation. For example, in secular studies they read about the Crusaders. So in the Hebrew department they explain to the children that there were plenty of Jewish communities wiped out by them. But still in the books they are heroes. We don't expect that the secular teacher will explain it to them, but the Hebrew teacher will.

In addition to the screening efforts of the schools, parents consider it their responsibility to be aware of what goes on in their children's English classes, and may petition the principal to change what they think necessary. For example:

... the trouble is that we do take too much for granted (concerning the secular curriculum). It's wrong and we definitely should go in and see what's going on in the school. . . . I could see from my past two daughters, and this daughter as well, that there was a lot that parents could have corrected. Let me give you an example. In English they asked my daughter to read certain novels. Even with _____ looking over these novels, still there were novels that I didn't want my daughter to be reading. And I had to make sure to speak up and get this through. . . . There are always things that we can't take our eyes off, so to speak.

An important way that such negative influences could be avoided or controlled and checked is for the parents to take an interest in what their children are studying. . . . And even my youngest, who is only in elementary school, came home with a view of something that the teacher said. I didn't like it, so I referred it back to the principal and she checked on her. . . . If you get an irreligious teacher, not only could she be plain irreligious, but she might have some negative or cynical views about religion . . . and doesn't even try to control its coming out. Now if she's teaching very young children, that's very bad. And I think it's only through parent-teacher communication, or parent interest in what's going on, that you can check this . . .

Students from Non-Lubavitch Families in Lubavitch Schools

The majority of students in the Yeshiva and *Bays Rivkeh* are from non-Lubavitch families. One of the *Bays Rivkeh* administrators remarked: "As I said before, Lubavitch can't put together that many. If it was only Lubavitch in the *Bays Rivkeh* it would just be ridiculous to open." Although numerically Lubavitcher students are a minority in the schools, the schools' spirit is Lubavitch oriented. Thus, together with the Jewish department teachers, students from Lubavitch families try to influence the students from non-orthodox homes toward *Yiddishkayt.* For example, the Yeshiva organizes trips to Lubavitch *Farbrengens* in New York for some of the students. In the *Bays Rivkeh,* the editors of the school's newspaper, being from Lubavitch families, write and insert articles which relate directly to traditional Judaism with a Lubavitch orientation. A Lubavitch parent expressed the views of many when she said: " . . . the children who grow up with the concept of Lubavitch can have ten irreligous kids in their class, twenty, and they'd be perhaps three, and they'd do beautifully."

As mentioned earlier, Jewish students from various backgrounds, religious and non-religious, are welcomed to the community's schools. Since Lubavitcher see it as part of their task to show less religious Jews the relevance and significance of orthodox Judaism, they view the school environment, which is conducive to working on younger people, as an optimal setting in which to accomplish this goal. With such a philosophy, Lubavitch schools are not selective as to the kind of Jewish student accepted. This is precisely the opposite practice in other chassidic and certain orthodox schools where student selectivity is regarded as necessary. The following, by the principal of a Lubavitch school, illustrates this:

It's much harder to find differences between us and the *Bays* _____ (an orthodox girls' school). I would say (there is) no difference in the instruction but there's a difference in the philosophy of the school. *Bays* _____ is a religious school for religious girls. In other words, there is, I don't want to sound fancy, but this is a ghetto-type attitude, a defensive ghetto. Let's say there's a hundred, two hundred families in X (name of city) who have children. I was one of them at the time. I didn't send my girl either to Coronation or to the *Folk Shulle* because it's not religious. I wanted a school for my girl which would teach her a way of life, so here is a school for us. But if my next door neighbour who is not religious wanted to send his girls to this school, under different pretexts or reasons, she would be refused. This girl would not be accepted because they would say: "The whole purpose of the school is to create a religious atmosphere for our girls, they should live out their life at home and at school without conflict. If we introduce in the school girls from non-religious families who can come and say that they drove in a car on *Shabbess*, we'll have conflicts." This is *Bays* _____. It's a healthy attitude, it's a very relaxed way, no problems, a smooth ride. As you know, Lubavitch in general, and therefore *Bays Rivkeh* which is part of it, are absolutely open to anyone and I do not discriminate against any child. On the contrary, I have many children from homes where parents know nothing about Jewishness, practise very little, and thanks to G-d we have never yet had a case in the Lubavitcher Yeshiva or here where an outside boy or an outside girl, misled a boy or girl of ours philosophically. But we do know of cases where outside boys and girls came in looking sarcastic and became very serious.

The presence of non-Lubavitch children ensures that both schools provide a progressive secular education that compares favourably with that in other schools. Although many Lubavitcher would prefer an entirely religious curriculum, they recognize that this is not feasible for the community at present.

While most of the students in both schools are from outside this chassidic group, the majority come from families in which at least the Sabbath and *Kashruth* are observed. The Ashkenazic students in the school are mainly from observant homes, but students from Sphardic families are, with minor exception, not religious. Although many parents may not be as strictly observant as Lubavitcher and may not share many of their chassidic customs and views, most are interested in providing their children with the kind of education offered by Lubavitch. Others are drawn to the Lubavitch schools because they are afraid that social trends in the public schools will be a harmful influence on their children.

In spite of the students' varying backgrounds, the schools are engaged in a socialization process whereby all students are impressed with the importance of observing the tenets of orthodox Judaism. For example, all Yeshiva students are expected to wear a skull-cap and a fringed ritual undershirt and to observe *Kashruth* and the Sabbath. Some students find this very different from their home life and consequently resist the regulations, but Lubavitcher are tolerant in dealing with them as they realize the importance of creating the right atomsphere. As one of the principals put it:

You know, the general outlook of Lubavitch is to harmonize, to respect everyone's feelings. For example, we ask the children to come in the morning to *davn* (pray). With some children we are lenient and we know that we can't expect much from them. Our outlook is to accept and to

understand, and the boys should understand each other.
. . . We would never allow a boy from a *frum* (orthodox)
background to criticize one from a non-*frum* background.
We try to create a brotherly atmosphere in class in order to
understand each other and feel for each other, to understand everyone is a Jew.

Although both schools attempt to generate an atmosphere of
harmony and toleration, they are not always successful in
preventing conflicts between students and their non-observant
parents. The in-coming non-observant students are gradually
made aware of Jewish laws and practices and are taught that these
are applicable to all Jews. In time they realize that there are
rewards to be gained by altering their behaviour to conform to
these expectations and are prepared to do so. The parents, on the
other hand, may resist their children's eagerness to follow certain
laws and customs and/or have little interest in altering their lifestyle. The nature of such conflicts are described by a *Bays Rivkeh*
administrator:

. . . there were some parents who knew about *kashress*
(*kashruth*) and *Shabbess* (the Sabbath) and all that, so
putting their children into a school like this created a
conflict because the child said: "Why don't you do it?"
There are some parents who didn't know anything, but
wanted to expose their children to some Judaism, and the
conflict was even bigger. The most frequent thing, I think, is
that the children come home with the *dinim* (laws) about
the holidays, the *Shabbess* (the Sabbath) and the parents
say: "We don't do that at home." And the children say:
"Well, why don't you? My teacher told me . . . " And that
makes for conflict.

The schools' principals and other personnel try to mediate such
conflicts, but the outcome is not always certain:

Sometimes the children accept the parents' explanation.
. . . If the children are strong enough in their beliefs and the
parents are really wishy-washy, the children will convert the
parents. But sometimes parents just don't care enough.
. . . We try as much as possible to speak with the parents
and to speak with the children to tell them: "Well, if you

can't do it all, then do as much as you can and, you know, slowly it'll come." But it doesn't always work.

For some parents the only solution is to remove their children from the schools. In the course of this research I have encountered parents who in anticipation of these difficulties decided not to enroll their children in the Lubavitch schools.

The presence of non-observant students in the schools also works in the opposite direction as Lubavitch students are exposed to potentially negative influences. As one parent remarked: "Many of our own were fearful of the influence of these outside children on ours; the language they speak, the way they dress, the way they conduct themselves, even the refreshments they bring in." In spite of such concerns, however, Lubavitcher believe that their efforts at exposing young Jews to orthodox Judaism is so necessary that they are willing to take the risk. The *Rebbe's* encouragement and concern in this matter leave these chassidim with little doubt of its importance. When the issue of non-Lubavitch students in Lubavitch schools was brought to the *Rebbe*, reports a Lubavitcher, the *Rebbe* stated: "You have nothing to fear. In the merit of trying to influence these other children who need the help, you will be protected and nothing will happen." The *Rebbe's* remarks appear to have been proved correct, as the following two comments by administrators of the *Bays Rivkeh* and Yeshiva indicate:

So far, I think we've been quite fortunate. We haven't had any problem like that. . . . The influence is not that strong. The children, and perhaps this is a credit to our own, are so strong, they believe so strongly that what they are doing is correct, that there isn't too much of an influence on them.

No, we don't feel that (our children will be badly influenced). We feel that it is the opposite, that we are strong enough to influence the child that comes from a non-observant home. . . . There has never been a case where I could say a religious child from a religious home was badly influenced and went off the way. The opposite, yes.

Although Lubavitcher believe their *derech* (approach) to orthodox Judaism is the most complete and personally satisfying, they are anxious but reluctant to impose their system of beliefs on elementary grade students from non-Lubavitch families. Consequently, efforts to influence younger students from non-Lubavitch families toward orthodox Judaism and Lubavitch are limited.

The Bays Medresh

In addition to the two schools maintained by the community, the Yeshiva includes a *Bays Medresh* (Rabbinical College) where students (*bocherim*) between the ages of fourteen and twenty-two study. The number of students in the *Bays Medresh* is usually maintained at between fifty-five and seventy. Depending on their age and background, some of these *bocherim* have completed high school and might even have attended college for a time, while others have received only a religious education. Whereas the older *bocherim* study in the *Bays Medresh* full time, that is, without the interruption of secular studies, some of the younger ones attend high school courses at the Yeshiva as part of their afternoon curriculum. Unlike the community's schools which draw students only from Montreal, the *Bays Medresh* includes students from cities across the United States and Canada. Although Lubavitch has established Yeshivas in a few other cities, *Bays Medresh* facilities are not always available or the parents and son, in consultation with the *Rebbe*, may decide it is preferable for the boy to pursue his studies at a Yeshiva away from home. A number of students from either non-orthodox or non-chassidic family backgrounds who have become attracted to Lubavitch are also encouraged to enroll in a Lubavitcher Yeshiva.

The Yeshiva's facilities include a dormitory within easy walking distance of the Yeshiva which consists of several apartments in an apartment building, and serves as sleeping quarters for students from other cities. Although students from Montreal live with their families, the two groups spend the majority of their time in the *Bays Medresh* or elsewhere in the Yeshiva. A student describes a typical learning day:

> The schedule of the day consists of getting up at seven o'clock, coming to the Yeshiva here. If you're on time, going to the *mikveh* (ritual bath), if you're not on time— later. Learning *chassidess* for an hour, then preparing yourself for *davening*. If you didn't go to the *mikveh* before,

you go. *Davn* at nine o'clock. You have till ten thirty to finish your breakfast. Ten thirty upstairs and then *Gemoreh* or whatever you are learning till a quarter to two. Quarter to two—*mincheh*—(afternoon prayer). Two o'clock—lunch hour till three. If you've got to go shopping, buy something, or write a letter, you do it then. Three o'clock back to studies. Six thirty—*myriv*—(evening prayer), in the winter. Supper—again you get an hour. Seven thirty—*chassidess*. Nine thirty you're free.

The typical day is so structured that *bocherim* are expected to spend almost all their time either in the Yeshiva or in the dormitory, which is considered part of the Yeshiva. They are immediately immersed in a religious atmosphere and adhere to the *Bays Medresh* learning schedule. Although their decision to attend the Lubavitcher Yeshiva is voluntary, the Yeshiva's administrators exercise direct control over their everyday activities. In addition, they are under the informal supervision of other *bocherim* with whom they are in continuous contact. As a result, the pace of their status passage into *Yiddishkayt* and Lubavitch is more rapid.

While the younger students at the Yeshiva are taught *Yiddishkayt* and to be observant Jews, *bocherim* in the *Bays Medresh* are groomed to be Lubavitcher chassidim. They study *chassidess*, regularly travel to attend the *Rebbe's Farbrengens*, and are exposed to stories and incidents about Lubavitcher chassidim and *Rebbeim*. The Yeshiva is where one learns to be a Lubavitcher and therefore where *bocherim* are expected to spend the majority of their time. *Chassidess*, chassidim, and *Yiddishkayt* are seen as a way of life, as opposed to a set of separate activities, which for the *bocher* can best be observed and discovered in the Yeshiva. Two *bocherim* describe the importance of the Yeshiva in discovering this way of life:

Well, first of all, I'd say that by living in the Yeshiva you pick up the warmth that *chassidess* has to offer within *Yiddishkayt*. It is very difficult for somebody, a student, to live a way of life. Generally a student who lives at home goes to school and he knows that at five o'clock or whatever time it may be, he's out of school and then he's back at home in his different world and he forgets about school until the next morning. This is a very big obstacle in picking up a way of life. You go home and your mother tells you that you've got to visit relatives, you've got to do this, you've got to do that. All these things take away from the Yeshiva. Whereas while you're in the Yeshiva, whatever you're doing, whether you're eating or you're sleeping, or you're *davening* or you're learning, or you're going to put on *Tefillin* with other people, or you're going down to campus to arrange for a *Pegeesheh*, or whatever you're doing, you're always doing it with other *bocherim*, in a chassidic atmosphere and you pick up the *Yiddishkayt* and the *chassidishe* warmth that Torah wants a person to have.

Another *bocher* put it like this:

You can sit and learn and learn and learn and, believe me, that's very important. You have to do that. But I think that's only part of it. You can have a lot of knowledge but there's more to Lubavitch than that. You have to learn how to be a certain type of person with certain attributes. You have to learn manners, and the place to get all this is right here (in the Yeshiva). Just look at some of the people walking around this place. You know them, people like Rabbi_____ , Reb_____ , Reb_____.
Where else can you get this if not here? You learn a lot just by watching these people.

There is only a slight difference between the *bocherim's* formal and informal activities in the Yeshiva for one is really an extension of the other. The formal activities consist of the classes the *bocherim* are expected to attend as students of the Yeshiva. As mentioned, the *bocherim's* learning schedule is intensive and they are expected to satisfy its demands daily. *Bocherim* recognize that to live *Yiddishkayt* fully, studying the Torah and its commentaries is necessary, and that to understand the system of Chabad *chassidess* at a progressively deeper level, learning *Tanya* is essential. In addition, they appreciate that the Rabbis who teach them and supervise the classes are best qualified to determine when a student is ready to graduate to a more advanced class. A student meant this when he said:

. . . *chassidess* and chassidism is a way of life that can't possibly be lived in its fullest sense in a nine-to-five day or even in a nine-to-nine day. It can only be done by living in a Yeshiva, and being completely dependent on the *hanholleh* of the Yeshiva, on the Dean, *Mashpeea* and *mashgiech* of the Yeshiva as your guidance counsellors.

Along with the scheduled classes, informal activities occupy the *bocher's* time. These consist largely of sitting around and talking about such things as the *Rebbe's* latest *sicheh* (discourse), encounters made during *mivtzas Tefillin*, secular ideas, or whatever is of popular interest at the time. Such discussions might originate in the *Bays Medresh* and carry over to the dormitory, might last from a few minutes to several hours, and might include only three or four *bocherim* or quite a large group. While the *bocher* should be interested in gaining knowledge about *Yiddishkayt*, which results from his formal study classes, he should also be concerned about learning a way of life. This comes mainly through informal encounters and discussions about attitudes, feelings, and beliefs toward fellow Jews. As *bocherim* insist, however, one can take greater advantage of these encounters by living in the Yeshiva than at home. Two students discuss the benefits of these kinds of gatherings:

> For instance, guys pick up much more than they do from their studies, they pick things up in their dormitory when they see how an older guy, a good guy, conducts himself on his own, you know, in his own private time, in his own personal life. He sees the convictions or whatever it may be and he gets a lot more out of that, or else, you see before he goes to sleep, . . . you start the bull sessions and you get into personal things which we call a minor *Farbrengen*—two guys get together and this cannot be done at home.

> Wherever there's a common interest, that's where you get together and the common interest is here, in the Yeshiva—learning in general, even bull sessions. The kinds of bull sessions that go on here are of common interest. They might have to do with what the *Rebbe* said today, or with stories, or with secular ideas, but it's still common interest. . . . The kinds of things that you can pick up here, not that they are as important as learning, the formal learning that you do, but they seem to complement the learning that goes on.

The Yeshiva, both as a school and community institution, tries to shape the minds of those who go there regularly. For the younger students this takes the form of providing a traditional Jewish interpretation of creation and stressing the importance of orthodox Judaism. Students at the high school and *Bays Medresh* levels are expected to assume an orthodox Lubavitch perspective of the world and one'e role in it. The optimal situation is one in which the teachings of the Yeshiva and the religious practices in the home are complementary. Although one could study the Yeshiva's curriculum at home, being enrolled as a Yeshiva student is regarded as mandatory for becoming an orthodox Jew. As a *bocher* said:

> The *Rebbe* spoke about this at a *Farbrengen*. In the old days it used to be different. The person can be the most religious person and he will not send his kids to the Yeshiva. The kids go to college and everything else. The person could be the most religious person and not go to the Yeshiva and everything would be alright. And the home would be enough for them. Today it's not like that. Today it's impossible. You can come from the most religious home but if you don't go to a Yeshiva, forget it. You haven't got a chance. That's the way it is because the Yeshiva is the backbone, it's the nucleus, it's the central point. It's very true. When you think about it you'll see how true it is.

Summary

The Yeshiva is, therefore, best seen as both an assimilative and anti-assimilative institution. As the former, its schools provide students with a Torah education, its congregants inform nonorthodox Jews about orthodox Judaism, and Lubavitcher keep one another informed on matters concerning the *Rebbe* and Lubavitch's work in the community. To encourage Lubavitch men and boys to live within the spirit of Lubavitch, the Yeshiva is used both as a place where one can *davn* and learn and where one meets for informal chats. As an anti-assimilative institution, it attemps to channel its youth into an orthodox and Lubavitch way of life and away from the fads and fashions of the surrounding culture. While the Yeshiva serves as a base from which Lubavitcher make contact with non-orthodox Jews, it also acts as an insulator against the dominant social values of the larger society.

As one *bocher* said:

> There are various reasons besides the fact that to learn
> Torah a Jewish boy should go to Yeshiva—that's one thing.
> Of course, it's not an argument that Jewish kids should be
> given the best possible religious education available. There
> you have right away the Yeshiva. ... And it's more, of
> course, than a place just to learn Torah. ... Here you have
> a living example of the epitome of the old chassidim. Rabbi
> _____ is an example. ... Secondly, there's the
> environment. ... As far as I'm concerned and as far as
> others are concerned in general, ... the environment in the
> world today is very bad. ... Kids, generally, nowadays,
> should be brought to the Yeshiva. They go out into the
> world and they're faced with tremendous ideas which are
> floating back and forth and someone who's fresh, it'll really
> hit them. You have to face it with an armour of Torah. The
> environment in the Yeshiva, on the other hand, is Torah
> oriented, Chabad oriented. If they go out, including just
> going shopping downtown, they'd know continuously, they
> know what is right as far as Torah is concerned, know what
> they see in the world is not necessarily correct ...

Lubavitchers' network of activities in the Yeshiva, for both
ballebatim and students, appears to separate them from the surrounding non-Lubavitch community and to serve as a non-
assimilative barrier to channel Lubavitchers' everyday lives and
help maintain their chassidic identity. In the case of students
from non-orthodox backgrounds, the Yeshiva's curriculum aims
to instill in them a positive feeling toward traditional Judaism and
encourages them to become observant Jews.

In contrast to the larger society in which the schools tend to
set the children apart from adult society, the Lubavitch school is
not a children's world separated from adult society. Since the
Lubavitcher Yeshiva is utilized both by students and adults, the
former are continually in contact with adults from the community. The two age groups *davn* in the same *shul* and meet at
many of the community's celebrations and *Farbrengens* so that,
in fact, the school is part of the adult's cultural world.

So far the emphasis has been on the fact that, in order to
persist, the Lubavitch community must create and maintain a
distinctive identity and, at the same time, provide its members

with a tenable way of life. The community's tenability is, however, directly related to its relationship with the larger Jewish community whose financial contributions and interest in traditional Judaism support Lubavitch institutions. An outcome of these chassidim's contacts with outsiders is their possible exposure to situations which may threaten and be in opposition to their distinctive way of life. Lubavitchers' solution to this dilemma is a series of proselytizing activities in which they seek to attract newcomers. In addition, these activities permit them to a large extent to control their contacts with outsiders and ensure that they will focus mainly on religion. Although these chassidim's proselytizing efforts do not attract many newcomers to the community, some people do decide to alter their way of life and become integrated into the Lubavitch community. The remaining chapters of this book will focus on the interaction between Lubavitcher and non-Lubavitch Jews, their proselytizing activities, and the way possible converts are initiated into the ways of the Lubavitch community.

Footnotes

[1] In contrast to the Yeshiva, the *Bays Rivkeh* provides all students with a secular education.

[2] Ashkenazim—Jews of central and eastern Europe. The Ashkenazim have come to develop a set of distinctive customs and rituals, different from those of the Sphardim, the Jews from the Mediterranean countries and North Africa.

[3] For example, it is usual for these students to form close friendships with one another. As one Yeshiva student put it:

> There are those kids who take a *vos darfstu gayn in Ainglish* (why study secular subjects) attitude. You know, what do you need it for? And any kid who comes in (to secular studies) is looked down upon. He is going English to a large degree, and is looked down upon.

Chapter Six

Lubavitcher and Their Neighbours: Gentiles and Jews

Since they are not institutionally complete Lubavitcher must establish certain relationships with the larger society. Their dealings with non-Jews are not extensive and are engaged in fleetingly and impersonally. They do, however, need the support of the larger Jewish community, especially to help finance such activities as their schools and summer camps. Contact with non-Lubavitch Jews is also necessary to fulfil Lubavitcher's obligation to observe the Torah's precepts and encourage non-observant Jews to return to the orthodox faith. As Mauss (1967) and others have shown, a relationship must be two sided; that is, there must be benefits accruing to both sides if the relationship is to be lasting and fruitful. What then are the benefits that the larger community receives as a result of its relationship with the Lubavitcher chassidim? For some, Lubavitch's schools, summer camps, and other organized activities ensure that their children are exposed to a traditionally orthodox view of life and are given a secure base for their future religious observance. The majority of Jews familiar with Lubavitcher regard them as ultra-orthodox or super-Jews, and recognize that their presence is desirable as a standard of strict orthodox observance. Although most non-observant Jews have minimal contact with Lubavitcher, they use Lubavitcher's presence in whatever manner they consider fitting. This is similar to what occurred in Williamsburg when the chassidim arrived. The presence of these orthodox Jews led to the establishment of kosher butcher shops which less observant Jews were glad to patronize, although they had not been sufficiently concerned about the dietary laws to establish such shops themselves. (Kranzler, 1961:61-62)

This chapter will focus on the nature of Lubavitchers' contacts with the larger community. The mutual benefits gained by Lubavitcher and the larger Jewish community, the Lubavitchers' role as models to this community, and three activities through which

Lubavitcher attempt to initiate and sustain contact with other Jews will be discussed. The chapter concludes with an examination of Lubavitchers' ties with the surrounding non-Jewish community.

The Relationship Between Lubavitch and the Larger Jewish Community: Mutual Benefits

Although the larger Jewish community has, to a great extent, been responsible for the tenability of the Lubavitch community since it was established in Montreal in 1941, the benefits accruing to non-Lubavitch Jews, though often intangible, have been considerable.

The presence of the Lubavitcher in Montreal signifies to many, especially non-observant Jews, that orthodox Judaism still flourishes. As such, it may be said that these chassidic Jews serve as orthodox Jewish role models. As early as 1941 the Montreal Yiddish newspaper wrote:

> ... till now one can only say that Canadian Jewry can have no regrets that they helped the Yeshiva students to immigrate to Montreal. Tremendous moral strength has been added to the city; young people have something to say to Canadian Jewry, and will unrelentingly use their influence to further orthodox Jewish life in this country. (*Der Keneder Odler*, October 31, 1941) (translated from Yiddish)

Although a majority of Montreal Jews neither have nor wish to have sustained contact with Lubavitcher, they recognize these chassidim's contribution to the Jewish population. One non-observant Jew expressed the general feeling when he mentioned:

> I really have nothing to do with them, but I'm pleased they're around. You see, there are plenty of orthodox Jews in this city without the Lubavitcher. Take the other chassidim, for example, and a lot of others who aren't chassidic. But Lubavitcher put a lot of work into getting people to understand their position. Even though you're not observant, to them you're still a Jew and they care about you. They also remind you that you're a Jew and that's important too.

147

Many non-Lubavitch parents, wishing to provide their children with an orthodox education and to immerse them in an orthodox Jewish environment send them to Lubavitcher institutions which they regard as less extreme in their teaching methods and attitudes regarding orthodox Judaism than some chassidic groups. In addition, students at Lubavitch schools and summer camps are likely to attend other Lubavitch functions such as rallies, parades, and youth group meetings. Although the majority of these students are from families in which a degree of orthodoxy is practised, several come from backgrounds where orthodox Judaism is completely absent.

Although Lubavitcher eagerly welcome all Jews, most of the people using their institutions come from orthodox families. The establishment of these institutions can therefore be seen as attempts to fill a void in the Jewish community in general and the orthodox segment of this community in particular. The founding of the Lubavitcher Yeshiva and *Pardess Channeh*—the Lubavitch girls' camp—are excellent examples of this, as a Lubavitcher affiliated with this chassidic community since 1943 remarked:

> Well, at the time, Jewish education in Montreal was at a very low state, low level. Even the Talmud Torah, as we know it now, was on a very small scale. The idea of parochial education, day schools, was not very much known. . . . You see, at the time, many of the parents, I would say most of the parents, were first generation immigrants and they themselves did not have any education as far as English education is concerned. Then, I would say in the beginning of the forties, it was just after the thirties and the recession and all this, I suppose that people did not even have the money to send their children to private schools, like a day school, like a Talmud Torah or a Yeshiva. There was no Yeshiva in the first place. So it was something that everybody did, send their children to Protestant schools. And, of course, not too many children visited afternoon schools. It was mostly, as it's known now, a *Bar Mitzveh* education. So when Lubavitch opened their doors many of the children joined. . .

The opening of the Lubavitch girls' camp was also partly due to the absence of such an institution in Montreal. Although there are many co-educational Jewish camps available nearby, none was considered suitable for girls from strictly orthodox Jewish homes. Camp *Pardess Channeh* was organized to provide a summer camp for these girls, though others were also welcome to attend. A camp administrator said:

> In Montreal you probably know ... that there is no religious girls' camp whatsoever around. Now we've been dreaming about having a girls' camp for I wouldn't even know the number of years, but at least twelve or thirteen years. Either there was no place or there was no one to run it or there was no site ... whatever there was, there was always something. ... I don't think I'll have trouble filling the camp next year. I think this camp will be around for a long time. I mean it was important that there be such a camp. There was a great need for it.

Lubavitcher do not, however, restrict their services to youth; programs and activities are also available for interested adults. The Lubavitch women's groups and drama group readily welcome interested outsiders and all Jews are free to pray at Lubavitch, attend the Lubavitch study classes, and ask Lubavitcher's advice about Judaism.

In return for these services to the larger Jewish community, Lubavitcher receive a sizeable proportion of their revenue from outside support. Although Lubavitcher contribute a certain amount toward the maintenance of their institutions, this outside revenue is of considerable importance as was suggested by several Lubavitcher:

> Do you know what it costs to keep the Yeshiva going, the *Bays Rivkeh*, the camps, the youth groups and whatever else there is? I don't know the exact figures, but it's plenty. But how much can Lubavitcher pay? I mean there's a limit. So we need to get contributions from the outside— you know, from people who may not use the Yeshiva themselves but, for whatever reason, have feelings for it.

The degree of such outside support could be gathered by attending the Yeshiva's fund-raising dinners and banquets where approximately half of the guests were not Lubavitcher. At one such affair, for example, more than five and a half thousand dollars was pledged by those in attendance. Although many of the guests maintained only a peripheral relationship with the Yeshiva, their financial contribution was necessary to assist the Lubavitch institutions meet their obligations.

Many Jews in Montreal believe that chassidim support themselves from donations solicited for their Yeshivas. It is not unusual for Jews to ask: "Do these chassidim work for a living?" or "Who supports these Jews? Where do they get money?" While many Lubavitcher are aware of this image and sometimes refer to it in conversation, they quickly disclaim its validity. They admit, however, that some Lubavitcher's occupations are directly concerned with collecting money for the Lubavitcher Yeshiva. When one such Lubavitcher was asked about the sources of the community's fund-raising, he replied: "The money comes from donations, from different people, Jewish and non-Jewish." He also claimed that "each Jew has a hidden need for Torah" and regarded financial support to the community as "a partnership between the scholar and businessman." As he put it: "The businessman by giving money helps people to learn and study and gets some of the benefits from this." Although data on the Lubavitch community's fund-raising in the larger Jewish and Gentile communities are scarce, it appears that since their arrival in Montreal, Lubavitcher have attracted people who today are expected to contribute regularly to the community. The full-time fund-raisers are expected to ensure that monetary pledges are fulfilled, to canvass in the larger community for additional sources of support, and to assure the community's supporters that their contributions further the observance of *mitzvess*.

This monetary support from outsiders is essential for the schools and summer camps, which contribute to the tenability of the community's way of life. Lubavitcher's ability to maintain both a boys' and a girls' school, for instance, enables them to provide their children with a special Jewish education, and thus helps to ensure their acceptance of the Lubavitch way of life. The programs at the two summer camps are best viewed as an extension of the schools' Jewish curricula for the basis of both is the practice and understanding of precepts regulating orthodox Jewish life. As in the schools, the children from Lubavitch families attending the summer camps are in the minority. Camp *Gan Yisroel's* registration for the 1970 season, for example, included only between 30 and 40 per cent of children from Lubavitch families, the remainder coming from the larger Jewish community. When the Camp Director was asked if *Pardess Channeh* included only Lubavitch girls, he replied:

> No, you see, the funny thing about it was that we really never got the camp before because in the past, . . . let me put it this way, Lubavitch over here would not be able to put together more than . . . thirty-five to forty kids of camping age altogether. . .

Outsiders are, therefore, crucial to these institutions' viability. With Lubavitch schools in particular, it is precisely the presence of students from non-Lubavitch families which ensures that the schools retain enough of a secular curriculum to qualify them for "associate status" rank and financial support from the state.

Lubavitchers' relationship with the larger Jewish community also enables them to perform various *mitzvess*. Whereas certain *mitzvess* are usually observed privately, such as reciting the appropriate prayer before eating or abiding by certain Sabbath regulations, others are easily fulfilled in the presence of non-observant Jews. If, for example, all Jews in Montreal observed *Tefillin* or recited the prayers related to the holiday of *Sukkess*, there would be no need for Lubavitchers' *Tefillin* campaign or their Sukkehmobile. Because of the large number of non-observant Jews in the community the Lubavitchers' proselytizing activities result in a greater stress on observing various *mitzvess*. Proselytizing in the larger community is also consistent with the *Rebbe's* constant reminder to his chassidim that non-observant Jews must be contacted and pursuaded to conduct their lives in an orthodox manner. Since Lubavitchers' self-conception centres on their execution of the *Rebbe's* advice and requests, the community's relationship with the larger Jewish community becomes central to maintaining its distinctive identity.

Lubavitcher are set apart, and set themselves apart, from chassidim of other groups by their efforts to establish contact with non-observant Jews and to direct their attention to orthodox Judaism. They have organized strategies to penetrate this community and to infuse it with a feeling for traditional Judaism. Three of the more important campaigns they used are the *Tefillin* campaign, the Encounter with Chabad, and Lubavitch summer camps.

Relationship With the Wider Jewish Community: Lubavitcher as Role Models

To understand Lubavitchers' proselytizing activities in the larger Jewish community it is essential to focus on how they acquired and retain their role as super-Jews. Strict observance of orthodox precepts is necessary but insufficient by itself. The Satmarer and Tasher chassidim, for example, while strictly observant, are isolated from and hardly seen by the larger Jewish community and therefore cannot serve as a role model. To assume such a role, one must necessarily come into contact with the larger Jewish community in situations that emphasize Jewishness. The *Tefillin* campaign, Encounter with Chabad, and the summer camp programs are activities which, although not intended primarily to convert people to Lubavitch, aim to convince non-observant Jews that Lubavitcher are only different from them in degree and not in kind. This emphasis on quantitative rather than qualitative differences lessens the chance of non-observant Jews becoming alienated and reinforces their belief that they are part of the Jewry that the Lubavitcher typify. Thus, while meeting and conversing with other Jews, Lubavitcher continually emphasize *madraiggess*—levels—in *Yiddishkayt*, and stress that their attainment of a particular level of *Yiddishkayt* is accessible to all willing to practise orthodox Judaism:

> I mean, really, what is the difference between us? O.K., I might have reached a higher *madraiggeh* (level) of *Yiddishkayt* but that's because I practise the *mitzvess*. But you could reach a higher *madraiggeh* too if you begin to put on *Tefillin*, observe *kashress*, *davn*. I mean everyone should be interested in reaching a higher level of *Yiddishkayt*. O.K., so I'm at step two and you're at step one, but you can reach step two if you work at it.

The *Tefillin* campaign, for example, emphasized that others can easily embark on the same path as Lubavitcher with a simple start. This campaign, the Encounter with Chabad, and other

Lubavitch organized activities are best regarded as public, observable super-Jewish activities.

Lubavitchers' pursuit of proselytizing activities emanates from their shared belief that those Jews whose practice of traditional Judaism does not conform to the orthodox version must be persuaded to regulate their lives by the Torah's precepts. This belief has been central to all the Lubavitcher *Rebbeim* and has also been reiterated by the present Lubavitcher *Rebbe*. A story told by a Klausenburger chossid highlights Lubavitchers' proselytizing zeal:

> I'll tell you an example. There's a storm at the water, a gale. Anybody who goes near the water drowns. Someone is drowning. Here are the thoughts of three people: One says, "I don't care. I'll jump in even if I drown. I'll give up my whole body." Another says, "I'll run away. Look at the terrible storm. He's lost but I can save myself if I run away." The third person answers—he gets himself down to the water and he sets himself strong. He throws a rope and calls out: "Catch it and I'll pull you out."
>
> Lubavitch is like the first. Their way is to give out everything to pull in. They'll live in the worst community in the world, even though the person can get spoiled himself, even though something could go wrong with his children. Satmar is like the second: "If I see a person not religious, not only will I not have anything to do with him, but I'll chase him away." We (at Klausenburg) put down a Yeshiveh, make it as orthodox as we want. If a man who is not religious sends us his son, we take him in. If he wants to grab on to us, we take him in. We don't chase after him. . . (Mintz, 1968:154)

Other activities the Lubavitcher have organized to draw Jews into the orthodox fold include the Institute for Brides and Grooms to inform young couples about the Jewish laws regulating marriage, *Messibbess Shabbess* groups to maintain younger boys' and girls' interest in orthodox Judaism, *Chanekkeh* (Feast of Lights) and *Purim* (Feast of Lots) rallies, a *Lag Bo'Oymer* Day Parade (children's festive day) and a women's drama group. As indicated, the common feature of all these activities is that they are organized for the express purpose of bridging and eventually closing the gap presumed to exist between the orthodox and non-observant Jews in the community. A Lubavitch woman explains how the drama group helps achieve that goal:

> ... the drama group attracts women that aren't Lubavitcher really. They seem to like this (the group) very much. This year we have a few women who ... have a feeling for Lubavitch, they sympathize, but they're not religious, they don't keep *Shabbess*. ... Once they're in it they get to know the other women and we become friends and we don't feel we have to stay away from anyone if they're not religious. As long as they're Jewish we associate with them. We may not be able to eat at their houses, but we could still be friendly and talk to them and meet with them. And this way we have an open door to their houses, to them. [The group started] as a fund raiser. We didn't realize it would have this effect. But now we feel this part of the play is just as effective, is just as important as the money part because either way we're gaining. [brackets mine]

The Lubavitcher devote a great deal of energy and enthusiasm to these activities as a comment by a Yeshiva student after a *Lag Bo'Oymer* outing shows: "Wow, can you imagine what we did today? We got a thousand kids who have probably never made a *brocheh* (blessing) in their life to make a few *brochess*. That's fantastic!" Lubavitch sponsored activities are not intended to recruit converts to their chassidic group as indicated by the absence of a prolonged and sustained drive to process non-orthodox newcomers into Lubavitch. The activities ought, instead, to be regarded as strategies to persuade those contacted of the significance of traditional Judaism. A Lubavitcher expressed this well when he said:

> Look, the idea is not to get hold of someone and say: "Hey, you have to become a Lubavitcher because that's the best thing you can do." What we're really after is that people should realize that we have to lead our lives according to the Torah. This is what has kept the Jews together for so long.

The *Tefillin* Campaign

The *Tefillin* campaign, while not organized exclusively by the

Lubavitcher chassidim, was initiated by the Lubavitcher *Rebbe* and became associated with Lubavitch. It started shortly before the outbreak of the Six Day War in June 1967 when the Lubavitcher *Rebbe* urged his followers throughout the world to ensure that as many Jews as possible observed *Tefillin*. The following notice, also translated into other languages, was displayed prominently wherever Lubavitcher gathered:

> In view of the present situation in the Holy Land, the Lubavitcher *Rebbe*, Rabbi Menachem M. Schneerson, has emphatically reiterated his appeal concerning the specific need—*to strengthen and disseminate the observance of the mitzvah of Tefillin among Jews*.
>
> The *Rebbe* emphasized that the fulfillment of this *Mitzvah* in addition to its essential aspect as a Divine Commandment which must be observed for its own sake, is even more imperative at this time not merely for its protective quality as indicated in the Torah, "and they shall fear you"—the fear that is instilled in the hearts of the enemies as a result of the observance of this *mitzvah* . . . —but even more so for the Divine strength which the *Mitzvah* of *Tefillin* bestows upon its defenders *to vanquish the enemy in the course of battle*.
>
> The Lubavitcher *Rebbe* appealed that:
>
> a) Each and every Jew should scrupulously observe this *Mitzvah* every weekday. Also, one should have his *Tefillin* examined periodically as stated in the Code of Jewish law.
>
> b) By every possible means everyone should spread and foster the observance of this precept among his fellow Jews, especially those in the military defense forces, their relatives and friends, by explaining to them the vital importance of this *Mitzvah*.
>
> May it be G-d's will, concluded the *Rebbe* in his appeal, that in the very near future the current situation will be a thing of the past, for peace shall reign over the entire world, especially in the Holy Land about which it is stated: "*And I will grant peace in the land!*" and that every Jew should be able to study Torah and observe the *mitzvot* in peace and tranquility.

Announcements regarding the campaign appeared in both the English and Yiddish press. One, appearing in a Yiddish newspaper in Montreal, read in part:

. . . Millions of Jews have been saved miraculously. Now let us add millions of Jews who will add to their *Mitzvah* observance, beginning with the *Mitzvah* of *Tefillin* . . . (from a proclamation of The Lubavitcher *Rebbe, shlita*)

Shortly before the outbreak of the "Six-Day War" last June the Lubavitcher *Rebbe* . . . initiated an unprecedented *Tefillin* campaign . . .

This campaign has received the support of the most prominent religious leaders both in Israel and the Diaspora. Already, thousands of Jews who formerly neglected this *Mitzvah* are observing today as a result of this campaign.

. . . In Montreal—a *Tefillin* campaign is being proclaimed by the undersigned religious leaders of our Community, beginning this week of Parshat Yisro (February 17th). We call upon our Jewish brethren, from teenagers to senior citizens, who have until now not observed this *Mitzvah* regularly to commence to do so this Sunday morning, preferably at Services held in their synagogue. Anyone in need of guidance and assistance is invited to call one of the undersigned of the *Tefillin* Campaign headquarters. . .

The above text was signed by thirty-two Rabbis in Montreal representing different synagogues and religious affiliations within Judaism. In addition, a section of a pamphlet circulated by Lubavitcher read:

In Montreal, the religious leaders of the community proclaimed that starting *Parshas Yisroi* Feb. 17, there will be a strengthened effort to make the Jewish populace aware of the importance of this *Mitzvah*. Lectures and newspaper articles are being devoted to this subject. Hospitals and organizations, offices and homes are some of the places where visitations have accomplished undreamed of results. Many, inspired by this, have decided to continue putting on *Tefillin* daily; thousands are responding to this call as the campaign steadily expands.

The main objective of the *Tefillin* campaign was to persuade Jews of the significance of *Tefillin* observance in Jewish life. While all Lubavitcher displayed an interest in the campaign's progress, the older Yeshiva students were primarily responsible for the proselytizing activity it entailed. They established "*Tefillin* booths" at strategic Jewish locations such as the Young Men's Hebrew

Association. In addition, invitations were extended to people to perform this *mitzveh* in the Yeshiva.

In spite of the importance of the campaign, the Yeshiva students only participated in it in their spare time during their lunch period and primarily Friday afternoons when their studies end earlier. Two older Yeshiva students (*bocherim*) recounted episodes about their activities:

> . . . We would ask people to put on *Tefillin* for Israel. Sometimes we would go to the person's house in the morning, or sometimes we would even go to the factories or stores. It's really fantastic how many people we got. Have you ever heard of (name of restaurant)? We even got him to put on *Tefillin*. There are so many stories about the number of new people that we got to put on *Tefillin*.

> When we started it was really an all out effort. We still learned but everyone was really involved. The stories from the campaign are really something. We used to go down to the St. Lawrence to the Israeli ships. This was once every two weeks or once a month. And, after a while, we really got to know the people there. And so we would come on the ship and we would say: "Oh, he's a good guy, let's get him." . . . Another time we were on our way to New York and the bus broke down. . . . it was near a college town. So we got off the bus and we *davned* (prayed) and then we went looking for people. It's something (*Tefillin*) which has gotten in everyone's veins, it really has.

Although *bocherim* were the most energetic participants in the campaign, all Lubavitcher were encouraged to become actively involved. The involvement, however, took different forms as those who felt bashful or insecure about approaching others assisted by offering to drive Lubavitcher to their *Tefillin* routes, helping distribute literature related to *Tefillin*, or contributing financially toward the campaign's expenses. A Lubavitcher, teaching at an English high school, remarked:

> I'll be very open with you. At the beginning I was very skeptical about it. I mean why should anyone believe that people would begin to put on *Tefillin* again? But then slowly I began to hear stories and also saw new faces at the services. I thought: "Maybe the idea isn't so far-fetched

after all." You know I'm a teacher. . . . So one day I decided to take along with me a pair of *Tefillin*. This was done secretly and I would approach a few boys and say: "Excuse me, may I know if you have already put on *Tefillin* today?" I knew beforehand what their answer was going to be and then I would say: "Would you mind if you took five or ten minutes to put on *Tefillin*?" They would usually say "Yes" mostly because I was the teacher... But then, more and more students would come to put on *Tefillin*.

All the *Bays Medresh* students actively participated in the campaign in their spare time and all had a *Tefillin* route which, as one student explained, was, "anywhere from a certain street downtown to standing outside _____'s bookstore and just asking people if they want to put on *Tefillin*." Another *bocher* described it this way:

> ... It actually means that you have two or three blocks and along these two or three blocks you have about eight stores where they put on *Tefillin*. So you establish a route, where somebody with less English can go next week and say: "I'm here again to put on *Tefillin*." And the guy'll say: "Oh, sure." Establishing that route means coming in and hammering and hassling with the guy. No put on, yes put on, getting thrown out.

Two or three *bocherim* were responsible for their own particular route for a few months. Sometimes the route was already organized and they had information about the people to visit, but often they had to establish a new route and initiate contacts with new people. Once a *Tefillin* route was established they then had to find a suitable place for people to put on *Tefillin* for they recognized that less people would agree to observe the *mitzveh* if they were the object of curious stares from onlookers. One Yeshiva student said:

> ... If you're asking people in the street you have a problem. You can't put on *Tefillin* with them on the street. You have to have a place. You have to have a place nearby where you could put on *Tefillin* with them inside, in the back room somewhere. . . . You know, I can't imagine a grocery enjoying people putting on *Tefillin* in the store.

While initiating and maintaining a *Tefillin* route, the Lubavitcher had to learn to cultivate a convincing argument to persuade the people approached to agree to perform the *mitzveh*. Part of a conversation with a Yeshiva student illustrates this:

> ... Each person has his own set [speech]. What I mean is that you can't come in to somebody and say: "I'm here to put on *Tefillin*. Roll up your left sleeve." ... I'd walk in, I would say: "Good afternoon" or "Good morning, are you Jewish?" And some people say: "No, I'm sorry." I'd say: "It's O.K." Some people will say: "Yes, can I help you?" You see, when we're trying to put *Tefillin* on somebody, we're going to use the best approach. If it's around a holiday, like if it's around *Chanekkeh*, we're going to tell them: "Listen, *Chanekkeh* is approaching. Being as it's a Jewish holiday, we've got to show our solidarity to Judaism. Why don't you put on *Tefillin*?" If something happened in Israel last week, I'll say: "Listen, our brothers are having a tough time in Israel and the Lubavitcher *Rebbe*, he's a very great leader among the Jews, said that putting on *Tefillin* helps our soldiers fight in Israel. Would you like to help us out and put on *Tefillin*?" Or I might say: "How about doing a *mitzveh*? When was the last time you put on *Tefillin*?" You have to warm up to a person. [brackets mine]

A student, whose *Tefillin* route was by a store which sold religious articles, remarked:

> Well, we don't just look for a customer to come in. We stand outside. Any passerby who looks like he's Jewish is asked ... if he wants to participate in *mitzveh's Tefillin*. You know, would he like to? And a lot of them think you have to give money right away and so you have to get that settled with. A lot of people are surprised at this. And so they say: "Fine." This is great and so you take them into the store to put on *Tefillin*. If they don't really like the idea too much we ask them why and you try to get them into a discussion.

The *Tefillin* campaign's ultimate objective was more encompassing than simply convincing others to observe *Tefillin*. Lubavitcher hoped that once the person began observing *Tefillin* regularly, the practice of additional *mitzvess* would follow naturally. This is nicely illustrated by the following:

> ... Like, for instance, last year for the *Pegeesheh* (Encounter with Chabad), we went to visit _____ (person's name)... And we were sitting there and she was telling us: "Oh, by the way, you guys are Lubavitcher? I want to tell you something very interesting. Some of your fellows came to my husband on Decarie ... and they put on *Tefillin* with him and they came again and again and he started putting on *Tefillin* every day and he asked if there is anything that can be done, that a woman can do, and they told him: "Yes, she can light the candles Friday night." You guys are really doing a wonderful job.

There are various religious and mystical reasons why *Tefillin* observance was selected as the basis of a campaign for *Yiddish-kayt*, but the choice was ultimately made for a practical reason. Compared with other salient precepts such as *Kashruth*, family purity, and Sabbath observance, *Tefillin* is relatively simple to observe and requires little time to perform. In addition, it demands few, if any, initial changes in the person's lifestyle.

> ... Why necessarily *Tefillin*? ... why didn't we pick *kashress*? Why didn't we pick ... ? Because it's an automatic thing. It's not hard, it's easy. It's not like you have to go into a guy's house and say: "Listen, throw out all your dishes." You can argue with them and you're not asking for money, you're not telling them to give, you're just asking them to put on *Tefillin*. And it's a positive thing that can be done on the spot, immediately.

or:

> ... one of the reasons why *Tefillin* was picked was because it's a positive thing to do at the moment. A normal person would not refuse this too vehemently because he doesn't lose anything by it at the moment. Tell him: "Go start *kashress*, go keep *Shabbess*," these things are hard. He'd have to give up in other things. On the other hand, all you're asking him to do at the beginning is to put on *Tefillin*.

Tefillin observance is regarded as a critical step in a process whereby the person is urged to become more observant. Lubavitcher hope that the regular practice of *Tefillin* will encourage non-observant Jews to observe additional *mitzvess* and will establish a contact with them that can be maintained:

> You want to remain in contact with him because eventually it would be great if these people would, of course, not only just put on *Tefillin* but would observe *kashress* and become *baal tshuvess* and *shoimrai Shabbess* and everything. But that's a very long range goal. But the beginning, the first part, is to get him to put on *Tefillin*.

or:

> ... And we sit with them and we explain our view and they become quite receptive after a time and afterwards they'll start putting on *Tefillin* on their own. That's generally the goal. The eventual goal, of course, is that that can lead to other things.

The element of time is an important feature in the process of leading a person to traditional Judaism. Lubavitcher are aware that the observance of new precepts can be a trying experience both for the individual and those close to him. Consequently, they try to ensure that the person himself will monitor his degree of increased observance. I was once told, for instance, that if "you tell someone to put (*Tefillin*) on every day right away, chances are it won't happen. Generally it takes a lot of work."

Although *Tefillin* is observed only by men, women have also been given a role in the campaign. Shortly after the campaign's initiation, a release from the Lubavitch News Service claimed:

> ... The *Rebbe* said that although *Tefillin* is observed by men only, women can also take part in the campaign by influencing those who are obligated to observe the *Mitzvah*, and by contributing funds for the distribution of free *Tefillin* among those who cannot afford to purchase them.

I once asked a Lubavitch woman what kind of work women could do in the *Tefillin* campaign. Her reply fell into line with the *Rebbe's* instructions:

> They've raised money. They gave their own money, whatever they managed to save up in the bank, and they've paid for *Tefillin*, to buy *Tefillin* for those who don't have and can't afford and want to put on *Tefillin*. But at the same

time while this *Tefillin* campaign came out the women and the girls were giving their money. For a pair of *Tefillin* I think they gave an amount, let's say, eighteen dollars. ... Ya, they were up in arms. "What are we going to do?" This is what they were told. They can give their money and in this way they can have a share in the *mitzveh*.

Since the campaign's outset, the importance of *Tefillin* has been repeatedly stressed by the Lubavitcher *Rebbe*. Lubavitcher chassidim have tried, as a result, to persuade non-observant Jews in Montreal to observe the precept. Their degree of success is determined by their manpower resources and the amount of time devoted to proselytization. Although both are limited, Lubavitcher have labelled the campaign an overwhelming success. Success, however, is not defined solely by the number of people who consent to observe *Tefillin*. Such a definition is too restrictive for it detracts from an important aim of the campaign—to emphasize to Jews the urgency of guiding their lives in accordance with Jewish law.

Encounter With Chabad

Unlike the *Tefillin* campaign which was aimed at all males over the age of thirteen, the Encounter with Chabad program was intended for college and university students, and, again it was designed to expose them to orthodox Judaism and attract them to its principles. Lubavitcher consider it the main vehicle for establishing contact with Jewish students of post-high-school age.

The Lubavitcher chassidim's concern for Jewish students at universities and colleges reflects their *Rebbe's* views on Jewish youth—a topic to which he has addressed himself on numerous occasions. The Lubavitch leader once wrote in reply to a letter:

Fortunately, one has been able to clearly discern a new trend among our young Jewish men and women, especially academic youth who come closer to the world of ideas and thought. Being children of The People of the Book, of essentially spiritual and holy people, they are by nature and heredity inclined, subconsciously at least, towards the spiritual. Their disillusionment and dissatisfaction have prompted them to search for a new way of life which would give them a sense of terra firma under their feet, make their life meaningful and put their mind at peace with themselves. Some of them have been fortunate in making fateful encounters, by design or "accident" (everything is, of course, by Divine Providence) which have put them on the right track. Others, unfortunately, are still groping in the dark. It is the momentous duty and challenge of our day to help these young Jewish men and women to find their way back to the "fountains of living waters" to quench their thirst for *life*. We of the Lubavitch have made it our "business" to do all we can to help them. (Teachers Programme, Vol.2, 1970:336)

The Encounter with Chabad programs, organized by the Lubavitch Youth Organization, "serve the Jewish college community with varied programs designed to enlighten the student in a straight manner on the meaning and significance of Torah Judaism in the modern world." (A Thought for the Week, Vol.3, No.10, 1969) The programs' objective was to convince the participants that it is necessary to practise traditional Judaism, while attempting to refute the popular claim that many Jewish laws are irrelevant and ought to be altered to conform to today's society.

The Encounter program in Montreal began four years ago, in February, 1970. Several older Yeshiva students, with the nominal support of a few Rabbis, directed the Encounter's publicity and made the other necessary arrangements to organize the event. Advertisements were inserted in the press, were broadcast on the radio, and appeared on university and college notice boards and in store windows. An advertisement in one of the university dailies read:

An Encounter With Chabad Chassidism
An invitation to Jewish College Youth to experience a joyful, authentic Shabbos within a Chassidic milieu

When: Weekend of March 5—March 7
What: An opportunity to live, study and discuss in a
             Chassidic environment inspired with joyful
             heart warming song and dance
Why: To give students seeking a meaningful commit-
             ment a chance to explore Torah Judaism and
             Mysticism and to see how Chassidism can be
             the answer

Where: Rabbinical College of Canada
- Participants will be housed with Chassidic families
- No prior background or commitment necessary

An invitation to Jewish College Youth to experience a joyful, authentic Shabbos within a Chassidic milieu

As the advertisement indicates, the Encounter's program was intended to allow participants to explore an atmosphere of orthodox Judaism and chassidism primarily through lectures and discussions. For instance, one of the schedules included:

Fri. March 5th:
3:00 –	5:00 P.M.	Arrival and registration
	6:15 P.M.	Introduction to Encounter
	6:30 P.M.	*Kabbolas Shabbos*
	8:30 P.M.	"The Identity Crisis"

Sat. March 6th:
	9:00 A.M.	Chassidus—A Study in Chassidic Philosophy
	10:00 A.M.	*Shachris* (morning service)
	3:00 P.M.	"The Status of Women in Judaism and Chabad"
	4:00 P.M.	*Shalosh Seudos:* Chassidic Discourse, Talks, and Melodies
	8:30 P.M.	*Melave Malke*—Main session "Chassidism, the Mystical Aspect of Judaism"
	11:00 P.M.	Chassidic Song and Dance
	12:00 Midnight	*Farbreng-In* (Chassidic Gathering) getting "high" Chassidicly

Sun. March 7th:
	10:00 A.M.	*Shachris:* Explanation of *Tefillin*
	11:30 A.M.	Breakfast: Closing session: "Who am I?"

The lectures and discussions were oriented toward a Lubavitch perspective in that they stressed particular issues Lubavitcher feel are critical to all Jews. Thus, for example, a lecture on "The

Identity Crisis" related to Lubavitcher's concern over recent trends in Israeli law regarding conversion of Gentiles to Judaism.

To complement the program's intellectual emphasis, participants were housed with a Lubavitch family for the Sabbath. This was designed to show students how a Lubavitch family celebrates the holy day, and also to give them an opportunity to establish a more personal relationship with a Lubavitch family. The family, in turn, was able to impress upon someone with a limited knowledge and practice of orthodox Judaism the profits to be gained from living a fully orthodox Jewish life.

As it was hoped the sessions would be informative and thought-provoking, older Yeshiva students and older girls and women were available at all times to answer informal questions. Lubavitcher had anticipated that the kinds of questions they would be asked would be on the lines of what is the relevance of the Torah's laws in today's society, why God did allow six million Jews to perish since Jews are identified as His chosen people, or is there a proof for God's existence. Such questions present only minor difficulties to the majority of Lubavitcher since the *Rebbe* has addressed himself to precisely these matters on numerous occasions and his replies are well-known to his chassidim.

Although the Encounter's organizers wanted to attract a large audience, they hoped that the majority would not already be committed to orthodox Judaism. During preparations for the first Encounter one of the students said: "I hope we don't get too many of the Yavneh (a religious organization on the university campus) crowd. They're alright. They know where they stand. A few, fine, but not too many." Another said: "I hope we get a couple of radicals and extremists. Do you know X (a student believed to be a radical)? He's coming for sure and he's going to get some of his friends." Of the thirty students who participated in the first Encounter, approximately half were observant. While attendance for the Saturday night session was considerably larger than the number of registered participants, over half the audience was comprised of members of synagogue groups and young orthodox Jews. These people did not, unfortunately, spend the Sabbath with a Lubavitch family which was a basic purpose of the program.

Lubavitcher view the Encounter as a catalyst for stimulating contact with college and university students. During the weekend of the Encounter little formal effort was made to win people over to Lubavitch. The only formal proselytizing occurred on Saturday night when a table, arranged in the main auditorium, displayed Lubavitch literature and music. During the Encounter, however, participants were informed that Lubavitch was anxious to arrange a study group for those interested and that individual tutelage was available.

The Encounter provided an opportunity to establish an initial contact in a setting in which traditional Judaism was stressed. Since the program relied on formal sessions, individual attention was hardly possible. When, however, anyone accepted Lubavitcher's invitation to study *Yiddishkayt*, his individual needs were considered and planned for. The men students typically met with an older Yeshiva student or adult at a prearranged time and place. During the first meeting they would arrange their course of study which would mainly be determined by the person's Jewish background. They might decide to concentrate on the *Tanya* (Lubavitch philosophy), the weekly reading of the Torah, or reading and discussing the *Rebbe's* discourses. Women students would usually meet at a Lubavitch woman's home where they too would embark on a course of study relevant to their Jewish background.

Again attendance was not considered the only criterion by which to judge the Encounter's success. Equally important were Lubavitcher's impressions on how well they had established contact with those that attended. One Lubavitcher, disappointed with the Encounter's apparent lack of organization and poor attendance, voiced his complaints to one of the organizers. The latter replied:

What do you think, that it's so easy? And let's say that of those who came three will now start putting on *Tefillin*. Do you think that's such a little thing? And let's say that one or two will begin to come here once a week to learn. This is also something. I grant you that it would have been better had more people attended but the question has to do with what was accomplished.

The Encounter with Chabad program has been reportedly successful wherever it has been organized. As an article in the Yiddish press, written by a Lubavitcher, stated:

Today as one visits Lubavitch, regardless of where these visits occur . . . one can see young men, who a few years earlier, were members of S.D.S. or other leftist activities, or concerned with similar events, with little to do with Jews and Judaism and almost lost and forgotten. Today you can find these same people immersed in Torah study, observant of Torah and mitzvess and conducting themselves accordingly. (translated from Yiddish)

Although the program began only four years ago in Montreal, it has served as an effective vehicle for contacting non-observant Jewish college youth. Some Lubavitcher argue it will have to be better organized and publicized to profit from its potentially high return, but the program has already resulted in numerous relationships between Lubavitcher and non-religious Jewish students.

Lubavitch Summer Camps

During the summer vacation period Lubavitcher concentrate their efforts on their summer camps to initiate and maintain contact with Jewish youth. A main objective of these summer camps is to attract youth whose contact with orthodox Judaism is minimal and to influence them in a traditionally Jewish direction. As one camp administrator stated:

This camp is not entirely built around Lubavitch campers, although we have them as well. I'm interested in keeping a nice number of Lubavitch campers to keep the atmosphere chassidish. But the main objective in founding this camp, going on with the camp, was strictly for kids from a non-Lubavitcher origin, for kids even who have no background in *Yiddishkayt*.

Three summer camps are organized by the Montreal Lubavitch community—a boys' camp, *Gan Yisroel*, a girls' camp, *Pardess Channeh*, and a day camp, *Messibbess Shabbess*. The first two are situated in the Laurentian mountains, north of the city, while the latter is at the Lubavitcher Yeshiva.

The Lubavitch camps' main attraction is that the campers are exposed to a traditionally orthodox way of life. Although there are many Jewish summer camps in the same area, the Jewish content in their programs is planned for specific periods and centres on cultural phenomena. When religion is incorporated into the programs as, for example, the organization of Sabbath services, it too is treated as an aspect of Jewish culture. The Lubavitch camps, on the other hand, introduce no distinction between the religious and secular content of the programs as the various everyday activities are intended to be infused with traditional Jewish ideals. A brochure on *Gan Yisroel* claims:

> (*Gan Yisroel*) ... was established to fulfill the long-felt need for a summer camp where Jewish boys can relax and enjoy the summer vacation in an atmosphere of Torah-true Judaism... The program of studies, as well as the daily religious services, are designed so that the children themselves participate with zeal and devotion.

The religious atmosphere itself is one of the main incentives for many parents to send their children, but it is the implications accompanying such an atmosphere that are more important for other parents. They select the Lubavitch summer camps as they feel assured that the influences of sex and drugs believed to prevail in many camps are totally absent from the activities organized by Lubavitcher.

A primary purpose of all three camps is to attract and exert a maximum influence on the youth from non-orthodox homes. For example, at a Lubavitch organized rally during the Feast of Lots (*Purim*) one of the prizes consisted of a month's vacation in *Gan Yisroel*. As the winner's name was to be announced, a Yeshiva student whispered to me: "If a Lubavitch kid wins this prize, then they're (Lubavitch) crazy. What sense does that make? I think that last year a kid from Lubavitch won. That's stupid." As is the case in the Lubavitch schools, there is little apprehension among Lubavitcher that the presence of non-Lubavitcher in the summer camps will prove damaging to their children. Instead, it is commonly accepted that the camps' staff, consisting of Lubavitcher, together with the Lubavitch and other orthodox campers will influence those from non-orthodox homes toward accepting traditional Jewish practices. Speaking about *Gan Yisroel*, an older Yeshiva student remarked:

> ... they're interested in influencing non-observant Jews. So, for someone who isn't religious who wants to send their kids, it gives them an opportunity to send them. That's one of the important, well, that's the purpose of the whole Lubavitch movement, so that camp functions in that respect, in that they get people to go there and influence them. One of the purposes of the camp, no doubt, is to have a camp for ... Lubavitcher, but that's in a certain way secondary.

In 1971, the day camp registered one hundred and ten campers of whom approximately fifteen were students from the Yeshiva. *Gan Yisroel's* registration for the 1970 season totalled almost two hundred of whom only 30 per cent were from Lubavitch homes. Girls from Lubavitch families in *Pardess Channeh* in the summer of 1973 comprised 10 per cent of the one hundred and fifty campers.

Each of the camps' programs is guided by the belief that the summer vacation period must not distract Jewish youth from learning about orthodox Judaism. On the contrary, the Lubavitcher *Rebbe* has recently re-emphasized the importance of providing youth with facilities in which their religious education could be continued during the summer months. A recent release of the Lubavitch News Service quoted the *Rebbe* as saying:

> During the summer months many Jewish institutions are closed and teachers are away. In many instances youth are left to roam aimlessly through neighborhood streets, and are often exposed to the lurking dangers of degenerate elements. This ominous threat and waste of invaluable time can be transformed into a constructive recreational and educational boon.

Following the *Rebbe's* statement, the Montreal community issued a directive to the camp directors that, in line with the *Rebbe's* instructions, emergency expansion measures should be undertaken to accommodate additional campers. In addition, in line with the Summer Torah Educational Program (STEP) organized by the educational branch of the Lubavitch movement in New York, announcements appeared in the Lubavitcher Yeshiva and were posted in other Jewish institutions as well as advertised in the city's newspapers:

> *to the Jewish residents of Val Morin and vicinity*
> Take a giant S T E P forward for a creative summer. A Summer Torah Educational Program has been established by the New Lubavitcher Yeshiva of Val Morin. We are introducing unique types of study clubs for Jewish youth of *all ages,* and will provide an opportunity for you and your children to make new friends, while enjoying a diversified educational program. Why not take part in one or more of our programs?

1) *special Sunday program*—experience practical Judaism through putting on Tefillin and learning about our Torah and Mitzvos.

2) *special shabbos program*—for boys and girls ages 6-12 every Saturday at 4:00 P.M.

3) *daily drop-in centre*—come in any time of the day and learn about Judaism and Chassidism. Private tutoring also available for anyone interested,

All programs will be held at the Yeshiva, located at Sternthal Cottages, Ave. 12

All services are absolutely free of charge

To continue the children's Torah education the camps' programs include formally scheduled activities during which religious instruction is offered. Each morning in *Pardess Channeh*, for instance, one of the Rabbis speaks briefly on a topic pertaining to Jewish religion, such as "making a *brocheh* (blessing)." After breakfast the camp is divided into study groups for an hour where themes centring on the Jewish religion are discussed. In the day camp, which caters to children between the ages of six and nine, the boys' program includes study classes from nine till ten o'clock which are organized around the class's knowledge of orthodox Judaism, and consisted of *"aleph bays"* (alphabet), *Sidder* (the prayer book), *Chumesh* (the five books of Moses), and *Mishnai-yess* (portions of the Mishna).

These formally organized instructional classes are complemented by the other daily activities all of which are organized on a religious basis. Much of what the campers are taught, in time becomes interwoven with the routine of their daily activity. Campers are immediately encouraged and expected to participate actively in a variety of religious observances. Thus, for example, all campers are taught and expected to recite the appropriate blessings corresponding to the particular situation and occasion; and participation in prayer, an optional component in most Jewish summer camps, is presented as an integral part of the daily activity.

The camps' activities are presented in such a manner that orthodox practices and expectations and familiarity with Jewish history and the work of the Lubavitcher *Rebbeim* are continually emphasized. While such emphasis and reiteration is neither intended nor appears to detract from the excitement and stimulation of the activities, Lubavitcher believe that their positive influence on the campers is inevitable. The infusion of religious influences with camping and other Lubavitch organized activities is exemplified in the following excerpts taken from some of the songs often sung at the camps:

> *Yeshiva*, Oh! That's the place for me,
> We learn *Gemorah* and *Mishnaios*, *Chumash* and *Rashi*,
> *Yeshiva*, That's where I want to be,
> We learn and play every day,
> Enjoy it, all the way.

> When we get up in the morning and see,
> We say the *Mode Ani*,
> The way of every Jewish boy,
> *Naigel Vasser*, is next on the list,
> To wash our entire fist,
> And that's the way to start the day with joy,
> We put on *Tzitses* every day,

> To chase the *Yaitzer Horah* away,
> And to remind us of our Holy Torah!
> After Bar-Mitzvah, we put on *Tefillin*,
> It's like an injection of penicillin,
> To keep us healthy through the *Avoda*.
>
> . . . .

> We only eat a Kosher diet,
> Non-Kosher food we'd never try it
> To be healthy Jews is our main goal
> Non-Kosher food is harmful for body and soul.

> Shabbos is a day of rest
> We don't do any labors
> We just get dressed in our best
> And attend *Shul* with the neighbours
>
> . . . .

> In the city of Lubavitch
> Dwelt a *rebbe* of great fame
> Whose Chabad Chassidic teachings
> Set the world all aflame.

> With body weakened and weary
> In Russian dungeons of despair
> His spirit rallied forth
> With strength beyond compare.

His sacred work in the states
Devotion for the young and old
Have revived the Yiddish spirit
Returning millions to the fold.

And Lubavitch marches on
With the *Rebbe* of our time
Always treading greater paths
Molded in the sands of time.
. . . .

And when the *Moach* understands
What Hashem of him demands,
Then it compels and commands
Both the heart and the hands
Not only to feel but also to do
What G-d expects of every Jew.

So live and rejoice, glorious team,
For the *Alter Rebbe* taught your theme
Through Chabad, with your *moiach*
And inspired by the *Rebbe's koiach*
Moishiach and *all* that is now concealed
Will speedily be revealed.

The informal approach to educating the campers can also be seen at camp bonfires and during rest periods when stories about the *Rebbe's* concerns and accomplishments are related. In the course of informal discussions with campers, counsellors often emphasize the importance of following the Torah's precepts and encourage their campers to conduct themselves accordingly. Murals and posters decorating the dining and recreation halls also serve as constant reminders of the importance of Torah observance. While some of the murals depict themes relating to the *Rebbe's* teachings, other posters and drawings have such captions an "Work All Six, Rest on Seven, As it is Done in Heaven," "Teach Torah to our young generation, Ensure the future of our nation," "Fight Assimilation with a Torah Education."

As with the *Tefillin* campaign and the Encounter program, the purpose in attracting non-orthodox youth to Lubavitch summer camps is to impress upon them the significance of their Jewish heritage. It is not, claim Lubavitcher, to convert them into Lubavitcher chassidim. Since the expressed aim is to imbue the individual with a feeling for traditional Judaism, the camp setting is seen as the optimal place to accomplish this goal as intensive contact can be maintained with the campers.

> You see, there's another difference between camp and the city. It has to do with the atmosphere in the home. For example, a kid can come from a home where it isn't religious, but even then, she's only there [in school] seven to ten hours each day. No matter how religious the atmosphere in the school is, she comes home and this might kill everything. It depends on the friends she has on the block. So whatever she absorbs in school for eight hours, she can lose in the three or four hours before she goes to sleep at night, or on Sunday or on the weekends. While at camp, they're, I wouldn't say locked up, but they're encompassed in an atmosphere for twenty-four hours each day, for four weeks or eight weeks—one atmosphere, and the same friends. . . . And everyone knows that what a kid can pick up in camp, they'll never pick up in school. [brackets mine]

Another advantage of the camp setting lies in the opportunities it provides for imparting certain kinds of religious-oriented information to the campers. The summer months present both a variety of religious occasions and other situations which can be used to teach the children about traditions and practices with which they might be unfamiliar:

> You see, summer is a time when you really have time to [teach]. You have the three weeks which start the days of mourning for the *Bays Hamikdesh* (Temple), you have *Tisheh B'ov*, you have joyous occasions, you have fast days. It's enough time to swing quite a number of things in there. During the summer you can have things that a kid wouldn't learn in the city. For instance, an *Ayrev*. On *Shabbess* you're not allowed to carry anything. In camp, if you make an *Ayrev* around the camp, you can carry things. This is a law the kid wouldn't find out about if she didn't see it in camp . . . In camp you have the opportunity of giving kids another *din* (law) which they would never know in the city. You're not allowed to spill water on grass on *Shabbess*, because if you do this, then, not necessarily, but this can help the growth of the grass. In other words, on *Shabbess* you're doing something to make grass grow. Here you can spill water [pointing to the gravel], while there you can't. Now a kid should know this. She can live all her life in the city and she'll never know that. [brackets mine]

In contrast to summer camp, acquiring knowledge of *Yiddishkayt* in the Yeshiva during this period often seems abstract and unrelated to everyday life and therefore has less impact on the person. Whereas one can gain theoretical knowledge about orthodox Judaism in the city, camp provides the opportunity to "live" *Yiddishkayt*. A Yeshiva student put it like this:

> Camp is the best place for this person (to whom we're trying to teach *Yiddishkayt*). He lives Judaism better than he does in the Yeshiva. I used to get them to go to New York for a couple of weeks because in the Lubavitch Yeshiva you can't do anything to fit the person. The person has to go to school and the Yeshiva is too much of a change. You can't just keep him there and just study with him. You have to let him live *Yiddishkayt* which is at camp.

The Lubavitcher summer camps in Montreal give these chassidim the opportunity to initiate relationships with Jewish youth and their parents. Although one of the objectives of summer camp is to attract new students to the Lubavitch schools, this goal is only realized occasionally. Lubavitcher do not take this to indicate that the summer camp experience is not effective for they firmly believe that although the positive impact may not be immediately apparent, it will, in time, manifest itself:

> . . . you see, if I'm planting a tree and am putting in the seed today, when it's going to start to grow depends on many things. But you know one thing—it's going to grow. We have, according to the Talmud, one thing that we are guaranteed—that any work, any investment that a person makes into any human being . . . will not return empty-handed. In other words, some result is going to hit.

Lubavitchers' involvement with the larger Jewish community is not restricted only to children and college students but extends to all non-observant Jews of all age groups. Their proselytizing fervour does not, however, extend to the relationships they have to enter into with the surrounding Gentile community. In contrast, these are marked by distance and an absence of emotional commitment. We now turn to an examination of these relations.

Contact with the Wider Non-Jewish Community

Some religious communities, fearing contact with outsiders will threaten their identity, insulate themselves from relationships with others not of their own kind. Although Lubavitcher recognize the potentially harmful consequences of contact with non-observant Jews, they are determined to befriend such Jews to attract them to traditional Judaism. They must also, however, establish relations with the surrounding Gentile community. These relations are, however, mainly dominated by financial, social, and legal considerations.

Since it is situated in a Gentile society, the Lubavitch community and its members have to enter legal and social relations with non-Jews. At the various levels of government, for example, Lubavitcher pay taxes, although as a synagogue group the community's Yeshiva, girls school, and summer camp properties are tax exempt. To be granted "associate status" with the Protestant School Board in Montreal, the Yeshiva and *Bay Rivkeh* administrators are required to provide evidence that their schools satisfy the Protestant School Board's criteria for standards of physical structure, curriculum, and admission policy. Associate status entitles the schools to receive grants of four hundred dollars per public school pupil and six hundred dollars per high school pupil for teaching secular subjects. Finally, as citizens and residents of Canada, Lubavitcher are governed and must abide by the same laws as all others.

Breton's institutional completeness concept (1964) refers to the extent a community is able to provide for its members' various needs. The degree to which the community succeeds at this task limits its dependence on native institutions. The Lubavitch community has a high degree of institutional completeness which reduces its contact with non-observant Jews and Gentiles. The community does not, however, provide some services, such as janitorial staff for the Lubavitch schools, teachers for secular studies, medical and other professional services, household appliances, clothing and decorations.

Lubavitcher usually choose which stores they will shop at for clothing and various household necessities for purely practical reasons. I never heard a Lubavitcher remark that certain stores were preferred as they were "Jewish" or others avoided because they were owned by Gentiles. Instead, they use the stores that are known to provide a decent service and offer the desired goods. An older Yeshiva *bocher* remarked:

> A few of the *bocherim* get their suits made by this *goy* (Gentile) on _____ _____ street. We bring him the material and he makes the suit. His price is very reasonable and the work is done very well—no complaints. There's a Jewish tailor not far from the Yeshiva. I'd go there except that he wants to charge almost twice as much.

Certain stores are known to stock the styles of clothing that are acceptable to Lubavitcher. Since Lubavitch women are expected to wear skirts that reach to the knee, they have frequently had difficulty in finding stores which stock such styles. As one of these women recalls:

> It sure is very difficult [to shop for clothes]. And at the end, most of the time, the only place that you can find them is where . . . people put it out on their racks, what they made four or five years ago. . . . but, if we would go for the latest style, during the winter when we went shopping, we came home with nothing most of the time. We couldn't find anything. It was at the sales . . . we found everything because, like I said, they were getting rid of their very old styles. [brackets mine]

When they find such stores, Lubavitch women will buy there regardless of whether the stores are owned by Jews or Gentiles. Such pragmatism also governs their shopping for items such as radios, record players, kitchenware, and other household furnishings.

Another area where Lubavitcher and their children must sometimes enter relations with non-Jews is in the schools. Again for pragmatic reasons most of the teachers hired to teach secular subjects are Gentiles or non-observant Jews. As with the purchase of clothing and household furnishings, Lubavitchers' contact with various professional institutions is also guided by practical considerations since the community is unable to produce its own doctors and lawyers. The professional's recognized competence and qualifications rather than his religious affiliation is the major criterion for requesting his services. A Lubavitcher's preference for a Jewish physician usually stems from the fact that he is unable to express himself adequately in English, and believes that Jewish doctors may speak and understand Yiddish and are naturally more sympathetic and understanding. Although Lubavitcher generally prefer to go to a Jewish hospital if possible, they will readily agree to being admitted to a Gentile institution if they consider the staff and facilities there are more highly specialized.

Since they are living in the Province of Quebec, the majority of Lubavitcher are exposed to and become familiar with the demands and expectations of the French-Canadian population. The topics of Quebec separatism and cultural autonomy are not often brought up in conversation in the Yeshiva, unless introduced by outsiders, but Lubavitcher are concerned, as are all non-French speaking people in the province, with how their lives will be affected by new provincial laws and other government practices. Most Lubavitcher are familiar with the current events in the province as, to a greater or lesser extent, they read Yiddish or English newspapers, or listen to the radio. As many have to come into contact with Gentiles in their business transactions they can often gather the tenor of French-English relations from these passing conversations. As one Lubavitcher remarked, reflecting the views of many:

Of course I take an interest in what goes on in the Province. I mean one Government is better or worse for the Jews and I think everyone here is concerned about this. Just as you'd find anywhere else, some people here [in the Yeshiva] are very up on the situation and can tell you which political figure said what, when and where, while others know that there's something cooking but have other things on their mind. But, in general, people here find out—even those who you would never imagine would have a clue about such things. [brackets mine]

Interest in and concern for political affairs at the federal level of government is also a matter with which some Lubavitcher chassidim are more familiar than others. Like other religious minorities such as the Hutterites and Mennonites, for example, or many recently and not so recently arrived immigrants to this country, Lubavitcher are appreciative of the religious freedom to be found in Canada, as well as the opportunity to attain a comfortable standard of living. In light of these concerns, however, the extent of Lubavitchers' political involvement begins and ends with the casting of their vote during municipal, provincial, and federal elections.

As a religious minority group the Lubavitcher express no interest in either maintaining or strengthening ties with other religions and religious denominations. The interfaith dialogue, increasingly prevalent in today's society as members of various religious groups attempt to gain a richer understanding of their neighbours' religious practices and behaviour, has been strongly criticized by the Lubavitcher *Rebbe*. In a letter written in response to an inquiry on the subject of interfaith discussions, the *Rebbe* wrote in part:

> One of the consequences of the said state of affairs is also the misconception prevailing in some quarters regarding the so-called "interfaith" movement. The "brotherhood of mankind" is a positive concept only so long as it is confined to such areas as commerce, philanthropy, and various civil and economic aspects of the society, wherein peoples of various faiths and minority groups must live together in harmony, mutual respect and dignity. Unfortunately, the concept of "brotherhood" has been misconstrued to require members of one faith to explain their religious beliefs and practices to members of another faith, and in return to receive instruction in the religion of others. Far from clarifying matters, these interfaith activities have, at best, added to the confusion, and, at worst, have been used with missionary zeal by those religions which are committed to proselytizing members of other faiths. (Teachers Programme, Vol. 2 1969:342)

The Lubavitcher see all other religions and followers of other religious persuasions as a single "other" category—Gentiles—and only make minimal distinctions between different sects if it is necessary for social and economic exchanges.

The main feature characterizing Lubavitchers' relations with the surrounding Gentile community is lack of personal involvement. While some Lubavitcher retain an acquaintanceship with non-Jews, either for business or political motives, Gentiles are never befriended and invited home. The relationship is never intimate and is maintained simply as a result of the mutual benefits it offers to both parties. Lubavitcher see no reason for engaging in friendships with non-Jews as they believe there is nothing in common between the parties. In addition, there is the possible risk that the association will effect the Lubavitcher negatively by influencing his ideas about his way of life. It is, therefore, understandable that Lubavitch children are forbidden to foster such relations.

Chapter Seven

The Community's Proselytization Work:
A Latent Consequence

The usual purpose of proselytizing in any community is to add to the ranks of the social system so that it may either maintain or increase its membership. This generalization does not, however, appear to apply to the Lubavitch community for two main reasons. First, despite the Lubavitchers' proselytizing activities, few outsiders are attracted to the community. Second, the community's birth rate is high enough for the community to maintain its membership without new recruits. Proselytizing is, however, important to the Lubavitch community because it supports their religious beliefs and reinforces the community's tenability. In the preceding chapter such proselytizing activities as the *Tefillin* campaign were described as ways in which Lubavitcher came to be seen by non-observant Jews as super-Jewish role models. In the present chapter, another aspect of Lubavitchers' recruitment-oriented activity will be shown to have ends other than that of expanding the ranks.

If any religious community intends to persist, it must actively address itself to the assimilative influences threatening its members. Chapter Five focussed on the Lubavitch schools and emphasized how the community attempts to inculcate in the young its distinctive way of life. Closely related to the concept of persistence is that of the community's possible expansion by attracting outsiders. The effects that outsiders contacted by proselytization have on the community under study can also be seen in terms of the contribution they make to the tenability of the community's way of life. Lubavitcher's rationalizations for engaging in proselytizing work appear, however, to centre on their concern for other Jews and only secondarily stem from either the threat of assimilation or the desire to increase their ranks.

The Religious Context of Recruitment

The Lubavitch community's relationship with other Jews is best understood by presenting this religious movement's attitudes and feelings with respect to non-Lubavitcher. Its perspective toward non-Lubavitch Jews has characterized Lubavitch throughout its history and, today, is one of the chief characteristics that distinguishes it from other chassidic groups.

The essence of the Lubavitch movement's teaching is *Ahavas Yisroel*—love for one's fellow Jew. The *Alter Rebbe*, founder of the Lubavitch movement, once said:

> Ahavas Yisroel means to love a Jew regardless of whether he is able to learn or not. The manner of love in Ahavas Yisroel should be a brotherly one. Brotherly love, i.e., love to a brother does not cease or change, because it is natural. One cannot divorce himself from a brother, since he and his brother are the same flesh and blood. Just as the love of the Torah is shown by valuing and keeping precious the "mantle"— the cover of the Sefer Torah, so too should our attitude be to our brethren in the Mitzva of Ahavas Yisroel. (*Di Yiddishe Heim*, Vol.4, No.3:18)

The *Alter Rebbe's* interpretation of *Ahavas Yisroel* has become the foundation of Lubavitcher's conduct. All the Lubavitcher *Rebbeim* have reflected this basic philosophy in their devotion to and interest in Jews regardless of their degree of religious observance. They have all insisted that one is to love a Jew not because of his future, that is, what can be accomplished with him in the realm of Torah and *mitzvess*, but because of what he is now. The present Lubavitcher *Rebbe* emphasized the importance of this philosophy when he asserted:

> There are various incidents related about the *Rebbe, my father-in-law*, regarding his efforts to perform acts of kindness, even for individual Jews, whether in a spiritual or a material matter. This was done even to the neglect of his own material and spiritual concern, and for persons utterly remote from his lofty spiritual degree . . .
> Each individual is required to know that if he desires for himself the ability to "call out G-d's name,'' then he must inspire others to do so. One is not required to provide

knowledge for the other person, but must cause him to "cry out." This person may have been utterly ignorant, but you must see that he cries out . . . that G-dliness and the world are one, that G-d constantly animates and sustains all of created existence. (*Di Yiddishe Heim*, Vol.10, No.3:13)

Among the chassidim, Lubavitcher are unique in their efforts to establish channels of communication with less orthodox Jews. Realizing that their commitment to orthodox Judaism means they represent a minority among Jews today, they are nonetheless convinced that even their small numbers can make an impact on their fellow Jews. To help attain the goal of preserving the orthodox precepts while simultaneously drawing less religious Jews into the orthodox fold, the Lubavitcher *Rebbe* sends his chassidim to Jewish communities to serve as his emissaries. Mintz writes:

> To help further that end the Lubavitcher Rebbe sends Rabbis to synagogues that need leaders, readers to congregations where there is a lack of learned men, and shohtim [ritual slaughterers] to communities where there is a need to maintain orthodox standards for the slaughtering of cattle. (1968:153) [brackets mine]

Lubavitch's efforts are not only directed at American Jewry in large cities, but representatives are also sent to outlying Jewish congregations throughout the world. *Di Yiddishe Heim*, the Lubavitch women's quarterly publication, contains articles focussing on the necessity to accept the task of disseminating orthodox Judaism. It is worth examining a few excerpts from these articles:

> More and more women are journeying forth with their husbands in the shlichus [assignment] of the Rebbe Shlita. This was the underlying spirit at the home of Rebetzin Jacobson. Rabbi and Mrs. Gorelik, were leaving for Milan, Italy, as emissaries of the *Rebbe* Shlita.
> Bessie herself, one of our old-time chaveros, [female friends] knew what this would mean—leaving her home and her friends—everything that had been part of her life here. Yet, she also clearly saw what it meant, to help bring Jews closer to the life of Torah. This, overpowered any doubts that may have arisen in her mind. Our shluchim [emissaries] understood that this was to be their mission, and

were thankful for the opportunity which would enable them to do that one favor, for that one Jew, who might be waiting for the light of Torah to be shown to him. This, in itself, would be an accomplishment. To bring warmth, to bring a good word, to kindle a spark of light somewhere in the darkness . . . (*Di Yiddishe Heim*, Vol. 1, No. 1:13) [brackets mine]

Another story tells of Miriam and her husband who intended to settle in a small town in Europe "in order to establish a Jewish religious centre, to teach and spread Judaism among those unfortunate ones who had strayed far from the path of Torah." (*Di Yiddishe Heim*, Vol.2, No.4:17) The same issue included an interview with a Lubavitcher Rabbi who had moved to Australia with his family to head the Lubavitch activities there. He is quoted as saying:

We hope to carry out the wishes of our *Rebbe* Shlita. We hope that many, many more people will go on assignments to strengthen Yiddishkeit in remote places and that some of them will choose to join us in Australia, for Yiddishkeit has no limits and knows no bounds. And as those who have already gone know, they will find contentment in their work and great happiness in knowing that they are fulfilling a shlichus—which will bring us closer to the coming of Mashiach. (*Di Yiddishe Heim*, Vol.2, No.4:20)

If one of the major goals of Lubavitcher chassidim is to draw Jews closer to traditional Judaism, a primary prerequisite for this is to establish contact with non-observant Jews whenever and in whatever way possible. During the Fourth Annual Convention of the *Neshai Uvnos Chabad* (Lubavitch women's groups) one of the resolutions passed read:

Every group should try to organize periodic special meetings, in which Jewish women of all backgrounds should be invited. Fundamental laws and ideals of Judaism, such as Shabbos, Kashrus, etc., should be explained at these meetings. (*Di Yiddishe Heim*, Vol.1, No.3:20)

When Lubavitcher women in Montreal were once asked to sell books of raffle tickets, they were reminded that such an activity was also intended to establish contact with women who might later start attending the women's groups meetings. An indication of the success of the first *Lag Bo'Oymer* parade in London, England, was not only the appreciation expressed by the children but also that "several mothers of the children showed a keen interest in the Movement and have already enlisted in the Ladies Section." (*Di Yiddishe Heim*, Vol.2, No.3:21)

Lubavitch philosophy teaches that no Jew is ever wholly lost to God. Within every Jew there is a point of authentic religious faith, *"dos pintelle Yid,"* which is the reason for the Lubavitch movement's missionary zeal. (Weiner, 1969:145) A Lubavitcher expressed this idea when he said:

> You know, I've met a number of Jews who say that they don't really care about being Jewish, *Shabbess* and *kashress* aren't for them—they don't need it. But one day a Lubavitcher is going to bring these people back because no matter how hard they try to lose their Jewishness, *dos pintelle Yid* is still going to remain and once you reach that point in a person, and you'll reach it eventually, you're going to make an impression on him.

An appreciation of Lubavitch's emphasis on this matter helps to understand their relationship with other Jews in the larger community.

A characteristic feature of many religious communities is their effort to insulate themselves from the influences of the surrounding culture. One approach to a religious community's persistence is to examine the nature of its boundaries as it attempts to insulate itself from outsiders. The Tasher chassidim, for instance, continually discourage their Yeshiva students from conversing with outsiders. Similarly, the Satmarer chassidim prefer to be left alone and do not encourage interested onlookers who sometimes appear at their Yeshiva. As both chassidic groups believe the effects of such contact, especially for the younger persons in the community, are negative, they insulate themselves from the surrounding Jewish and non-Jewish communities. Since Lubavitcher chassidim, unlike other chassidic groups, are engaged in attempting to attract individuals to orthodox Judaism, they have no desire to achieve any sort of physical isolation. Because of this, Lubavitcher's proselytizing is not condoned by other chassidic Jews who believe that " . . . Hasidism is meant for only a select few for fear it will be diluted, and . . . because they question the merit of inducting American novices into such an intense religious life." (Mintz, 1968:154) Mintz continued:

> The Lubavitch movement is growing steadily, with clearly defined purposes of educational proselytism. ... While the other courts accept donations from non-observant Jews as a matter of necessity, the Lubavitcher maintain that it is part of their program to draw in the nonreligious—or, to put it another way, to develop what is good in the nonreligious as well as the religious for the overall good of the Jewish community. (1968:155)

The Lubavitch community in Montreal has organized various activities to satisfy people of varying intellectual levels and widely different age groups. A Lubavitch woman mentioned the available activities for women:

> ... well, there's a P.T.A. that works for the Yeshiva; those are parents of the students. And we have projects throughout the year. We sponsor a *Chanekkeh* evening, the *Chanekkeh* festival that takes place every year and that has a little campaign with it for *Chanekkeh gelt* for the Yeshiva. We send out the invitations and prepare the place for it, the hall, and we prepare entertainment with children. And we have a P.T.A., a lady's auxilliary that's part of the girls' school. And we have an organization called *Nachess*. ... They work for the dormitory students ... and go personally into the dormitory to see how things are ... and if the students are happy and ... there are other organizations like that. There's the drama group which we have ...*Neshai Chabad* ... mostly a learning group ...

While the above activities are organized mainly for themselves, Lubavitcher hope that outsiders will also be attracted to participate. The drama group provides a good example:

> It's funny that a lot of the people who became actresses in these plays were of a very different background, really, from having very little to do with Lubavitch. . . And at the end, the warming up toward Lubavitch and the airing of questions and views was, I think, more successful ... than in any of our direct attempts through these study groups ...

185

Another example is the Junior *Neshai* group (young Lubavitch women's group) which, according to one member "was originally supposed to be for the religious women themselves to get together and to encourage themselves about religion . . . so that they wouldn't begin to feel that it's a drag. . . " Several of the women attending the group's meetings, however, are from backgrounds with minimal *Yiddishkayt* content.

Certain activities, however, are specifically intended for those from non-orthodox Jewish families as, for instance, the Institute for Brides and Grooms, the Encounter with Chabad, and the *Messibbess Shabbess* groups. Although Lubavitcher also participate in them, the purpose of these and other such programs is to confront the participants with their Jewish heritage, expose them to traditional Judaism, and attempt to correct their misconceptions about it. By examining the *Messibbess Shabbess* program we can see how this is partly accomplished.

The program's main aim is exposure to *Yiddishkayt*. The groups, reserved for boys and girls between the ages of six and twelve, meet on Saturday afternoons in as many as eight separate locations. The leaders of the boys' groups are younger Yeshiva students, while older students from the *Bays Rivkeh* and *Bays Yankev* schools serve as the girls' leaders. A former organizer of this program describes a typical Saturday afternoon meeting and its underlying philosophy:

> All right. As a group, the first thing is that they sing songs. [He names a few.] You're acquainted with these songs? They're very good songs. One's called "I ain't gonna work on Saturday" and the kids learn the songs. Then they're told about the *Parsheh* (weekly reading of the Torah) of the week, what it is, the meaning of it and of the different holidays, what they have to do for the holidays. Then they'll have refreshments and play games. Also, before refreshments they hear a story with a moral. At the end, the main objective, well there's a dispute about what the objective of *Messibbess Shabbess* should be. I always feel it should be to get the kids to a summer camp. Or if the kid doesn't attend Yeshiva, to attend Yeshiva. That everyone holds with, the kids should walk into a Yeshiva. . . . So most people who come to *Messibbess Shabbess* are going to learn a lot and they'll keep on making *brochess* (blessings). A *Rebbe* said that if a *Yiddish kind* (Jewish child) makes a

brocheh then the *malochim* (angels) could not but hear his *brocheh*. That's a big thing. It's worth the whole business just for that. So the most we get out of this . . . is to make a lot of *brochess,* to make a lot of *malochim* happy . . . [brackets mine]

The National Council of *Messibbess Shabbess* has printed a *Messibbess Shabbess* Leaders Guide, containing program suggestions for the group leaders. One program entitled "The Different Brochos We Make" begins with the following:

Last week, we taught you how to begin most of the *brochos* we make everyday. Before we teach you the different ways how to end the *brochos*, we will see how many children are able to recite the first six words by heart. (Have each child recite the first six words for the rest of the group.)

Now, we are ready to learn the different ways how to end the *brochos.* Though all *brochos* begin almost the same way, they all have a different ending. Now, this all depends upon what we are making the individual *brocho* for. There are many different types of *brochos* that we make every day. Here are a few:

1) *Brochos* for food and beverages
2) *Brochos* before performing a *Mitzva*
3) *Brochos* we say in our daily prayers

First, we will teach you how to make the *brochos* for food and beverages. The *brochos* which we will teach you today is a very easy one to learn. All you have to do is add only four words that you already know. . . . Children, now I am going to tell you when we are to make this *brocho*. This *brocho* is to be said before we eat *bread*. (Explain to the children that each week they will be taught how to make a new brocho.) . . . (1960:54)

While children from Lubavitch and other orthodox homes are familiar with these *brochess,* the success of the program, especially with children whose contact with *Yiddishkayt* is minimal, is considered a great accomplishment. As the *Messibbess Shabbess* leader said, having non-orthodox children make even a single blessing is "a big thing" and "worth the whole business."

Other activities reflecting a similar dimension include rallies held in the Yeshiva during the Jewish holidays—*Chanekkeh* (Feast of Lights) and *Purim* (Feast of Lots). Three years ago, for example, the *Chanekkeh* rally was attended by approximately three hundred children who were treated to a program of comedy skits and the traditional lighting of the *Chanekkeh* candles. The youngsters' names, addresses, and telephone numbers were recorded and then added to the mailing list for the *Purim* rally which is celebrated a few months later. These students were also invited to the *Messibbess Shabbess* groups. As with these groups, the main objective of the rallies is to attract children from non-orthodox Jewish homes and, even if only for one afternoon, expose them to orthodox Judaism.

Lubavitcher view the non-orthodox Jewish community as a body of people who, for whatever reasons, have not recognized the importance of practising orthodox Judaism. As a result, efforts must be initiated to strengthen these Jews' ties to their heritage.

Possible Motives for the Community's Proselytizing

System theorists have argued that recruitment for new members is a functional prerequisite of any social system. (Aberle *et al.* 1950) If the community cannot maintain its ranks through internal production, it will seek outsiders as recruits to maintain itself. The purpose of proselytization, then, is to attract new members to enlarge the community or to maintain its size. Although the Lubavitcher proselytize, they do not do so in order to expand, as few members are attracted to the community in this manner. In addition, the community does not lack for members as it has a high enough birth rate to maintain its numbers. As a result, the argument usually mounted for proselytizing does not apply to the Lubavitch community under study.

Another reason many religious groups need to recruit outsiders is that their numbers are depleted by members lapsing from the faith. To help retain a stable population figure, the community has to shop in the larger community for interested people to join it. The size of a community may decline as adults become dissatisfied and disappointed with the community's lifestyle and leave. It has already been argued that the Lubavitch community's ability to provide a tenable way of life for its adult members means that few if any leave the community. The Yeshiva strongly supports this tenability for adult members, and women's interest in the community's way of life is sustained by their social groups and their acceptance of an ideology related to their role as home-makers. These chassidim's frequent contact with one another, added to their common bond with the *Rebbe*, reinforces their identity as Lubavitcher while imposing social barriers for those who are contemplating leaving the community. Lubavitchers' daily affirmation of their way of life, accomplished through prayer, performing *mitzvess*, and contact with the *Rebbe*, enables the community to satisfy those within it and provides them with reasons to remain.

The size of a community may also decline if it is unable to offset the surrounding society's assimilative influences on its young members. The community may easily lose younger members through intergenerational conflict and intermarriage. When exposure to the surrounding culture is not controlled, family disorganization frequently results for the two generations do not share a similar perspective. Several studies have pointed to the kinds of cultural conflicts that develop between parents and their children when the latter are submitted to a secular education which, at points, openly contradicts their parents' living habits. (Gottlieb and Ramsey, 1964; Hapgood, 1902; Shibutani and Kwan, 1965; Wirth, 1928) The kind of socialization offered at home is often at odds with that taught in the school and this often results in serious disagreements between parents and their children over appropriate selection of mates. Lubavitcher, how-ever, do not generally experience such difficulties with their children. Their two schools enable them to screen the secular curricula carefully to avoid students' exposure to ideas contradic-tory to the ideology of traditional Judaism. In addition, the culture of the community's younger generation does not lead to the development of an autonomous social world that excludes adults. It is, in fact, closely linked to the perspectives and every-day assumptions governing their parents' lives. Finally, the com-munity's proximity to the much larger New York Lubavitch community ensures that young people of marriageable age will have a good possibility of finding suitable partners there, thus lessening the risk of intermarriage.

Although exact figures showing the community's growth rate are not available, it is safe to argue that its size has increased

189

rather than decreased in the last several years. This is based on several comments offered by Lubavitcher who emphasize that the community's growth is primarily due to large family size. As one remarked:

There's no question that Lubavitch in Montreal has grown in the last few years. You've probably noticed this yourself that Lubavitcher have large families. It's hard to say how many babies are born but it seems that all the time there's someone who's having a baby.

In addition, though not the main source of the community's growth, Lubavitchers' proselytizing activities have attracted several newcomers. Even though they invest considerable time in such activities, the overwhelming proportion of Lubavitcher's contacts with non-observant Jews is fleeting and success at winning such Jews to orthodox Judaism is, in fact, minimal. Since efforts at proselytization do not, apparently, yield benefits commensurate to the time invested, why are they continued? This question is especially relevant as it is mainly the younger people who engage in most of the proselytizing in the larger Jewish community which might be considered potentially harmful to the Lubavitch community's distinctive identity.

Who Does the Proselytizing? A Threat to the Community's Distinctive Identity.

The actual practice of proselytizing is not officially delegated to a specific age group within the Lubavitch community. Unofficially, however, the community's formally organized activities are primarily co-ordinated and administered by the older Yeshiva students (*bocherim*) studying in the *Bays Medresh*. The *Tefillin* campaign is an excellent illustration of the *bocherim's* involvement in proselytizing, for although all Lubavitcher were interested in the campaign's success, the older Yeshiva students were mainly responsible for the actual proselytizing activities. These students also regularly visit college campuses to contact Jewish youth, call on the orthodox synagogues in the city on Saturday afternoons to recount the *Rebbe's* discourses, serve as counsellors in the boys' camp and organize the Encounter program. The organization of these activities entails entering situations with outsiders—both Jewish and Gentile—which may expose them to ideas and appearances contradictory to their way of life. Unlike the *bocherim* of the Satmarer and Tasher chassidim in Montreal, who are strongly discouraged and sometimes forbidden to converse with non-observant Jews, Lubavitcher *bocherim* regularly devote periods of time to befriending Jews whose religious observance is minimal. As outsiders are invited to the Lubavitcher Yeshiva and are welcomed into their organizations and celebrations, the distinction between insider and outsider, so crucial to the very existence of a community, is obscured. It appears that Lubavitcher's proselytizing in the larger Jewish community could threaten the preservation of their distinctive identity by diluting the community's boundaries and the distinction between the insiders and outsiders. This threat does not, however, appear to decrease the Lubavitcher's proselytizing zeal, nor in fact to weaken the community. In spite of theories to the contrary, proselytizing appears to have beneficial consequences to the community that are almost incidental to the professed aims of most proselytization.

Proselytizing Activities—An Unintended Consequence

Our analysis so far has suggested that the usual consequences of proselytizing do not pertain in the Lubavitch community. It is rather the latent consequences that make it important to the community's persistence.

Festinger *et al.*, in their presentation of cognitive-dissonance theory in *When Prophecy Fails*, suggest that a consequence of a group's successful proselytizing is "reduced dissonance." (1956:28) If the group's central beliefs are either questioned or disbelieved by others, proselytizing is an effective means of reaffirming the members' identity with the group. As the writers assert: "*If more and more people can be persuaded that the system of belief is correct, then clearly it must, after all, be correct.*" (1956:28) In spite of the fact that they recognize that a large proportion of Jews in Montreal do not share their convictions about orthodox Judaism, Lubavitcher do not become discouraged, and continue to order their lives according to the precepts underlying traditional Jewish law. It is precisely the act of proselytizing in the larger Jewish community that reinforces the members' beliefs and enables the Lubavitch community to retain its identity. When a Lubavitcher attempts to influence and convince a non-observant Jew of the relevance of orthodox Judaism, he is, in fact, becoming influenced and convinced himself. As G.H. Mead noted, this results from the person's ability to act socially toward himself just as he acts toward others and thus to become the object of his own actions. (1934:199-246) An important consequence of Lubavitchers' proselytizing activity, therefore, is that by discussing and arguing with non-observant Jews about orthodox Judaism, the Lubavitcher *Rebbe's* accomplishments, or the everlasting significance of Torah observance, they expose themselves to certain information and reinforce their identity as Lubavitcher chassidim. As Festinger *et al.*, argue, the increased proselytizing activities of messianic movements whose prophecies have been disconfirmed would indicate that, as the larger Jewish community drifts away from the tenets of traditional Judaism, Lubavitchers' proselytizing efforts will increase.

In light of this argument, the involvement of older Yeshiva students in such activities is now understandable. These students, ranging in age from fifteen to twenty years, are the very people whose beliefs require strengthening. Their commitment to the Lubavitch way of life is less intense than that of the adults who have raised families and have chosen their friends from within the community. As they live with their parents and are thus exposed to their influence concerning Torah observance, the identity of the younger children as orthodox Lubavitch Jews is continually manipulated and reinforced. As the majority of *Bays Medresh bocherim* come from other cities and reside at a Lubavitch dormitory by themselves, they are the ones whose self-conceptions as Lubavitcher must be supported. Co-opting *bocherim* into recruitment is no doubt an important way to build their own belief systems. By teaching and becoming witness to their beliefs and by urging them on others, they learn to think of themselves as Lubavitcher chassidim. Lubavitcher *bocherim*, then, are not expected to isolate themselves, but rather to control the contexts in which they meet with outsiders. The context is always expected to assume a religious base, emphasizing religious differences and making religion an explicit focus of attention or barrier.

Another factor contributing to Lubavitchers' interest in proselytization has already been discussed in the context of the benefits they derive from their relationship with the larger Jewish community. Successful proselytization results in the presence of non-Lubavitch students in the Lubavitch schools and summer camps. Since such institutions are advantageous to the community and help ensure its persistence, Lubavitcher are prepared to invest considerable time and energy in proselytization work. Although attracting newcomers (*baal tshuvess*) to the Lubavitch community is again not one of the main purposes of Lubavitchers' proselytizing activities, they do have a considerable number of recruits who have to go through a period of instruction while they are becoming members of the Lubavitch community. In addition to adding to the community's population, these recruits provide concrete evidence that Lubavitchers' proselytizing efforts enjoy a considerable measure of success. A more important result of their proselytizing than either support of their institutions or new recruits is the positive effect that their activities have in maintaining the identity and tenability of the community.

Chapter Eight

Newcomers To The Lubavitch Community

Introduction

In this chapter the community is viewed as an institution which attempts to attract new recruits and instill in them a greater awareness of the Jewish way of life. The progress of newcomers from merely interested outsiders to fully fledged members of the Lubavitch community is seen as stages in a status passage. (Glaser and Strauss, 1971) Although there is a general strategy for initiating recruits into the Lubavitch way of life, the distinctive feature of Lubavitch proselytizing and teaching is that each recruit is dealt with on an individual basis, depending on his interest in and level of *Yiddishkayt*. The community does not have any formal control over the recruit's movement from one stage to the next, but leaves this up to the recruit himself.

The first step is to determine the recruit's level in *Yiddishkayt* so that his observance can be directed in an appropriate and efficient manner. This is followed by introducing the recruit to religious practices while simultaneously encouraging his dissociation from his previous lifestyle and his commitment to the Lubavitch community. The recruit's progress in matters pertaining to orthodox Judaism must also be continually assessed and encouraged through both formal and informal contacts.

Any outsider participating in Lubavitch-organized activities may be regarded as a potential newcomer to the Lubavitch community, but in fact, of those that come initially, only a small number express the desire to become strictly observant Jews or to join the Lubavitch community. Although there are some dropouts who no longer maintain any contact with the community, Lubavitcher do not consider them complete failures as any contact with orthodox Judaism is considered better than none at all. The chapter concludes by focussing on some community-organized efforts to assist newcomers in their attempts to meet and befriend Lubavitcher. These organized activities also ensure that newcomers have intensive contact with Lubavitcher which, they hope, will eventually commit the recruits to the community's way of life.

Stages in Becoming a Lubavitcher

In some institutions a recruit has virtually no control over the route of his status passage, in others this passage is partially shaped by the newcomer and fitted to his needs. Lubavitcher do not insist that the newcomer pass through a specific sequence of regulated steps within a given time before admitting him to the community. They do not use such formal membership devices as membership cards or even initiation ceremonies:

> ... you see, there's no rules and regulations. Like, we're not a club where, for example, if you wear a certain uniform, you're in. Like, we have girls who don't cover their hair, I mean they're *frum* (observant)—they keep the *mitzvess*. This is a very hard thing for them to attain. Nobody would ever say to them: "Don't come."

Another Lubavitcher said:

> Well, the technical definition of a Lubavitcher is a person who holds by the *Rebbe* one hundred per cent. But there are no membership cards. I don't even know if there's a mailing list of Lubavitcher.

The main points Lubavitcher consider in determining the status passage of a recruit are the individual's personal status, his interest in *Yiddishkayt*, and his level of *Yiddishkayt*. The *baal tshuvess'* (newcomers') passage into Lubavitch is determined to a great extent by where he is placed or places himself in relation to each of these categories.

The Individual's Personal Status

Although the individual's sex is important in determining which *mitzvess* he or she will be required to learn, age and marital status are more important in determining how difficult it may be for the recruit to become an observant Jew. These two criteria are, however, often closely linked, as in the following example:

> Take somebody who comes closer to *Yiddishkayt*, they'll

be different, depending upon the status of the particular person. If you're going to be working with somebody who's fifty, sixty years old, it means that he has to be changed. Even thirty, forty years old it means that he has to be changed. Not only himself, but his wife and his kids. He has to make his home kosher. His wife has to start observing *tahress hamishpocheh* laws. It's a big change. Take a kid, a university kid, it's much easier for him in different steps.

The following is from a discussion with a Lubavitcher student regarding how an unmarried university student may be drawn closer to *Yiddishkayt* and Lubavitch. As he suggests, less changes are generally involved for the single individual than for a married couple:

Well, let me start with the university kid. Obviously there has to be his first contact. It could be some Lubavitcher who met him at a school dance, possibly someone who put on *Tefillin* with him. Possibly he came to a *pegeesheh*, or a concert, and he gets interested. Why does he get interested? Undoubtedly he's missing something. He wants a meaning in life. He's dissatisfied with what society has to offer him. Fine, he comes. *Tefillin*? He doesn't dig the *Tefillin* with the leather boxes. He doesn't dig the whole business. O.K. he puts them on because a nice guy's working with him ... So they start learning. They learn a little *Tanya* (philosophy). Then he comes to a *Farbrengen* and he sees so many thousands of people and he sees the respect everyone has for the *Rebbe*. And he sees the way people are singing, the way people are quiet, and his heart starts feeling. Before, his head was working. Now his heart starts working. He says: "These guys have got something." Then he learns a little more. He wants to learn a little *Chumesh*. He learns *Chumesh* and he sees what *Chumesh* is, and he sees it interpreted by a *frumer Yeed* (observant Jew) ... Then he learns a little bit *Gemoreh*, and he learns a little bit more *chassidess*, and he realizes the significance of the six hundred and thirteen commandments, and he starts getting into the *mitzvess* more. And he starts appreciating what the *Rebbe* is. And while all along this line, there are hundreds of times, literally everday, he says to himself: "Man, what the hell am I doing here? These guys are nuts. These guys are out of their minds. I can't drive a car on *Shabbess*. These guys are crazy." They go through it everyday, but they hold on. They say: "Wait a minute, they've still got something to offer." And hardly anyone falls out if they're stable. I mean there are lots of nuts who've come and gone.

The situation, however, differs with a married couple where one is no longer working with one person but must include his or her spouse:

This girl came to me about four years ago; her husband had been *frum* (observant). She hadn't. He had married her because he was under the impression that she would want to become religious. She thought she wanted to become somewhat religious, but she didn't have any religious upbringing in her background, nor did she have too much education. But she liked him and she liked what he stood for, but she didn't know what it meant. When she got married she quit smoking on *Shabbess* and a whole lot of other restrictions which she wasn't too happy about. Now he was a Yeshiva boy, a rebellious Yeshiva boy, so he didn't mind marrying a girl of that type because he didn't care all that much for the Yeshiva. Anyhow, although he came from a religious home and he had always kept *Shabbess* and kosher and so on, all that he labeled "too much" was out. They were at odds with each other for the first year because she had to smoke cigarettes in the bathroom. In the end, after about a year, he decided what the heck and tossed in the ball and decided to become as non-*frum* as she was . . .

As age and marital status influence the shape of the newcomer's status passage, the community's socializers take this into consideration in their efforts to assist an individual in transition. I once asked a Lubavitcher *bocher* how this affected a recruit's training:

It depends on his age, and on who is dependent upon him changing. X had to change his wife with him so we're working on two people now. Mr. Y had to change his wife and kids, so we're working on a family. Z had to change himself.

Interest in Lubavitch

Lubavitcher do not see gaining an interest in *Yiddishkayt* and becoming attached to Lubavitch as a sudden total commitment. The newcomer is viewed as someone who is interested initially in only certain *mitzvess* and these are the ones he is encouraged to fulfill immediately. A Lubavitch woman put it this way:

> ... each person is different and has different interests. It depends what age group they're in, and how much they want to know. O.K., it depends on the person. It doesn't depend on me. And I can only tell that person what I know, and if I don't know anymore, I can say: "Go to someone else." It depends on how much you're interested ... you see, like in Judaism, it's not like you have to believe everything, or you have to accept everything, or you ... because nobody's like that. Nobody's perfect.

It is expected, however, that the newcomer will, in time, become curious about other *mitzvess* and the correct manner in which they ought to be observed. For example:

> You see ... as in anything that you do, you know, you get an appetite. When you eat you want to eat more. When a person stops eating he loses his appetite eventually. The same thing with *Yahadess* (Judaism). You begin with small things. You begin with the essential points of *Yiddishkayt* and then gradually you get an appetite for more, and you do the asking, and you're going to come up and say: "O.K. I have *kashress*, I have this, I have that. What can I do more?" Instead of I should be the guide of that person, he's guiding me really, because he's edging me on, so to say. He says: "I even want more things to do." And I say: "All right, if you want, do what I do, you know." ... So when you speak to a person and that person says "I'm interested in *Yiddishkayt*"—from your part you try to give him a basic understanding of *Yahadess*, and that's all you can do. You don't have to convert him really and say: "Become a Lubavitcher," but that person seeing that he's a Lubavitcher ... and has a special flavour of his *Yiddishkayt*, wants to become like that person eventually.

As we shall see, there is no fixed program and related time schedule to guide the newcomer's initiation. Once undertaken, teaching is pursued gradually so as to avoid imposing excessively difficult demands on the person.

Level of *Yiddishkayt*

Newcomers to Lubavitch come from a variety of religious backgrounds, ranging from strictly observant to non-religious, but they can generally be separated into at least four distinct types. First is the individual whose upbringing was orthodox although not chassidic. For example: "My family is *shoimer Shabbess* orthodox. I had an orthodox type of upbringing. I had Yeshiva education all along." The major difference between such a person and someone from a chassidic home, is that the former's parents were not affiliated with a chassidic *Rebbe*. A second type is the one whose parents were moderately observant and kept a kosher home and lit the traditional Sabbath candles. These and other Jewish laws, however, were not observed as strictly and faithfully as the newcomer now observes them. For instance:

> The whole family is (very kosher) . . . As far as *kashress* in the home, it has always been that way. Of course, there are different degrees of *kashress*, you understand, but God forbid there should be *trayf* (non-kosher) in the home. During my growing up years we weren't *shoimer Shabbess*. My father would never work on *Shabbess* but mainly we were leisurely on *Shabbess*.

A third type is the person with minimal religious training. Coming from a non-observant home with negligible religious education, his relationship with *Yiddishkayt* is tangential at best. The following is from a discussion with such an individual:

> I don't even come from a religious family. I couldn't even read Hebrew. (My parents were) raised in a Reform Temple. My father came here this week and he couldn't even read the "Shema" in Hebrew. My mother did light *Shabbess* candles, usually after *Shabbess* had already begun. But we had a *trayf* home. We didn't observe *Shabbess*.

The final type of newcomer is the convert to Judaism. His level of *Yiddishkayt* would generally be similar to that of the non-observant Jew.

In the course of his contact with Lubavitch, it is hoped the newcomer will become committed to its philosophy and orthodox way of life after a period of socialization in the community and desocialization from his previous lifestyle. Initially, however, newcomers range from those who can identify with *Yiddishkayt* immediately to those who know very little about it. As a newcomer from an orthodox background noted:

I didn't really have that many questions, because . . . when it came to *kashress* I had done enough of it in my home before, so I didn't need to ask questions about it in terms of my husband and myself.

The General Strategy

The initial central organizing principles of Lubavitch's strategy with new recruits are to make the person a more observant Jew and to bring him along at his own pace. Since the recruit submits himself to such processing voluntarily, Lubavitcher realize that the person is not committed to continuing and can back out at any time. Since, at least in the beginning, Lubavitcher exercise little if any control over the person, to insist that he follows a rigid initiation schedule does not seem a successful way to draw people into the orthodox fold and Lubavitch circles.

Lubavitcher do, however, encourage newcomers to perform certain basic precepts immediately. One of the first of these that males are urged to observe is *Tefillin*, while married females are impressed with the importance of attending the *mikveh* (ritual bath) regularly. The recruits are then themselves called upon to determine when they are willing and prepared to begin observing additional *mitzvess*. As such, there is no definite time period during which the recruit must be ready to adhere to the majority of laws and customs regulating an orthodox Jew's life:

I can think of a Lubavitch family right off, right off like this, that, I think ten years ago, they became interested in Lubavitch. And her sons were wearing beards and this woman, just last year, maybe a year and a half ago, she finally covered her hair. It took her ten years to cover her hair, but I'm sure that now she is doing it. . . You see, it's real. Now she's not doing it just to be like everybody else.

Lubavitcher have discovered that fanatical recruits who try to alter their lifestyle immediately and completely to conform to orthodox laws and chassidic traditions and customs are more

200

likely to experience personal and familial difficulties as a result of the abrupt dissociation. It is not surprising, then, that Lubavitcher suggest to recruits who are eager to perform as many *mitzvess* as possible to wait some time before accepting additional ones. A Lubavitcher explains the reason for this:

> We don't want to come and then label you . . . here, this is our group and you have to dress this way, and you have to put on this and that. . . As long as it doesn't come from his own feelings . . . what's the purpose? What's the use of it? Why put on a *shytl* . . . when you don't even feel the word *shytl*? What's going to happen later on, you're going to take off the *shytl*. You wouldn't put it on ever again, because once you have taken it off . . . so, therefore, with a *mitzveh*. Don't grab too many *mitzvess* together and then it will be too hard on you. So then you're going to drop them off. It'll be double hard to take them on again.

The recruit is initially encouraged to select a *mitzveh*, such as putting on *Tefillin*, which will not interfere drastically with his present way of life.

> I would say to a person . . . it wouldn't make any difference which *mitzveh* you want to do. Whatever appeals to you, whatever is easiest, and just the opposite, you never pick a hard *mitzveh* because then you're very discouraged. . . Not to answer the phone on *Shabbess* may be terribly hard and to keep *kashress* would be easier. . . You see, it depends on the person.

Although the recruit is permitted to progress at his own pace, he is, nonetheless, encouraged to perform additional *mitzvess*. Such encouragement only occurs, however, when the recruit is considered ready for advancement. While he selects those *mitzvess* he feels confident to begin observing, the Lubavitcher in contact with him has a planned "*mitzveh* route" which he hopes the recruit will eventually follow:

> . . . and chances are, and we hope that this person himself, the next main step will be *kashress* and *Shabbess* and we hope we wouldn't push him to *Shabbess* like we push him to *Tefillin*. This person himself . . . will himself decide to come (to *shul*) on *Shabbess*. Smoking will be difficult for

him to stop. Movies will be more difficult. To maybe not drive his car to the Yeshiva on *Shabbess* might be easier for him . . .

The Lubavitch strategy just described is a consequence of having recruits who are neither committed to nor identified with traditional Judaism. They are not committed because they can leave at any time and, at least in the beginning, lose nothing. They may not be strongly identified because they are not seeking to become fanatics but rather to become more observant; they may in fact have been approached through recruitment activities rather than be self-selected. As a result, Lubavitcher recognize the advantages of not exacting too many demands of newcomers since such demands may lead them to terminate their involvement with Lubavitch:

> I know when I deal with people. I deal, you you, with a lot of kids. I dealt with X, I deal with Y now. I know there are some things which I don't tell them to do because I know that he's not ready to do it, and he's just going to get up and take the next bus home. You cannot push anything on a person until he is ready.

The recruits are gradually encouraged to become more interested through discussions with Lubavitcher:

> . . . It depends on how he says it to you. If he comes in and he wants to have questions, you're not going to tell him: "You're not allowed to write on *Shabbess*." It'll scare him before you're started. He'll be chased off. We wouldn't start with *Tefillin* either except that the *Rebbe* explained *Tefillin* is the basis of the religion . . . There's no other *mitzveh* which we play up, you know. Rather, the best opportunity which we always looked for before the *Tefillin* campaign came up, is to try to learn with them, to try to get them learning something and then, as he learns, he'll want to hear more.

Determining the Person's Level of *Yiddishkayt*

The Lubavitch philosophy stresses that each Jew is, at any time, at a particular level of *Yiddishkayt* and his objective is to raise himself to the next higher level. Lubavitcher's initial concern with recruits is to determine their level in *Yiddishkayt*. This entails finding out about their history, including the type and extent of their Jewish education and degree of religious observance. Such information, which is vital for determining the shape of the person's passage, is determined in a variety of ways. Firstly, a recruit's appearance might provide some clues, for example, a young man entering the Yeshiva without a head covering, or a woman attending a Lubavitch women's meeting in a low-cut dress would indicate that they are unaware or unconcerned about the impropriety of their appearance. Yet gathering clues from a person's appearance is unreliable. The manner of dress does not give sufficient information about, for instance, whether the person observes the laws of *Kashruth*. In addition, a recruit may dress appropriately only when in Lubavitcher's presence, for example, a young man may wear a certain kind of *yarmulke* which suggests his head is always covered, or a woman might lower the hemline of a few of her dresses which she will wear only to Lubavitch functions. A more reliable way to learn about the person's background and religious practices is by engaging him in conversation. In the course of such conversation the person will probably be asked whether he observes *Tefillin* or the Sabbath. The question is often phrased in such a way so as to let the person realize that Lubavitcher are tolerant of their fellow Jews' shortcomings. For example:

> Lubavitcher: Do you try to keep *Shabbess*? Of course it depends on your background. Like sometimes the parents are not *shoimer Shabbess* and they just don't feel it's important enough and so in this case it's likely that the children will also not be observant.

Gaining this kind of information about the individual helps Lubavitcher determine how best to proceed to encourage him to become more observant.

Bringing the Recruit Along

Socialization

The recruit is familiarized with certain religious practices that are expected to instill in him an identification with traditional Judaism. This is best accomplished when the recruit begins to practice *Yiddishkayt* immediately. To link the person to Luba-vitch he is gradually informed about the Lubavitcher *Rebbe* and his views, and about events sponsored by this chassidic group. As a recruit, he is engaged in a simultaneous process of socialization into the Lubavitch way of life and dissociation from much of his previous lifestyle. This is intended to identify him with and commit him to Judaism from a traditional and Lubavitch perspective. At first, male and female recruits generally learn much the same precepts, for example, the laws regulating *Kashruth*, but, as they become more observant, certain features of the socialization process assume greater relevance for men or women.

A basic starting point for both is that they practise being more observant. A newcomer *(baal tshuveh)* emphasizes this point:

> Well, first of all the idea is not to become a Lubavitcher. The idea is to become a more observant Jew and this is what the Lubavitcher is after. . . . What is important is that someone becomes a Jew.

While they will eventually become familiar with and understand the traditions and customs linked to *Yiddishkayt* and Lubavitch, they are initially encouraged to behave as much as possible like an orthodox Jew. This may take the form of beginning to *davn* (pray), *davening* on a more regular basis, observing *Tefillin* or coming regularly to the Yeshiva. Although praying and observing *Tefillin* are relatively simple to perform they must be learned by those who have never previously practised these activities. A young man, recounting his first days in the Lubavitcher Yeshiva, recalls: "I *davned*, I learned how to *davn* . . . you know. To put on *Tefillin*, you know, that's a trick in itself at first." As the *baal tshuveh* becomes familiar with the precepts of orthodox Judaism, he is encouraged to choose among those he will find less demanding to observe initially:

> I remember when I stopped writing on *Shabbess*. I didn't do anything else. I didn't *davn*. I listened to the radio, I answered the telephone, but I didn't write.

While he is becoming acquainted with the details of Jewish law, the recruit is expected to incorporate as many of them as he sees feasible into his everyday life. He is impressed with the idea that *Yiddishkayt* is a way of life and not a mere series of acts to be performed at specified times. In time he becomes increasingly observant by performing additional *mitzvess* or performing the same ones more devoutly. As an instance of the former:

> . . . and we just decided to do one thing at a time. We started *benching*. That was the first thing that we did. Then we stopped driving on *Shabbess*. Then we took one additional step—we built a *Sukkeh*. We started to keep *kashress* properly. We stopped turning out the lights on *Shabbess*.

One may also become more sincere and serious in performing the same *mitzveh*:

> Since I got married, I've taken a lot of things more seriously. I didn't care too much the time I was learning before I was married. Now it seems more important to me. . . . I put on a *talless* (prayer shawl) when I *davn* and I guess I'm more serious. I think more of what I say when I *davn* than I did then. The urge to learn is there a little bit.

In Lubavitch circles, and among all chassidic and orthodox Jews, the woman's place is in the home for which she is held primarily responsible. An article in *Di Yiddishe Heim* states:

> The lady of the house cannot see herself apart from her home, her husband and her children. She understands her role as mother. She can find the time for her home and for her children. A mother sees the importance of putting aside time to talk to the children, read to them and review their lessons. She comprehends that the major part of the child's basic education rests with her, the *chinoch*—training—of the formative years, a period before school, is mainly the responsibility for the woman. (Vol.1, No.1:1)

Consequently she must familiarize herself with those laws which will ensure an orthodox home and family life. Two important sets of laws are those pertaining to *Kashruth* and family purity (*tahress hamishpocheh*). Married female recruits must learn certain things to help them manage their homes and themselves in an orthodox manner.

In keeping a kosher home, one must see to it that all food products, including the utensils in which the food is cooked and served, are pure. This involves learning how to be sure that a particular food product is kosher and where it might be purchased. For those who have not previously observed *Kashruth*, kosher food products will have to be substituted for those normally used:

> I wanted to know what butcher they buy from and where to buy fish and things like that... Some things were hard, like, I used to use these cheeses, this Kraft sliced cheese, and now there is this kosher cheese and it's about twice as expensive as this one. I'm not a stingy person, but somehow I couldn't. I wouldn't mind spending money on something that's healthier. It's hard especially since I thought both were the same.

Keeping informed about kosher food products is a continuous learning experience. New kosher products continually appear but, more importantly, old ones may disappear; that is, the ingredients of the product are altered so that it is no longer kosher. A recruit describes some of her experiences:

> And probably there were a few things that I had bought that I found out later on were no good... You bring in a product sometimes and you find out about it, and all of a sudden someone will tell you that this product is really dairy and it's not really kosher. So, it's a matter of learning every single day, and always watching what you bring into the house because there will always be something new that they'll change and you don't know when they're going to change a product in the market and put something in that is not kosher. So you always have to keep your pantry up to date and watch for these things.[1]

Along with the laws pertaining to *Kashruth*, the female recruits must familiarize themselves with laws relating to family purity. They begin to attend the *mikveh* (ritual bath) and study the laws accompanying attendance. With respect to these laws, both husband and wife will probably have to alter their sexual habits. During the period of the menstrual flow, for seven days after it has ceased, and until the woman has immersed herself in the *mikveh*, sexual contact between them is strictly prohibited.

In the process of becoming more observant the recruits learn not only about Jewish laws and traditions but about the Lubavitcher *Rebbe* and the kinds of attitudes and feelings his chassi-

206

dim display toward him. They are impressed with the *Rebbe's* supernatural powers and will hear accounts testifying to these extraordinary attributes. From the outset they will be encouraged to write to the *Rebbe*, either for a blessing (*brocheh*) or specific advice:

> Now, I was going this way and I was going that way and, of course, I discussed it with X (a Lubavitcher) and I talked to the *bocherim* about it. And what they suggested was that I write a letter to the *Rebbe*. I wrote a letter to the *Rebbe* but I never got an answer, and by this time I had already been accepted by *Shayrut La'am* (a program in Israel) and I didn't know what to do one way or the other . . .

Encouraging the individual to establish contact with the *Rebbe* is a Lubavitch strategy. Lubavitcher are always willing to assist recruits compose their letters and assure them of the advantages of establishing such contact. It appears, however, that recruits initially experience difficulty in accepting the *Rebbe* in the way other Lubavitcher do. This sometimes results in a reluctance to arrange for a personal audience with him:

> For some reason or other, I don't know what it was, it's something I just couldn't quite accept, because in my knowledge of Judaism it doesn't mean that just because you become an observant Jew you have to accept a *Rebbe*. With the chassidim it's almost part and parcel, especially with Lubavitch.

and:

> Their (Lubavitch) main objective is to influence you to become religious, and after he's religious, to become a Lubavitcher. A Lubavitcher is someone who has contact with the *Rebbe*. They got me to write. Writing is the next step. Then personal contact or at least to go to New York where the *Rebbe* talks. . . As a matter of fact, this weekend someone was trying to get me to go. . . . If I was really keen, I suppose I would go and try, . . . but I don't know. A Lubavitcher would do that.

The recruit soon realizes what other Lubavitcher would like to see of him and his consent to have a personal audience is taken both by him and others to indicate the beginning of a commitment to the Lubavitch orientation to *Yiddishkayt*. When the person first comes into contact with Lubavitch he is taught laws, customs, and traditions relating to Judaism and Lubavitch. As he applies what he learns to his everyday life he begins to identify with *Yiddishkayt* and sees himself trying to practise and observe traditional Judaism. The Lubavitch strategy recognizes the importance of first offering the recruit activities to build his identification with *Yiddishkayt*. In time, however, after becoming immersed in a Lubavitch milieu, recruits find themselves increasingly committed to this different, orthodox way of life. The transition from mere identification to identification with commitment is very gradual and is signalled by certain kinds of activities.

Dissociation From Previous Lifestyle and Commitment to Lubavitch

As recruits learn to be more observant they begin to feel compelled to display evidence indicating that they are taking this new way of life seriously. This may take the form of reallocating one's time to give more opportunity for religious-related activity. For example, where previously the recruit may have spent several hours at a movie, this time will now be devoted to learning about *Yiddishkayt*, participating in the *Tefillin* campaign, helping to co-ordinate an Encounter with Chabad, or some other related activity. The person may begin attending the Yeshiva or *davening* with a *minyen* (quorum). If possible he may particpate in a *sheeur* (study class) that meets regularly, or may become involved in some of the Yeshiva's social functions.

Along with the observance of Jewish laws and participation in Lubavitch activities, the recruit is encouraged to establish a relationship with the *Rebbe*. This relationship is likely to assume a different shape depending on the recruit's level of identification with traditional Judaism and the Lubavitcher chassidim. At the outset of his contact with Lubavitch he inevitably discovers the reverence Lubavitcher display toward their leader and the central role he occupies in their lives. He becomes acquainted with this information not through formal teaching but because the *Rebbe's* ideas, attitudes, and actions are a constant topic of conversation in Lubavitch circles. The recruit recognizes the *Rebbe* to be a holy man but remains sceptical of the powers that Lubavitcher claim are vested in his person. Since Lubavitcher regularly travel to New York to attend the *Rebbe's Farbrengens* and encourage the newcomer to experience a *Farbrengen* first-hand, he usually accepts their invitation albeit with some trepidation. During the course of his stay with a Lubavitch family while in New York he is again exposed to a series of stories testifying to the *Rebbe's* superhuman powers. Through contact with Lubavitcher he discovers the intensity of the *chossid's* relationship with the *Rebbe* and that the former regularly seeks the *Rebbe's* advice and blessings before proceeding on an important course of action. In time the recruit becomes interested in the *Rebbe* to the point of inquiring from Lubavitcher about "what the *Rebbe* said" or "what the *Rebbe* has to say" concerning various topics. During this period of interest in the *Rebbe* the recruit might "write in" to the *Rebbe* for a blessing, and might even agree to the arrangement of a personal audience with him. Unlike other Lubavitcher, however, he has not yet entrusted himself completely to the *Rebbe*. When faced with an important decision, for example, he may still rely primarily on his personal judgment for a suitable solution. It is only when the recruit places himself completely under the *Rebbe's* direction and is prepared to abide by his advice, however contrary it may be ot his own and others' thinking, that he is considered to be emotionally and intellectually committed to Lubavitch.

In the beginning the recruit's attachment to orthodox Judaism and to Lubavitch are tenuous. If he feels inclined to observe a precept he does; if he does not feel so inclined, he does not. Although during this time he becomes increasingly preoccupied with orthodox Judaism and Lubavitch, he still meets with his nonreligious friends who do not necessarily share his new found interests. In time, however, he begins losing contact with many of them. For instance, he will no longer meet with them on a Saturday afternoon to drive to a non-kosher restaurant. What further separates him from them is his feelings that he shares little in common with them. As one Lubavitcher expressed it:

> You know, you do lose contact . . . if I'm visiting X (name of city) having contact with [previous non-orthodox friends] or trying to renew contact with them is sort of futile because we have so little in common. You know, so little interests in common other than our family and home

and furniture. I did go to see one of my old friends when I was back last spring and we had a very enjoyable afternoon. But I don't think we could ever establish a close friendship together because there is so little to go on.

The alternative is to choose new friends with whom common interests are shared:

> I enjoy the friends that I do have and I have quite a few friends whom I'm quite close to here in Montreal and I enjoy their friendship and I depend on that very much. But it's meaningful to me. There is a definite exchange of interests and I think that there are things that we share, and these are very important to me, that I would be reluctant to do without.

The majority of new friends are likely to be from Lubavitch and it is with these people that the recruit finds most in common. It is they who teach him what he wants and is expected to know. Since they spend a considerable amount of their time in the Yeshiva, he is likely to do the same. His social life begins to centre around the Yeshiva and he begins to spend much of his time in the presence of Lubavitcher.

The female recruit also experiences a dissociation from her previous circle of friends. For her, increasing involvement in the Lubavitch community comes by way of attending meetings of one of the women's groups, getting involved in one of the Lubavitch women's telephone circles, or participating in the various other women's activities. Along with this, certain changes are expected and come about in her appearance. She may resist these changes initially but she is made to recognize the importance of conforming to certain standards of dress. She notices that Lubavitch women do not consider it necessary to keep abreast with the latest styles and fashions. Instead she is informed of the *Rebbe's* emphasis on *tzneeus*—modesty—in appearance. By seeing others she learns that one's hair is to be always covered in public, preferably with a *shytl*, that dresses are to be long-sleeved, high-necked, and of approximately knee length. Though it may be difficult to conform to these expectations with one's old wardrobe, the change gradually occurs. In the privacy of her home she may not be meticulous about the length of her dress or sleeves, yet when before others she tries to present herself appropriately. Conversation with two *baal tshuvess* help illustrate this:

> Well, it came about gradually. At first I didn't think anything about it. No one told me anything, but I gradually heard and learned that they wear their sleeves three quarter length. At first I didn't know. Even when I knew, somehow I don't feel it would be wrong if I came in short sleeves. Up until last year I would sometimes go. I have a lot of short sleeved dresses and I don't feel undressed if I wear them, although lately . . . all of a sudden . . . it just comes over you and you feel in their presence at least . . . this is how I should be dressed and I would feel uncomfortable if I did otherwise. . . Now, I try it. If I know somebody is coming over I'll probably wear long sleeves. If I do housework I have to wear a sleeveless dress and I'm often embarrassed if the bell rings and you have these men collecting. So I feel I'm not dressed properly.

and:

> Well, if I go out and forget my hat, I go back and get it. Or if I go out and realize that I'm wearing a dress that might be bothersome to someone, I will go back and get a sweater. I don't want to be disrespectful.

Male recruits also change their style of dress. The most important features that identify them and commit them to behave like orthodox Jews include wearing a hat and/or *yarmlke* at all times, a dark-coloured suit or appropriate substitute, a *talless kotn* (fringed undershirt), and in most cases a beard.

As the recruits gradually become more committed to *Yiddishkayt* and to Lubavitch, they tend to drop some of their former activities. Recruits learn that time is a precious commodity and that one must spend it productively. They learn that some of the activities they might be engaged in are regarded as unproductive. One recruit, for example, had given away his T.V. set:

> The fact is that there was in some way a religious motive, because you want to make and do the most with your time. You consider your time very precious, and we just felt that many times we just watched and we felt badly afterwards. We watched a program . . . and we felt that we could have spent our time doing other things. Life is short.

Newcomers to Lubavitch learn to reallocate their time in accordance with their new way of life. They realize that certain activities are regarded as either too time consuming or not compatible with a Lubavitch lifestyle and consequently try to refrain from them. For example, men grow to feel that time spent at movies ought to be put to more valuable use:

> ... and you have to recognize that to go to a movie for three hours and spend a half hour getting back, that's four hours. Now ... time is generally too valuable to find a block of time that's available.

or:

> You're not supposed to go to a movie... If you had the time you could do with others or with yourself, I mean, you could learn or do a good deed or go to put on *Tefillin* with somebody.

Since the person begins to think of himself as a religious Jew fitting into the Lubavitch community and is anxious to be so regarded by others he stops taking part in activities which may lead others to question his sincerity.

In these ways the recruit gradually assumes the Lubavitch attitude concerning the role and purpose of an orthodox Jew and realizes that continued participation in some of his previous activities is not in conformity with his new self-perception. He is now likely to focus his attention and devote his time toward practising to be a better Jew; that is, to elevate himself to a higher level of *Yiddishkayt*. The recruit is fully aware that he is drifting away from his past way of life since his change of status is undertaken voluntarily. Although a complete break with his past never occurs, his degree of contact with his former nonreligious friends and relatives slowly diminishes. His everyday social life is heavily influenced by Lubavitcher. They become his reference group and constitute the significant others in his immediate world. At this point, the recruit can be said to be socially committed to Lubavitch. The perceived costs of terminating one's involvement with the Lubavitch community or deviating sharply from the expected orthodox way of life are too great and the recruit becomes structurally locked into the community's lifestyle. (Becker, 1960)

Although it may be analytically possible to separate the recruit's intellectual and social commitment to Lubavitch, the two processes evolve simultaneously, one leading to or resulting from the other. Since the Lubavitch strategy allows recruits to set their own socialization pace, the status passage of becoming a Lubavitcher is mediated by innumerable contingencies influenced by the person's social and religious background.

Assessing Success With Recruits

In the process of meeting with recruits and instructing them in matters of *Yiddishkayt*, Lubavitcher wish to know if the former are practising what they learn and are becoming more observant. Unlike total institutions which can gain access to most aspects of their charges' everyday lives, Lubavitcher cannot nor want to exert such control over recruits. Certain activities can be seen to signify that the individual is assuming a serious attitude and is progressing satisfactorily. For male recruits, such activities may include attending the Yeshiva regularly, studying Torah with a Lubavitcher, going to the *mikveh* (ritual bath); for females the criteria are for example, altering their dress to conform with the standards acceptable within the Lubavitch community, buying certain food products at one of the kosher bakeries, and attending Lubavitch womens' meetings. If the recruit unit is a family with children of school age, enrolling the children in a Lubavitch school is taken as an indication of the family's serious intent.

While certain *mitzvess* are performed publicly so that the recruit's progress can be noted others are observed privately. For instance, Lubavitcher cannot check whether a recruit is observing the Sabbath properly or if a family is purchasing only kosher food products or keeping the laws of family purity for these *mitzvess* are observed primarily in the privacy of one's home. Certain situations, however, allow Lubavitcher to learn about the recruit's progress even in such matters. When a recruit meets with a Lubavitcher to study Torah or *Chassidess* (Lubavitch philosophy) the situation is conducive for the exchange of such information. The recruit is told at the outset that the study sessions should also serve as occasions where questions are asked and problems discussed. After a period of time both the Lubavitcher and the recruit feel free to acquire information from and about the other. At these times Lubavitcher can inquire about the recruit's observance of such matters as the Sabbath, *Kashruth* and, if married, family purity. At the same time the recruit is anxious to inform the Lubavitcher of his progress since their last meeting. In this manner the recruit's efforts at observing certain *mitzvess* are rewarded if only by the congratulatory remarks he receives from the Lubavitcher.

The recruit's progress in the observance of *mitzvess* is also judged by the nature of his questions. If certain questions are not asked about particular *mitzvess*, chances are they are not observed. Lubavitcher stress certain aspects of Jewish law sooner than others and it is expected that recruits will seek information concerning these. Such questioning, especially by telephone, indicates to others that the recruit is concerned about his progress in *Yiddishkayt*. It also informs Lubavitcher of their degree of success in drawing the person into the orthodox fold.

Although particular activities reflect a person's progress in *Yiddishkayt*, it is not actually possible to know if he observes those *mitzvess* he publicly avows. What is certain, however, is that the Lubavitcher knows the recruit is aware of those *mitzvess* he ought to be observing. The assumption made by the Lubavitcher is that the recruit has no reason to lie about his accomplishments in *Yiddishkayt* and thus ought to be believed. The reason he returns to the Yeshiva is because he wants to and not because of external pressures. Also, the recruit realizes that lying only commits him to observe additional *mitzvess* and exerts pressure on him to conform to new expectations which others now have of him.

Dropouts

Since passage into Lubavitch is initially a voluntary act, individuals are free to terminate the process whenever they wish. In fact, only a minority of those with whom Lubavitch comes into contact agree to change their lifestyle and begin observing Jewish law. As already mentioned, the Lubavitch strategy calls for these individuals to begin with the basic and "easy" *mitzvess* and, in time, to progress to additional ones requiring greater commitment. The majority of recruits travel the route of the status passage in typical fashion; that is, they conform to the kinds of expectations made of them by others in the community. Others, however, begin and continue to show progress but then reverse their field either by failing to progress or by discontinuing to observe those precepts practised to date. Thus another property of the status passage into Lubavitch is reversibility.

Recognized criteria constituting success or failure with recruits are not clearly marked as Lubavitcher do not consider that either complete success or total failure is possible. Complete success implies that further success is no longer possible and that the person has reached a level in *Yiddishkayt* which cannot be surpassed. The Lubavitch notion of levels, or *madraiggess*, mentioned earlier, strongly discourages this claim. At the same time, even those who have only come into contact with Lubavitch and have not begun to practise traditional Judaism are not considered failures. As one Lubavitcher said: "... I feel that whoever has come into touch with Lubavitch ... that no one comes out less from the experience." In other words, whatever contact a Jewish person has with *Yiddishkayt*, whether fleeting or continuous, it is better than no contact at all.

Those recruits who reverse their field give various reasons to justify their decision. A common reason is the person's inability or lack of desire to accept and maintain what are perceived as restrictions on their lifestyle. For example, a former Yeshiva student who recently left the Yeshiva to learn a trade and who has begun to dress quite stylishly remarked to me:

> You know, there are certain things that I enjoy doing which they [Lubavitcher] don't like. That doesn't mean that I can't do them. Now that I'm no longer here [studying at the Yeshiva] I do what I want and if they don't like it, it's too bad. I don't tell them how to run their life and they won't tell me how to run mine. Some don't like these pants because of these things [points to the flares] and others think this tie is too fancy. What's it their business what I wear? [brackets mine]

A Lubavitch woman, regarded as an experienced teacher of recruits, told me of an incident about a girl with whom she studied *Chumesh*. The girl made it clear at the outset that she did not believe in God but rather in Fate. The two had studied together for six months when one day the girl announced that a good Jew can only be a committed Jew and that henceforth she would observe the Sabbath and other *mitzvess* she learned in the course of her studies. "Recently," the woman said,

215

She decided to go away from it all. She had realized, she thinks at least, not to completely divorce herself but certainly to retreat. She feels that it had posed too many problems, and given her an insecure feeling and has made her belong nowhere almost. She can't really be friendly with her friends because they no longer share that much in common. She is not able to rip herself away enough from the past environment to face this type of restricted environment. She decided twice to go away, once to X [name of country], another time to Y [name of city] to go into a seminary and start really learning, but then it petered out at the end because she felt it would be much too much restriction on her. At this point she isn't ready. So there was only one answer for her—recede. I don't know how long she'll stay at that point. But here's a typical example. I think she's typical at least. [brackets mine]

Lubavitcher recognize that most of the people they encounter are not already observant Jews and few will become so. They are also aware that there is no guarantee that those whom they impress with the importance of traditional Judaism will live a fully Jewish life. The number of Lubavitcher Yeshiva graduates who either leave the orthodox fold or become lax in the observance of many precepts testifies to this. Even so, Lubavitcher claim to be unanimous in their belief that one should not feel discouraged in his efforts to draw people closer to *Yiddishkayt*, that a person's observance of even one precept if only for one occasion is superior to no observance at all. A recruit, then, does not have to become an orthodox Jew and Lubavitcher *chossid* to be considered a successful case. Convincing an individual who had no connection with Judaism to observe *Tefillin* is viewed as a great accomplishment. A woman expressed this idea nicely when she said:

... There's no insurance ... of what you're going to get done. Every little bit is better than nothing. A person is human and he's going to face the forces of the world which are so utterly against our forces and my husband keeps telling me: "Look, you know, every little bit is better than nothing and that is all we have to keep saying to ourselves and aim for the highest we can possibly get." It might not be very high but. . . .

Who Teaches the Recruit?

The Yeshiva serves as the centre where the male recruits learn much of what they are required to know. As it is also the community's social centre, they meet and become friendly with other Lubavitcher who teach them not only the various *mitzvess* but also *Yiddishkayt*.

The male recruits' learning is accomplished through two channels—one formal and the other informal. The formal channel consists of organized study sessions with a Lubavitcher. Since, at this point, the Lubavitcher's objective is to retain contact with the recruit, what they study is largely determined by the recruit's preferences. For example:

> I was once with B... I wanted to learn some *Chumesh*, he wanted to learn *Chassidess*. ... I told him we should be doing *Chumesh* better but he was complaining still to learn *Chassidess*, so we learned *Chassidess*.

Along with this, the recruit may learn about *Yiddishkayt* and Lubavitch by reading the Lubavitch literature which the *chossid* is eager to lend him. The second channel is informal in that information is not accumulated in a structured and systematic manner but through listening in on discussions concerning Torah or talking to Lubavitcher about specific questions.

The recruit typically becomes more involved in Lubavitch by attending the Yeshiva either to *davn* or study. In some cases he studies with someone whom he meets regularly:

> So he [the *Rebbe*] said, among other things, ... when I came back to Montreal I should get involved with this *bocher*. I used to go to study with him. You see, we lived way out in Y [neighborhood] and the Yeshiva was here, so there wasn't really that much contact except when I would go down to study ... [brackets mine]

or:

> I started by hooking myself on to someone and then found a teacher.

In other cases, although he does not meet with someone regularly, the recruit nonetheless visits the Yeshiva hoping to find someone with whom to study. Much learning is accomplished through informal contact with Lubavitcher. If a number of Lubavitcher, including the recruit, take on a *Tefillin* route, they may discuss the *Rebbe's* recent discourse while en route to their destination. This kind of learning may also occur when the recruit travels with Lubavitcher to attend a *Farbrengen:*

> . . . I would always go with a carload of people, and, you know, I always used to say I got more coming and going. Just general talking . . .

Often by simply sitting in the *shul* or elsewhere in the Yeshiva the recruit absorbs information from the general gossip and discussion:

> You know what a *Farbrengen* is. Not only in New York, but you get a number of people sitting around a table. There's a little bit of cake and a bottle of whiskey. Just talking. I can get a lot more out of that than a whole *sayfer* of *mymorim* or a whole *Farbrengen* in New York.

These informal gatherings not only bring recruits into contact with Lubavitcher, but they also help the recruit to learn what Lubavitcher consider worthy topics for discussion and to gain the Lubavitch perspective on them.

With the assistance of other Lubavitcher, the male recruit learns about *Yiddishkayt* at the Yeshiva. Unlike female recruits who often visit other Lubavitch women at home, the practice of meeting at home is uncommon among the men. The Yeshiva serves the men as the central meeting place in the community:

> . . . they (women) come over to our house or my wife goes elsewhere. This type of thing happens a lot more with the women than with the men. I can't imagine . . . going over and visiting at someone's house. I just never do, whereas getting together at the Yeshiva is a sort of standard thing.

As for the men, the learning process for the female recruits only commences after contact is initiated with Lubavitch women. While men may meet at the Yeshiva, no such central meeting place exists for the women and, consequently, other means must be found for acquainting female recruits with Lubavitch women. Whereas men are expected to set aside time for daily prayer and study, women are primarily expected to care for their homes and families, thus leaving them with little time to encounter other women. As a result, women use the telephone as a substitute for daily social encounters.

To initiate contact, the prospective recruit mentions to a Lubavitcher or someone in contact with the group that she is interested in learning about *Yiddishkayt*. She is, in turn, referred to or contacted by a Lubavitch woman who suggests arrangements for studying, either with someone privately or within a group:

> I was working ... and the first year they were always employing the Yeshiva *bochers* and I happened to meet one of the *bocherim* from the Lubavitcher Yeshiva. And I was discussing with him my desire to learn because I wasn't able to go out of town to learn and time was slipping by. And he mentioned the possibility for my learning privately with one of the Lubavitch women ...

During these "*Yiddishkayt* sessions" the recruit studies something appropriate to her level of Jewish knowledge. She will usually be taught *Chumesh* as well as *mitzvess* related to *Kashruth* and, if married, family purity. A recruit, already partly observant when she arrived at Lubavitch, remarked of her teacher:

> So like at the beginning ... she didn't want to push because she wasn't trying to get me religious because at the time, when I was going to her, I was already *shoimer Shabbess* and I was kosher. ... But there were certain things that I wouldn't have eaten after. So as far as trying to push any religion, no, she wasn't. But we just got to *Chumesh* and that was it, and we'd get carried away a little bit here and a little bit there.

Another recruit, at the time not observant, recalled:

> I used to go down about once or twice a week and she started learning with me, laws and things like that. And it started like that, and then I got really interested, you know. We used to do *Chumesh*, you know... But we did mostly laws because that's what I needed at the time.

Since not all female recruits receive private instruction, they learn about Jewish laws, customs, and traditions through meetings and telephone conversations. If married, the recruit's husband may relate what information he learnt at the Yeshiva. In the course of study, he too is familiarized with specific laws and they will review them together. This process was described as follows:

> The husband is usually encouraged to learn with another Lubavitcher in the evenings, and they go over these things [laws related to family purity] and they come across it and they ask questions and their questions are answered. It's this general process of learning that goes on and they become familiar with the law. In the evening when he returns home he will probably go over with his wife what he learned and they will discuss it and again if they have questions . . . [brackets mine]

The recruit helps decide what she will learn initially on the basis of her interests. Certain laws, however, such as family purity, are considered basic and she is pressured to learn about and observe those immediately:

> I mean, there were a lot of things when she first came . . . she didn't even observe *niddeh* (separation). She didn't go to the *mikveh*, and that point we just couldn't let go. So I spoke to her husband and she started to observe that, and she goes to the *mikveh* now.

Attending women's meetings is the most common way for female recruits to meet Lubavitch women. The women's group is called *Neshai Chabad* and the younger married women have organized the Junior *Neshai Chabad*. The majority of the members in both groups are Lubavitcher but non-Lubavitcher are continually invited and encouraged to return. The Junior *Neshai Chabad* meetings always centre on a different topic, such as the woman's duty at home, the importance of *Kashruth*, or baby care, and they serve as occasions when the recruits can discuss the difficulties they have had with other people who might share the same problems. These meetings also allow the newcomer to become aware of Lubavitch women's interests, the kinds of joys, hardships, or inconveniences they encounter as orthodox women and the measures adopted to find solutions. A recruit remarked:

> Well, you ask them questions and they answer your ques-

tions and you ask them for advice and opinions about how things are done. And then you have, well, just being in contact with these women. I guess you just sort of come into contact with them. This is one way in which you sort of grow into the batter more.

Contacts made at meetings may lead to additional contacts elsewhere. While meetings serve to bring recruits and Lubavitch women together, they also function as information centres which the former draw upon to acquaint themselves with pertinent gossip and general information. Considerable energy is, consequently, devoted to encouraging the recruit to attend the group meetings. Efforts are made to welcome and interest her and she is soon encouraged to assume certain responsibilities:

> ... I was very active in a group called *Bnos Chabad* ... and we were very interested in establishing this group and arranging lectures and arranging for speakers and meeting times and writing up the meetings afterwards and sending them out to the various girls. And I became active that way and I think, though, in general, that's what they try to do. ... Lubavitch is very good in drawing people in. . . They seem to have a knack for this type of thing and they make everyone who comes into the group really feel at home, mostly by working for the group.

Since much of her time is spent at home, and as some of her problems must be attended to immediately, the recruit telephones others for specific information. She might, for example, wish to question a particular Rabbinical ordinance (*hechsher*) or find out whether a product labelled as kosher is indeed so. The people most frequently called are those whom she has come to trust in areas pertaining to religious and personal affairs and second, recognized authorities on religious matters:

> Like, if I had a question to ask I would call X or anyone else. Mostly X. She was the one I sort of turned to all the time when I was first married. ... If I had a question I would just ask. I still do. I mean, sometimes it happens. You spill milk on a *flayshikeh* (meat) cup or something and you don't know what to do. You call up.

or:
> Ya, there were always questions. First we had an orthodox

Rabbi . . . and we began to consult another Rabbi, a Rabbi from Lubavitch. We usually consult him about questionable things.

For questions pertaining to *Kashruth*, the recruit may telephone the *Vaad Ho'Eer* Board. As a Lubavitcher remarks:

> . . . we have two Rabbis who are on the *Vaad Ho'Eer* Board, that is, the Rabbinical Council. Now they serve as a sort of . . . centre of information. Even if I want to get an O.K. on something or want to know something or more detailed information on how come or who's the one who's giving the *hechsher* [Rabbinical license] there, and so on and so forth, I'd call Rabbi Y or Rabbi Z, who, being there on the Council, will be able to give me all the information. So usually if they (recruits) had a question that could be answered like generally, like meat or what have you, like mustard . . . they could get in touch with these Rabbis. [brackets mine]

Although to a fairly large extent the recruit's instruction is through teaching and discussion, by observing how others behave she can learn what constitutes appropriate behaviour within the Lubavitch community. While attending a celebration in the Yeshiva for instance, she does not have to be told to refrain from mingling with the men since all other women are separated.

Whose are the Recruits?

Lubavitcher are continually initiating efforts to establish contact with new recruits for they consider it a *mitzveh* to show concern toward someone interested in *Yiddishkayt*. Most are willing, therefore, to help the person in any way possible, but there is no community institutionalized process which introduces the recruit to Lubavitcher. This lack of formality led a female recruit to remark:

> . . . but I think that they should put out something like a guide to a housewife, because you do things and you don't realize that you should do them another way. You think you're perfectly kosher and it really isn't. I feel that when people come in, they come from varying degrees of background. Some know what it's all about and some know nothing. I think there should be some sort of a guide,

certain basic things, like how that stove should be set up and how a sink should be set up . . .

Persons displaying interest in *Yiddishkayt* are contacted and invited to meetings and other social gatherings. Inviting the person and their family for the entire Sabbath, for example, serves as an excellent opportunity to establish lines of friendship.

> . . . maybe someone will come over to me and say: "You know, Mrs. so-and-so has shown a tremendous amount of interest in this particular group or this facet of Lubavitch and perhaps you would become closer with her. You know, to invite her and to become friendly with her."

or:

> Almost everything that exists in Lubavitch is almost as efficient as the _____ faculty here in its total disorganization. There's an ad hoc . . . you know, someone calls up so-and-so: "Well, I don't know. Why don't you call up so-and-so?" until something gets done which, in a sense, is as bad as it can be but it seems to work . . .

Learning groups and other social activities are on-going in the community, and are sufficiently diverse for recruits to find at least one compatible with their interest and level of *Yiddishkayt*. The Junior *Neshai Chabad* groups, for instance, meet regularly every second week, and every alternate week there is a study class in *Chassidess* (Lubavitch philosophy). The kinds of activities available to recruits were described by one Lubavitcher as follows:

> Well, it ranges from all age groups. . . Young ones have the *Messibbe* . . . and they have all different things that they can be connected with. They have learning groups of one sort or another for all ages. They have for the older girls, for the younger girls, for the newly married women, for the older women. They have groups which are directly affiliated with the Yeshiva, you know, parent-teacher groups and chapters connected with the Yeshiva, and those that make the rummage sale and the bazaars and the teas to raise money for the Yeshiva and the *Bays Rivkeh*. They have . . . the drama group that puts on plays each year, and so there seems to be a lot of groups and a lot going on during the course of the year.

There aren't enough days in the year for the person who wants to volunteer his services. No matter what capabilities a person has . . . they will put his efforts to good use in many different fields and it's principally not money raising because money raising is done by organized people. . . . Different people have different interests. Yes, there are some people who are interested in the camp. There are other people who are interested in the *Bays Rivkeh* and other people in the Yeshiva.

These contact situations serve a twofold purpose: on the one hand they bring Lubavitcher and recruits together, thus providing the latter with a feeling of community involvement. At the same time, these occasions easily lend themselves to discussions and to exchanges of attitudes and opinions between the newcomers and Lubavitcher.

Another channel through which Lubavitch initiates and maintains contact with newcomers is by inviting them to Lubavitcher religious and social functions such as weddings, *Bar Mitzvehs*, and *Farbrengens*. I asked a recruit if she and her husband were invited to weddings:

Always. They have a standard list of Lubavitcher. Every family has this list. That's the way they work it. . . . They invite, like, you know, the usual crowd, and they invite that standard crowd all the time to these affairs.

Newcomers are encouraged to attend *Farbrengens* at the Lubavitch headquarters in Brooklyn, New York. Lubavitcher consider this activity important for recruits as it permits them to experience Lubavitcher's relationship with their *Rebbe*. They hope the person will be impressed with the *Farbrengen* and maintain contact with Lubavitch. If a person agrees to attend a *Farbrengen*, Lubavitcher provide eating and sleeping accommodation, thus ensuring the newcomers will be immersed in a religious atmosphere. Lubavitcher see to it that newcomers will fit in and will become hooked into the various social and religious community activities. While different activities are available for men, women, boys, and girls, their ultimate objective—involvement with Lubavitcher and others who base their lives around *Yiddishkayt*—is similar.

Individuals attempting to organize their lives along a traditional Jewish line undergo a continual learning process. In the case of married couples, the female is likely to encounter more difficulty in accommodating herself to maintaining an orthodox way of life. Attending the Yeshiva, the male engages in more informal contact with Lubavitcher than does his wife and, while there, he is more likely to become involved in activities committing him to be with Lubavitcher. As well, others in the Yeshiva keep him attuned to the latest news from 770—the world headquarters of Lubavitch. While he becomes enmeshed in a network of Lubavitch relationships, his wife, on the other hand, finds herself mainly occupied at home with the children. A Lubavitch woman with much experience in assisting newcomers noted:

> ...a lot of the newly married couples, who have one or two children, who feel that their husbands have become quite entwined with the Yeshiva, some of them (husbands) who go to the Yeshiva to study in the evening, some of them will go out on a *Tefillin* campaign. ...Now, these women are stuck at home with the kids. They don't go out together hardly to a social function or so. ... What I have noticed is that men conform a lot faster and a lot easier, and at a much less dreadful process than the women do. The woman usually takes ... at least twice as long as the men, at least, with its aches and pains, so to speak. And I've seen this time and time again, whereby women sort of have it in, in some way, for what their husbands are doing and sort of can't go along with it all the way. They will, perhaps, in the end result, you know, after they've struggled through it point by point, but it's much harder on them.

Because there is no institutionalized rite of passage separating insiders from outsiders, recruits to Lubavitch can identify themselves with this chassidic group when they feel ready. This may be called gradual identification or creeping commitment. As such there is no definite point at which the person must make an important decision about his life or commit himself to a Lubavitch lifestyle. After a certain point is reached the recruit tends to feel that it would be more difficult to dissociate himself from the Lubavitch circle and return to his previous lifestyle than to remain committed to the community.

225

Footnotes

[1]The necessity to remain informed about kosher meat and dairy products is common to all Lubavitch and orthodox women. A Lubavitch woman, moving from a large city to a smaller one, might experience similar difficulties as the recruit:

> Alright. Now when I came to X [name of city], for instance, you want to speak about products in the supermarket. I didn't know most of the products because, as a matter of fact, many products in New York have a *hechscher* [orthodox dietary stamp of approval]. Hershey's cocoa has a *hechsher* in New York. It doesn't have one here. I really don't know about them. Even to this day I keep getting mixed up with . . . like Heinz has a *hechsher* in New York. Here they don't. . . . So you learn. . . . I think it's trial and error. Also, the *Vaad Ho'Eer* gives a listing partially, and you look for the C.O.R., M.K., O.U. let's say in the grocery store itself. In the home there are laws which you can learn. [brackets mine]

Chapter Nine

Conclusion

In the present study I have examined some of the strategies a minority religious community uses to persist successfully in an urban setting while surrounded by an alien culture. While numerous studies have focused on different kinds of religious communities, little explicit attention has been directed to the common strategies they use to maintain themselves. In an article distinguishing between successful (enduring) and unsuccessful (short-lived) nineteenth-century American utopian communities, Rosabeth Kanter (1968) describes "a number of structural arrangements and organizational strategies which promote and sustain commitment." In another article based on research into a group of mystics, Simmons (1964) suggests several processes that enable a community to maintain divergent beliefs. While each religious community undoubtedly retains its own unique characteristics, many of the strategies used to ensure its persistence are common to all for their aims are basically similar. Community members are socialized to fit a distinctive mold and are expected to see themselves as members of the community rather than of the larger society.

On important identity symbol in many religious communities is their style of dress which is used both to maintain their separation from the outside society and to reinforce a sense of their own continuity. The group attempts to link itself with its past history by adhering to the traditional garb of its ancestors. Another strategy is that of insulation from the surrounding culture, which is considered necessary to counteract the fear of gradual assimilation and eventual dissolution. Insulation does not necessarily refer to a spatial or ecological separation but also to a lack of social and cultural contact with individuals and ideas foreign to the group.

As we have seen in this study, although the Lubavitcher do employ both these strategies they are not as extreme as many other religious minorities, including the other chassidic groups. However, because of their common religious identity, all the chassidic groups share many similar features. For example, all are organized to ensure the perpetuation of Jewish laws, practices, and observances. While the goal may be the same, the way in which it is pursued is guided by each chassidic group's perspective on how threatened they are by the larger societal influences, and their co-ordinated program of action based on this understanding. Although like many other chassidic groups, Lubavitcher chassidim reside in the city, their philosophy respecting the maintenance and perpetuation of orthodox Judaism is unique. Unlike other chassidic groups and communities that avoid contact with the larger non-orthodox Jewish community since it is considered as threatening as the Gentile community, Lubavitch actively seeks out nonorthodox Jews to acquaint them with the tenets of orthodox Judaism.

Since Lubavitcher attempt to draw the larger Jewish community to orthodox Judaism, they are potentially exposed to harmful societal influences. Additionally, their particular views and different way of life make them easily susceptible to criticism. Although, as we have seen, the community's attempts to retain its distinctive way of life does present problems, its success at organizing and maintaining a distinctive identity and separate lifestyle is strongly related to its proselytizing activities with the larger Jewish community. This not only helps to strengthen the members' own religious beliefs and concept of their group identity, but also enables them to control and limit their contacts with non-Lubavitch Jews to a religious context and with Gentiles to necessary business transactions.

A comparison between religious-based communities and ethnic-based communities and the strategies they employ to maintain their distinctive way of life might also provide a useful insight into why they persist and how successful they are in persisting. An important feature in this respect is the extent to which they are aware of, and actively involved in, counteracting potential assimilative influences. Religious-based communities are characterized by a series of strategies actively intended to maintain the community's distinctive identity. As efforts are organized specifically for this purpose, religious communities are relatively successful at resisting the assimilative influences of the larger culture and group members are socialized to become integrated into the community's way of life. Although, on the other hand, ethnic-based communities may not actively seek to assimilate into the larger society immediately, they are not organized for the specific purpose of persistence and are not co-ordinated effectively to resist assimilation. The two kinds of communities can thus be distinguished by their active and passive resistance to assimilation. Active resistance to assimilation includes the organization of a series of institutions and activities to resist both the person's and the community's immersion into the surrounding culture. Such resistance is characteristic of religious communities. Passive resistance to assimilation, however, refers to the efforts of an individual or a family not to adopt the dominant culture deliberately. Unlike religious communities, the efforts of ethnic communities are not co-ordinated to ensure their survival over time.

As the above discussion implies, a characteristic feature of ethnic-based communities is that they are assimilative. While the first generation immigrants still retain much of the way of life of their native country, it becomes progressively less firmly grounded in the second and third generations. (Shibutani and Kwan, 1965) As the latter begin to take advantage of both educational and occupational opportunities for which their parents and grandparents were less well equipped, the ethnic group is gradually transformed. Religious communities, however, by strictly limiting the educational and occupational opportunities of their young, are able to exert greater control over them, thus ensuring that succeeding generations will not differ qualitatively from previous ones. Such communities' more marked success at persistence may be attributed to the *portability* of religious identity. Whereas ethnic identity tends to be grounded in the culture and lifestyle of the home country and is thus more difficult to retain in a new land, the religious community's identity is firmly rooted in doctrinal belief, supported by an explicit ideology regulating everyday behaviour regardless of geographical residence. As a result, immigrant communities are more likely to experience difficulties in defining and retaining their characteristic identity as succeeding generations become less familiar and develop a less intuitive rapport with their elders' native land.

Studies of religious communities sometimes conclude by

229

examining the penetration of outside influences on the community's way of life and the possible chances of the community's survival. While I have not addressed myself specifically to the latter point, I have attempted to show that the Lubavitch community in Montreal has, till now, successfully maintained its chassidic identity and should be able to continue in its task in the immediate future. While the community's financial constraints have, at times, confined its range of activities in the larger Jewish community, Lubavitcher's commitment to their orthodox way of life and to their *Rebbe's* teachings should provide the required supports to ensure this chassidic community's persistence.

In examining the strategies and the reasons why the Lubavitch community persists, I have taken what is known as the symbolic interactionist perspective. According to this view, the life of a group is not controlled by abstract forces but by the everyday activities of people responding to everyday threats and difficulties. If, for example, one examines a religious community in this way, its persistence must then be attributed to the individuals' collective actions to meet their life situations, as opposed to a set of forces acting on the community members and affecting them in a predetermined manner. Interaction among human beings depends on the fact that they do not merely react to each other's actions but rather interpret or define each other's actions before they act. As Blumer has noted, the response " . . . is not made directly to the act of one another but instead is based on the meaning which they attach to such actions. Thus, human interaction is mediated by the use of symbols, by interpretation, or by ascertaining the meaning of one another's actions." (Blumer, in Manis and Meltzer, 1967:139) The analysis of group life from a symbolic interactionist perspective must, consequently, include this process of interpretation.

Since the symbolic interaction position requires the researcher to address the process of interpretation through which the individuals under scrutiny construct their action, he must necessarily assume the role of the acting unit with whose behaviour he is observing. As a result of this, and since I have relied heavily on accounts provided by Lubavitcher themselves, the data may be regarded as subjective because they are based on such phenomena as experience, intuition, and empathy. Yet it is precisely these tools of humanism that can provide a true picture of the phenomena under study. Although these accounts might not be objectively or externally observable, they are, however, how the people in this study attempt to arrange their ideas and organize their experiences.

A further difficulty in using this perspective is that the researcher has to become accepted into the community that he is observing. I have already described how I approached the Lubavitch community in Montreal, but one aspect that is not often dealt with in sociological literature is how the researcher withdraws from the field. Since I experienced some difficulty in leaving the community I studied, I assume that other researchers have also encountered similar problems.

Clearly, all researchers will not find leaving the field equally difficult. The nature of one's commitments to the community, group, or organization determine the relative ease or difficulty with which the researcher will be able to sever ties and move out. Another consideration is whether or not the research has been officially sanctioned and made public to the participants of the study. If the research has been conducted covertly, terminating it should not pose any difficulty. Finally, if the researcher decides, for whatever reason, to remain "in the field" even after completing the research, potential difficulties relating to departure will be avoided.

When I first began visiting the Lubavitcher Yeshiva I only told one Lubavitcher that my main purpose in coming was to engage in research. When I would be asked: "What brings you here?" I would say: "I don't know, what brings other people here?" At no time did I try to obtain permission from the community leaders to conduct my research. I did not and still do not think that such permission would either have been granted or have made much difference. It soon became clear, however, that Lubavitcher were more willing to speak to me if they recognized that religious motives were responsible for my coming to the Yeshiva. As a result, while I started by wearing a white *yarmlke* which signified I only wore it occasionally, I switched to a knitted one and then to a black felt one, both of which gave the impression that I wore it all the time. I also began to observe *Tefillin*, studied with a Yeshiva *bocher* on a regular basis, and even travelled to 770 Eastern Parkway for the *Rebbe's Farbrengens*. These practices apparently convinced many Lubavitcher, but not all, that I was being drawn closer to *Yiddishkayt*. Many considered me to be a "successful case."

Some Lubavitcher suspected that my motives for taking an interest in *Yiddishkayt* were primarily academic and that once the research was completed I would disassociate myself from it. An indication of this attitude was given at a Lubavitch wedding, when a *bocher* revealed part of a conversation he had with one of my Lubavitch friends:

> ... you know I was speaking to _____, and he wondered if you would continue to come here after you finish school. He said he wasn't sure. Do you plan to come?

My standard answer to this kind of question was a variation of the following:

> In the beginning my interests in coming here were for school purposes. As I've continued I've come closer to *Yiddishkayt* and I now do things that I never did or thought of before. So, ya, I think my interests here extend beyond my research.

Most Lubavitcher who knew me believed that my interest in *Yiddishkayt* was more than fleeting. To convey such an impression I had to manage certain situations so that Lubavitcher would not doubt my sincerity. For instance, I would not drive near the Yeshiva on Saturday or other Jewish holidays; I always carried a *yarmlke* if I anticipated meeting Lubavitcher; I avoided certain restaurants so as not to be seen eating in them.

During the course of the research I may have appeared more concerned and interested in *Yiddishkayt* than I actually was. When the research was almost over I was faced with the dilemma of whether to terminate my association with the Lubavitch community, and, if so, how. I decided to maintain contact on a fairly regular basis for personal reasons. As a Jew I was positively affected by my experiences with this chassidic community. I had encountered and was befriended by individuals whom I had learned to respect deeply, and, therefore, wished to retain an association with Lubavitch. I could, therefore, see myself having to answer for my increased absence but not total disappearance.

Sociologists have given general and specific information on how to cope with difficulties encountered during the first days in the field. Their accounts have also included the strategies that were adopted to gain access to certain settings to obtain specific information. In cases where gaining access to a body of data has called for the researcher to engage in identity management while presenting himself to the subjects of the research, an account of how the data were collected should also include how exit from the field was accomplished. Such accounts would not only provide a more comprehensive view of the research project's natural history, but might also assist other researchers facing similar situations.

Recommended Readings

Those wishing to read other sociological and anthropological studies of chassidic communities are encouraged to consult the following:

Gutwirth, Jacques
>   1970 Vie Juive Traditionnelle: Ethnologie D'Une Communauté Hassidique. Paris: Les Editions De Minuit.
>   1973 "Hassidism Et Judaicité A Montréal." Recherches Sociographiques. XIV (septembre-décembre): 291-325.

Kranzler, George (Gershon)
>   1961 Williamsburg: A Jewish Community in Transition. New York: Philip Feldheim, Inc.

Mintz, Jerome
>   1968 Legends of the Hasidim. Chicago: University of Chicago Press.

Poll, Solomon
>   1962 The Hasidic Community of Williamsburg. New York: The Free Press of Glencoe, Inc.

Rubin, Israel
>   1972 Satmar: An Island In The City. Chicago: Quadrangle Books.

Shaffir, William
>   1970 "The Montreal Chassidic Community: Community Boundaries and the Maintenance of Ethnic Identity." Master's thesis, McGill University.

Sobol, Bernard
>   1956 "The M'lochim: A Study of a Religious Community." Master's thesis, New School of Social Research.

Several books focussing on the history of the chassidic movement including chassidic ideas and ideology include:

Aron, Milton
>   1969 Ideas and Ideals Of The Hassidim. New York: Citadel Press.

Lowenkopf, Anne
>   1973 The Hasidim: Mystical Adventures and Ecstatics. California: Sherbourne Press.

Mindel, Nissan
>   1969 Rabbi Schneur Zalman Of Liadi. Brooklyn: Kehot Publication Society.

Minkin, Jacob
    1935 The Romance Of Hassidism. New York: Macmillan.
Rabinowicz, Harry
    1960 A Guide To Hassidism. New York: Thomas Yoseloff.
    1970 The World Of Hasidism. London: Hartmore House.
Weiner, Herbert
    1969 91/2 Mystics. New York: Holt, Rinehart and Winston.

For those wishing to become familiar with chassidic tales and legends, the following material is recommended:

Ben-Amos, Dan, and Mintz, Jerome (editors and translators)
    1972 In Praise Of The Baal Shem Tov: The Earliest Collection
        of Legends about the Founder of Hasidism. Blooming-
        ton, Ind.: Indiana University Press.
Buber, Martin
    1956 The Tales Of Rabbi Nachman. Translated by M. Fried-
        man. New York: Horizon Press.
    1961 Tales Of The Hasidim. Translated by Olga Marx. 2 vols.
        New York: Schocken Books.
    1969 The Legend Of The Baal-Shem. Translated by M. Fried-
        man. New York: Schocken Books.
Langer, Jiri
    1961 Nine Gates to the Chassidic Mysteries. New York: David
        McKay Company, Inc.
Mintz, Jerome
    1968 Legends Of The Hasidim. Chicago: University of Chicago
        Press.
Newman, Louis and Spitz, Samuel, (editors)
    1963 The Hasidic Anthology: Tales and Teachings of the
        Hasidim. New York: Schocken Books.
Unger, Menashe
    1964 Chassidus un lebn ("Chassidism and Life"). New York.
    1955 Die Chassidishe Velt ("The Chassidic World"). New
        York: Hasidus.

The Lubavitch Kehot Publication Society has available a wealth of information concerning the philosophical underpinnings of this chassidic group, its historical development to the present time, and a description and explanation of its various activities in the larger Jewish community. This material may be obtained from the Kehot Publication Society, 770 Eastern Parkway, Brooklyn, New York, 11213.

Glossary

Ahavas Yisroel (Hebrew). Love for Jews.

Aibershter (Yiddish). The One above. God.

Aleph-Bays (Hebrew). The first two letters of the Hebrew alphabet. Refers to the alphabet.

Alter Rebbe (Yiddish-Hebrew). Refers to the founder of the Lubavitch movement—Rabbi Schneur Zalman of Liadi.

Am-ho'oretz (Hebrew). One unlearned in Torah matters. An uneducated man. Literally, people of the soil.

Ayrev (Hebrew). Literally, mixture. Symbolical act by which community or continuity of space or time is established for Sabbath purposes.

Baal-Tshuveh (Hebrew). Literally, to return. Used in this study to mean a newcomer to Lubavitch. (Baal Tshuvess. Plural.)

Ballebattim (Hebrew). Literally, householders; owners. The term is generally applied to the constituent members of a congregation. (Balleboss. Singular.)

Bar Mitzveh (Hebrew). Literally, son of good deed. The initiation of a Jewish boy into adulthood at the age of thirteen at which time he is expected to accept adult religious responsibilities.

Bays-Hamikdesh (Hebrew). The Temple in Jerusalem.

Bays Medresh (Hebrew). A place for study and prayer. Also used to refer to a school of higher religious studies.

Bays Rivkeh (Hebrew). The name of the Lubavitcher chassidim's girl's school.

Bays Sorreh (Hebrew). The name of a network of schools organized by the previous Lubavitcher *Rebbe*.

Bays Yankev (Hebrew). The name of a Jewish orthodox girl's school.

Beenoh (Hebrew). Second initial of the three letters composing Chabad; understanding.

Bentshn (Yiddish). To bless; to say the grace after the meal.

Bnos Chabad (Bnoys) (Hebrew). Lubavitch girl's club.

Bocher (Hebrew). A young boy; also unmarried male. (Bocherim. Plural.)

Brocheh (Hebrew). Blessing. (Brochess. Plural.)

Chabad (Hebrew). Initials of *Ch*ochmoh (wisdom), *B*eenoh (understanding), *D*aas (Knowledge). An acronym.

Challeh (Hebrew). Special white bread eaten on the Sabbath and other religious holidays.

Chanekkeh (Hebrew). Feast of Lights; Jewish mid-winter holiday.

Chanekkeh-Gelt (Hebrew-Yiddish). Money given to children as a Chanekkeh present.

Chassenneh (Hebrew). Marriage, weddings. (Chassenness. Plural.)

Chassidess (Hebrew). The teaching of chassidism.

Chavayress (Hebrew). Female friends. Members of a women's club. (Chavayreh. Singular.)

Chayrem (Hebrew). Ban, excommunication. (Charomim. Plural.)

Chinuch (Hebrew). Education.

Chochmoh (Hebrew). First initial of the three letters composing Chabad; wisdom.

Chossid (Hebrew). Literally refers to a pious, godly person. A follower of the chassidic movement. (Chassidim. Plural.)

Chumesh (Hebrew). The five books of Moses or Pentateuch, in popular usage.

Daas (Hebrew). Third initial of the three letters composing Chabad; knowledge.

Daf Yoymee (Hebrew). Daily page of Talmudic learning.

Davn (Yiddish). To pray; davening (praying); davned (prayed).

Deenim (Hebrew). Laws. (Din. Singular.)

Derech (Hebrew). Way; approach.

Dvaykess (Devekuth) (Hebrew). Religious ecstacy.

Dos pintelle Yeed (Yiddish). The inner Jewish feeling, or spark.

Ek (Yiddish). End, extremity.

Essreg (Hebrew). Citrus fruit. Used with loolev—a palm-branch flanked with sprigs of willow and myrtle—during the Sukkess holiday.

Farbrengen (Yiddish). Literally, to spend time. A chassidic gathering.

Flayshike (Yiddish). Referring to meat products or utensils.

Folk-Shulle (Yiddish). Name of a Jewish parochial school.

Frum (Yiddish). Observant, pious.

Frye (Yiddish). Free-thinkers.

Gan Yisroel (Hebrew). Name of the Lubavitch boys' camp.

Gemoreh (Aramaic). The portion of the Talmud explaining the Mishneh. In Lubavitch it stands for Talmud.

Goilem (Hebrew). Artificial man, such as the one created, according to legend, by the Maharal in Prague in the 16th century. A simpleton, a fool.

Goyish (Hebrew-Yiddish). Non-Jewish. The word may include derogatory implications for non-Jews and Jews alike.

Hanholleh (Hebrew). Leadership; administration.

Hechsher (Hebrew). Rabbinical approval concerning the manufacture of foods; permit.

Hislahavess (Hitlahavut) (Hebrew). Rapture; ecstacy; exaltation.

Kabboless Shabbess (Kabbolas Shabbos) (Hebrew). Literally, receiving of the Sabbath. Refers to Friday evening service inaugurating the Sabbath.

Kaftn (Yiddish). Long overcoat, fastened by a girdle, traditionally worn by chassidic Jews. Commonly referred to as a Surtuk in Lubavitch.

Kohl (Kahal) (Hebrew). The people of a community; the public.

Kashress (Hebrew). The dietary laws.

Klai Koidesh (Klai Kodesh) (Hebrew). Literally, holy utensils. Those (one) holding ecclesiastic office.

Koiech (Koiach) (Hebrew). Strength. (Koichess. Plural.)

Lag Bo'Oymer (Hebrew). Children's festive day. Thirty-third day between the second day of Passover and the holiday of Shvooess. According to Talmudic and Midrashic sources, many of Rabbi Akiva's disciples died of a plague during this period. The plague ceased on the day of Lag Bo'Oymer.

Limudai Koidesh (Kodesh) (Hebrew). Studies of holy subjects.

Loolev (Hebrew). A palm branch flanked with sprigs of willow and myrtle. Used with essreg (citron) on the Sukkess (Feast of Tabernacles) holiday.

Madraiggess (Hebrew). Levels. (Madraiggeh. Singular.)

Maftir (Hebrew). One who concludes the reading from the Law which precedes reading a portion of the Prophets. The reading of the Haphtorah in the synagogue.

Malochim (Hebrew). Angels. (Malech. Singular.)

Mashgiech (Hebrew). Supervisor. Mainly a supervisor of Jewish dietary laws in an institutional kitchen. In a Yeshiva refers to an educational supervisor. (Mashgichim. Plural.)

Mashpeea (Hebrew). Exerting influence. In chassidic Yeshivas refers to the head of chassidic studies.

Mecheetzeh (Hebrew). Partition. In orthodox synagogues usually used for the separation of men and women.

Melaveh Malkeh (Hebrew). Literally, "the ushering of the queen." The evening meal marking the conclusion of the Sabbath.

Mentsh (Yiddish). Literally, person. Decent person.

Messibess Shabbess (Hebrew). Sabbath gathering of Jewish youth.

Mikveh (Hebrew). Ritual bath. Usually used by chassidic men on days preceding holidays and the Sabbath and by women after menstruation. An absolute requirement of an Orthodox community.

Mincheh (Hebrew). Afternoon prayer.

Minyen (Hebrew). Necessary quorum (of ten) for the public performance of congregational services.

Mishnayess (Hebrew). Code of Jewish law. Refers to the book of oral law. (Mishneh. Singular.)

Misnagdim (Hebrew). Name for the opponents of the chassidic movement.

Mitzveh (Hebrew). A prescribed religious command; a good deed. (Mitzvess. Plural.)

Moiech (Moach) (Hebrew). Mind. (Moichess. Plural.)

Moide Ani (Hebrew). A prayer said in the morning upon awakening.

Mosheeach (Moishiach) (Hebrew). Redeemer. A descendant of the House of David that is hoped will come and deliver Jews and the world.

Mymorim (Hebrew). Treatises; written articles. In chassidic literature refers to chassidic Torah said by the Rebbe. (Mymer. Singular.)

Myriv (Hebrew). Evening prayer.

Nachess (Hebrew). Initials of *N*eshai *Ch*oyvevai *T*oyreh. Women Torah lovers.

Niddeh (Hebrew). Related to the precepts governing a woman's conduct during her menstruation period.

Olaynoo (Hebrew). Literally, "it is upon us." Last portion of the prayer.

Pardess Channeh (Hebrew). Literally, Channeh's orchard. Name of the Lubavitch girls' camp.

Parsheh (Hebrew). Weekly reading of the Torah; also section of that reading read to the individual called to the Torah.

Parshess Yisroi (Parshas) (Hebrew). The section of the Pentateuch containing Exodus chapters 18-20.

Payess (Hebrew). Earlocks, side-curls. (Payeh. Singular.)

Pegeesheh (Hebrew). Meeting; encounter.

Purim (Hebrew). Feast of Lots. The holiday celebrating the deliverance of the Jews from the persecution of Hamman, as recorded in the Book of Esther.

Rabonim (Hebrew). Rabbis. (Rov. Singular.)

Rashi. Initials of Rabbi Shlomo Yitzchaki, author of an 11th century commentary on the Bible and the Talmud, which is studied along with the sacred works themselves.

Rebbe (Hebrew). Used particularly for the religious, charismatic leader of a chassidic group—often referred to as a Tzaddik—in distinction from Rabbi, who serves as the official head of a congregation.

Refooeh Shlaimeh (Hebrew). Complete recovery.

Saifer (Hebrew). Used particularly for sacred books. (Sforim. Plural.)

Shabbess (Hebrew). Sabbath.

Shabbess Mevorchim (Hebrew). That Sabbath when a new month is inaugurated.

Shachris (Hebrew). Morning prayer.

Shaleshudess (Shalosh Seudos) (Hebrew). Literally, three meals. Late afternoon meal on the Sabbath.

Shammess (Hebrew). Name of the synagogue sexton who superintends the synagogue.

Shayrut La'am (Hebrew). Israeli version of the Canadian University Students Overseas.

Sheeur (Hebrew). In this study used to mean lecture.

Shleeta (Hebrew). Initials of sheyeechyeh l'oyrech yomim toyvim, omayn, meaning he shall live good long years, amen. Among chassidim, refers usually to a Rebbe.

Shlimazel (Yiddish-Hebrew). Unlucky person.

Shleechess (Shlichus) (Hebrew). Mission; assignment. (Shleechessn. Plural.)

Shoichet (Hebrew). Ritual slaughterer. (Shochtim. Plural.)

Shoimer Shabbess (Hebrew). A Sabbath observer. (Shoimrai Shabbess. Plural).

Sholem Alaychem (Hebrew). Literally, peace be upon you. Hello.

Shteebl (Yiddish). A moderately sized chassidic house of prayer. (Shteeblech. Plural.)

Shtikl (Yiddish). Literally, piece or part. In this study used to mean partly.

Shul (Yiddish). A house of prayer.

Shulchn Orech (Hebrew). Literally, a set table. Code of Jewish Law.

Shytl (Yiddish). A wig worn by orthodox women after marriage, in fulfillment of the prescription that a married Jewish woman must not walk about with her hair uncovered.

Sicheh (seecheh) (Hebrew). A discourse. (Seechess. Plural.)

Sidder (Hebrew). Prayer book.

Simcheh (Hebrew). Literally, joy. Celebration of any kind. (Simchess. Plural.)

Simchess Toyreh (Hebrew). The last day of Sukkess celebrating the end of the yearly cycle of reading the Torah.

Sukkess (Hebrew). Feast of Tabernacles. Jewish fall holiday.

Tahress Hamishpocheh (Hebrew). Literally, family purity. Laws pertaining to Niddeh (viz.)

Talless (Hebrew). Prayer shawl.

Talless Kotn (Hebrew). Literally, "small prayer shawl." Worn by a religious Jew (also boys) either under the shirt or jacket.

Talmid (Hebrew). Student; pupil. (Talmidim. Plural.)

Tanach (Hebrew). Bible.

Tanya (Aramaic) The book written by Rabbi Schneur Zalman of Liadi, the first Lubavitcher *Rebbe*, dealing with the philosophy of the Chabad movement.

Tefillin (Hebrew). Phylacteries. Religious objects containing excerpts from the Bible worn on arm and forehead during morning services on weekdays.

Tisheh B'ov (Hebrew). The ninth day of Av. A Jewish day of fasting and mourning in commemoration of the destruction of the first and second Temples in Jerusalem.

Tomchei Tmimim (Hebrew). Literally, supporters of the righteous. Name of the Lubavitcher Yeshiva.

Trayf (Hebrew). Not kosher.

Tzaddik (Hebrew). An extremely righteous man; usually synonymous with Rebbe.

Tzneeus (Hebrew). Modesty in appearance and in conduct.

Tzugekumenne (Yiddish). Newcomers.

Vaad Arbe Arotsess (Vaad Arba Aratzot) (Hebrew). The Council of Four Lands. An autonomous Jewish governing body in eastern Europe in the 16th-18th centuries.

Vaad Ho'Eer (Hebrew). Community Council.

Velt (Yiddish). World.

Yahadess (Hebrew). Jewishness.

Yarmlke (Yiddish). A skullcap. (Yarmlkess. Plural.)

Yaytzer Ho'Ro (Hebrew). Evil Inclination. Counterpart to the Yaytzer Tov—Good Inclination.

Yecheedess (Hebrew). Literally, privacy. Used in connection with a private audience with a chassidic Rebbe.

Yeerass Shomayim (Hebrew). Literally, fear of heaven. Fear of God.

Yiddishkayt (Yiddish). Literally, Jewishness. Refers to a Jewish way of life within traditional Judaism.

Yiddish Kind (Yiddish). Literally, Jewish child. A Jew.

Yom Kipper (Hebrew). Day of Atonement.

Bibliography

Aberle, D. F., A. K. Cohen, A. K. Davis, M. J. Levy, Jr., and F. X. Sutton. 1950 "The Functional Prerequisites of a Society." Ethics. 60 (January): 100-111.

Becker, H. S., Blanche Geer, Everett C. Hughes and Anselm L. Strauss. 1961 Boys in White: Student Culture in Medical School. Chicago: The University of Chicago Press.

Becker, H. S. 1963 Outsiders: Studies in the Sociology of Deviance. New York: The Free Press.
1970 Sociological Work: Method and Substance. Chicago: Aldine Publishing Company.

Blum, 1952 "Getting Individuals to Give Information to the Outsider." Journal of Social Issues 8, No. 3: 35-42.

Blumer, H. 1967 "Society as Symbolic Interaction." In Manis, J. G. and Meltzer, B. N. (eds.) Symbolic Interaction: A Reader in Social Psychology. Boston: Allyn And Bacon: 139-148.

Breton, R. 1964 "Institutional Completeness of Ethnic Communities and the Personal Relations of Immigrants." American Journal of Sociology. 70 (September): 193-205.

Dubnow, S. M. 1918 History Of The Jews In Russia And Poland: From The Earliest Times Until The Present Day. I Friedlaender (tr.) Vol. 2. Philadelphia: The Jewish Publication Society of America.

Festinger, L., H. W. Riecken, and S. Schachter. 1956 When Prophecy Fails. New York: Harper and Row.

Gans, H. J. 1962 The Urban Villagers. New York: The Free Press.

Glaser, B. G. and A. L. Strauss. 1967 The Discovery of Grounded Theory. Chicago: Aldine Publishing Company.
1971 Status Passage. Chicago: Aldine Atherton, Inc.

Graetz, H. 1939 History Of The Jews. Vol. 5. Philadelphia: The Jewish Publication Society of America.

Gutwirth, J. 1970 Vie Juive Traditionnelle: Ethnologie D'Une Communauté Hassidique. Paris: Les Editions De Minuit.

Hostetler, J. A. 1968 Amish Society. Baltimore: The John Hopkins Press.

Kanter, R. M. 1968 "Commitment and Social Organization: A Study of Commitment Mechanisms in Utopian Communities." American Sociological Review 33 (August): 499-517.

Kranzler, G. 1961 Williamsburg: A Jewish Community in Transition. New York: Philip Feldheim, Inc.

Liebow, E. 1967 Tally's Corner. Boston: Little, Brown and Company.

Lofland, J. 1966 Doomsday Cult: A Study of Conversion, Proselytization, and Maintenance of Faith. Englewood-Cliffs: Prentice-Hall, Inc.

Matza, D. 1969 Becoming Deviant. Englewood-Cliffs: Prentice-Hall, Inc.

Mauss, M. 1967 The Gift. New York: W. W. Norton and Company.

Mead, G. H. 1934 Mind, Self and Society. Chicago: The University of Chicago Press.

Merton, R. K. 1957 Social Theory And Social Structure. New York: The Free Press.

Mindel, N. 1969 Rabbi Schneur Zalman of Liadi. Brooklyn: Kehot Publication Society.

Minkin, J. S. 1971 Romance of Hassidism. California: Whilshire Book Company.

Mintz, J. 1968 Legends of the Hasidim. Chicago: University of Chicago Press.

Newman, L. I. 1963 The Hasidic Anthology: Tales and Teachings of the Hasidim. New York: Schocken Books.

Orne, M. T. 1962 "On the Social Psychology of the Psychological Experiment: With Particular Reference to Demand Characteristics and Their Implications." American Psychologist 17 (November): 776-783.

Parsons, T. 1951 The Social System. New York: The Free Press.

Poll, S. 1962 The Hasidic Community of Williamsburg. New York: The Free Press of Glencoe, Inc.

Rabinowicz, H. M. 1960 A Guide to Hassidism. New York: Thomas Yoseloff.

1970 The World of Hasidism. Hartford: Hartmore House.

Redekop, C. W. 1969 The Old Colony Mennonites: Dilemmas of Ethnic Minority Life. Baltimore: The John Hopkins Press.

Rosenthal, R. and R. Rosnow (eds.) 1970 Sources of Artifact in Social Research. New York: Academic Press.

Rubin, I. 1972 Satmar: An Island In The City. Chicago: Quadrangle Books.

Shibutani, T. 1955 "Reference Groups as Perspectives." American Journal of Sociology 60 (May): 562-569.

1961 Society and Personality. Englewood-Cliffs: Prentice-Hall, Inc.

Shibutani, T. and K. M. Kwan. 1965 Ethnic Stratification: A Comparative Approach. New York: Macmillan Company.

Simmons, J. L. 1964 "On Maintaining Deviant Belief Systems: A Case Study." Social Problems 11 (Winter): 250-256.

Skolnick, J. H. 1969 Justice Without Trial: Law Enforcement in a Democratic Society. New York: John Wiley & Sons, Inc.

Strauss, A. L. 1969 Mirrors and Masks: The Search for Identity. San Francisco: The Sociology Press.

Volkart, E. H. (ed.) 1951 Social Behavior And Personality: Contributions of W. I. Thomas to Theory and Social Research. New York: Social Science Research Council.

Weiner, H. 1969 9-1/2 Mystics. New York: Holt, Rinehart and Winston.

Whyte, W. F. 1943 Street Corner Society. Chicago: The University of Chicago Press.

Young, P. V. 1932 The Pilgrims of Russian-Town. Chicago: The University of Chicago Press.

Lubavitch Publications

Der Chaver. Montreal, 1942.

Challenge. London: Lubavitch Foundation of Great Britain, 1970.
Used by special permission.

Di Yiddishe Heim. New York: Council Neshai Ub'Nos Chabad.
Used by special permission.

Mesibos Shabbos: Program and Guide. Brooklyn: The Mesibos Shabbos Department of the Merkos L'Inyonei Chinuch, 1960.

Teachers Programme. London: Lubavitch Foundation, 1969.
Used by special permission.

Der Keneder Odler (The Canadian Jewish Eagle): Montreal.

7371-3
5-35